PEAK DISTRICT CLIMBS — FOURTH SERIES

Volume 3

peak
limestone
stoney

Series Editor: Geoff Milburn

Guidebook Team:
Andy Barker
Malc Baxter
Mike Browell
Chris Craggs
Richard Davies
Neil Foster
Gary Gibson
Dave Gregory
Chris Hardy
Adey Hubbard
Chris Jackson
Mark Kemball
Trevor Langhorne
Simon Nadin
Mark Pretty
Jim Rubery

Keith Sharples
Alan Wright

Diagrams: Phil G
Executive:
Nat Allen (Secret
Mike Browell (Bu
Dave Farrant
Neil Foster
Gary Gibson
Dave Gregory (Vice-Chairman)
Graham Hoey
Chris Jackson
Geoff Milburn
Keith Sharples (Artwork)
Ian Smith (Chairman)

Produced by the Peak Committee Guidebook Executive for the
British Mountaineering Council
First Edition: 1987

BRITISH
MOUNTAINEERING
COUNCIL

ISBN   0 903908 11 5

GV
2
99.44
.672 **CONTENTS**   (Line drawings in italics)
P42
1987

	page
Introduction	4
Acknowledgements	9
The Crag Environment	12
Technical Notes	19
Mountain Rescue	22
General Notes	22
STONEY MIDDLETON DALE	23
Stoney Middleton	23
Map – Stoney Middleton	30
Garage Buttress	34
Windy Buttress	44
Tower of Babel	51
Dead Banana Bay	54
Wee Doris Wall	60
Pearly Gates Buttress	65
Prayer Wheel Wall	68
Carl's Wark	74
Mortuary Steps Buttress	78
Slurper Wall	81
The Quarry	84
Cucklet Delf	87
Stoney West	88
Hidden Quarry	92
Horse-thief Quarry	116
Horseshoe Quarry	117
RAVENSDALE AREA	
Cressbrook	133
Ravensdale	142
Flying Buttress	146
Raven Buttress	152
THE CASTLETON AREA	165
Winnats Pass	165
Cave Dale	169
Pindale Quarry	178
Bradwell Dale	179

	page
THE BUXTON AREA	184
Peter Dale	184
Smalldale Quarry	185
Peak Dale Quarry	189
Bibbington Quarry	190
Harpur Hill Quarry	195
Grin Low	204
Aldery Cliff	206
Aldery Cliff	210
Ashwood Dale	217
Cow Dale	220
Staden Main Quarry	222
Joint Effort Wall	228
Charas Wall	232
Staden Lower Quarry	235
Deep Dale	242
UPPER WYE VALLEY CRAGS	257
Great Rocks Dale	257
White Wall	262
Previous Editions	271
Guidebook Pattern	272
Index	273

PHOTOGRAPHS

Front Cover: Ian French on Cabbage Crack, Stoney Middleton.
Photo: Chris Wright

First Colour Photo: Liam Grant on Scoop Wall, Stoney Middleton.
Photo: Keith Sharples.

Frontispiece: Graham Parkes on Circe, Stoney Middleton.
Photo: Chris Craggs.

Inside Rear Cover: Graham Hoey on an early repeat of Systems
Malfunction, Chee Dale.
Photo: Ian Smith.

Rear Cover: Nigel Slater beginning Pickpocket, Stoney Middleton.
Photo: Keith Sharples.

INTRODUCTION

---

*'One point remains, limestone still conjures up an
image of Kilnsey Overhang, pegs and paraphernalia to
many climbers. Some, not all of them strangers to the
area, still refuse to recognize standards on limestone,
and persist in decorating past free climbs with extra
pitons. One may welcome the addition to the collection
of a new Charlet, Simond or "offset", placed guiltily by
some previous party in the only move above Severe,
but one does tire of seeing lines of piton marks on
climbs previously done free. Extra pitons on a
Derbyshire limestone free climb are no better and no
worse than pitons on Froggatt, or Chamonix-style
wedges in the last pitch of the Dinas Mot Direct Route,
where most of us would agree they have not even
amusement value. Progress lies somewhere in the other
direction, one in which a number of ambitious youths
refuse to go. It lies in the use of less defacing aid and in
the development of climbing techniques beyond that
engineering ability which is open to every reasonable
human being.'*

Paul Nunn, 1966

Perhaps the first people to scramble on Derbyshire limestone
were the local quarrymen and miners, and some of the first
awkward moves were probably made underground in various
shafts and caverns as miners worked in flickering candlelight in
dangerous positions. Eventually in the early 1900s climbers such
as Henry Bishop, J.W. Puttrell and E.A. Baker began to explore the
Derbyshire crags in a methodical fashion and despite epic ascents
of routes such as the Dargai Crack and High Tor Gully the general
opinion tended to be that the majority of limestone is lethally
loose and totally unfit for rock-climbing. As John Laycock wrote in
1913:

*'The writer is satisfied that mountain limestone is
beyond the border line of safety as that is understood by
all the best and most experienced climbers ... It is safe
to assume that all holds on mountain limestone are
loose.'*

Henry Bishop on the other hand wrote in 1910:

> 'It has been urged against mountain limestone that its
> treacherous nature unfits it for the climber's attention.
> But the few who have really studied its idiosyncrasies,
> and who have learnt to treat it with deserved respect,
> will retort that it offers absolutely the finest training in
> the art of deciding by observation and actual test, as to
> the stability or otherwise of each apparent hold.'

One exception was the Dolomitic limestone of Harborough and
Brassington, which the early explorers quickly appreciated for its
abundance of holds, but a guidebook was not produced until 1950
when Eric Byne's Climbing Guide to Brassington Rocks was
published by the Midland Association of Mountaineers.

While the exploration of the gritstone edges continued steadily
throughout the Twenties and Thirties there were very few
tentative steps on limestone apart from the odd memorable
ascent such as Frank Elliott's breakthrough on Aurora at Stoney
Middleton.

In the Thirties according to Eric Byne:

> 'Meanwhile the limestone stayed decorously hidden
> away in the dales or shyly skulked amongst the trees. A
> few of us rather shamefacedly paid surreptitious visits.
> We saw the possibilities and vowed to exploit them, but
> there was always someone to say "It's suicidal; the
> whole bloody crag is tottering." So the limestone crags
> were left, and anyway there was so much to do on grit,
> and we liked the wild sweep of the gritstone hills and
> moors and the excitement provided by baiting furious
> gamekeepers, while lack of transport made access to
> limestone far from easy.'

After the Second World War however members of the Rock and
Ice Club began to explore on limestone and eventually in the late
Fifties, coinciding with the pegging activities in gritstone quarries,
there was a big push to peg and bolt some of the outstanding
lines on limestone. As Paul Nunn later commented:

> 'Ivy, fearsome hanging blocks, loose holds, grass, earth,
> brambles and the occasional tree all succumbed to
> reveal some of the best climbs in Derbyshire.'

> 'A justifiable fear of the unknown and of a moderate
> degree of rock-instability left some climbs littered with
> everything from the house-brick wedge to the stainless-
> steel micro-piton. Fortunately Harold Drasdo, Joe
> Brown and later Graham West re-established the
> practice of climbing these steep rocks free and did much
> to oust the other approach.'

Although various mechanical aids were used to overcome the most intimidating lines there was still a philosophy that climbs should be done free wherever possible and this was reflected in Graham West's guide 'Rock Climbs on the Mountain Limestone of Derbyshire', 1961, which contained over 80% of free climbs. In the early Sixties as the masses began to gain confidence they tended to go for ' . . . a good meal of limestone dust, on Sin, Skylight or The Thorn', and interest began to increase in the crags of Cheedale, Water-cum-Jolly, the Lower Derwent, Dovedale and the Manifold Valley.

> 'Crowds mill in Stoney Middleton on warm Sundays, just as they buzz round the buttresses of Robin Hood. In the frosty pre-dawn gloom, parties race for Mecca, The Big Plum and Bastion Wall, three classic artificial climbs. Perhaps here, Das Bluejeans may train not only to climb up rows of pitons, but also to race early-rising Germans to the foot of the ladder!'

As the Sixties progressed the number of routes increased steadily and two interim guidebooks appeared: Climbs on Derwent Valley Limestone by Doug Scott in 1965 and Stoney Middleton Dale by Geoff Birtles. Work was at an advanced stage for the proposed Northern Limestone guidebook and Paul Nunn took over the project from the Editor, Eric Byne. Nunn commented in 1968:

> 'There has been more development in this speciality in ten years than in any comparable earlier period. Those wishing to strip ivy, release suicidal blocks into space and discover anew will soon need to expend their rapacious energy elsewhere. Though problems remain, little that is obvious can survive for long.'

The main problem however was in obtaining financial backing and Nunn cynically proclaimed:

> 'The most bitter question remains. "Where is a guide?" To the last thousand climbs. Those who lost their way two years ago continue to grope. The visitor can scarcely do that. Only a financial bottleneck holds back what is probably the most demanded unpublished guide in England. As one who shares the responsibility and attempts to co-ordinate the work it seems too frustrating for words.'

Eventually the Climbers' Club came to the rescue and The Northern Limestone Area guide of 1969 was followed by The Southern Limestone Area guide in 1970. Sadly, and no fault of the guidebook team, the guides were well out of date by the time they appeared and throughout the early Seventies there was doubt as

to which lines had been climbed or freed. By 1973 Dave Gregory
had taken over as Series Editor of the Peak guides and while the
guidebook team was working on the gritstone guidebooks for a
new series there was an unprecedented surge of activity on the
limestone crags. This was documented in a 1977 supplement,
Recent Developments, by Steve Bancroft, which included
technical grades and a healthy debate took place on grading
systems. Consequently Chris Jackson's guide to the Northern
Limestone included the controversial 'E' grading system which
had had time to settle down in areas such as Wales.

In the Eighties there was a decision to amalgamate limestone and
gritstone guides on an area basis rather than produce a new
Southern Limestone guide. Although there was a small amount of
criticism at the time this decision later proved to be right and
Dave Gregory finished his fine run of guides with the Derwent
Valley Area in 1981. In the same year Geoff Milburn took over as
Series Editor for the Staffordshire Area guide to pave the way for
a new series.

During the early Eighties routes were being produced at such a
rate that a Peak Supplement was prepared by Gary Gibson and
the members of the Guidebook Executive. This temporary
measure in 1983 was to provide valuable information for a further
boom in new routes leading up to the current guidebook.

The original 'dream' was to have four gritstone guides to the Peak
District and one bumper limestone guide. Several factors worked
together to shatter this ideal. Firstly, as a result of intense training,
particularly on indoor climbing walls and in gymnasia, super-fit
young climbers increased climbing standards dramatically giving
E7 routes and technical grades up to 7a. There was also a
scramble to grab any remaining lines and to eliminate aid from
even the hardest of the old artificial routes. Raven Tor for example
was finally transformed into a free-climber's paradise – for those
with the ability to take advantage of it. One price was paid to gain
admission to some of the more blank pitches – bolts were used by
some climbers. Others fought to prove that these were not
necessary and the debate still continues. A second factor which
increased the volume of material was the need to give more detail
about limestone routes rather than provide the bare minimum
about the line of the route. Checking large numbers of unpopular
routes also took time – a great deal of time – and some guide-
writers wilted along the way. At a late stage there was also a
feeling that the time had come to document as accurately as
possible the history of Peak limestone. The final result is far from
complete and corrections will have to be made when climbers

read the finished product. Nevertheless a start has been made which should make the next guide-writers' task that bit less onerous.

The grading of hard limestone routes has proved to be a nightmare, mainly owing to the subjective nature of such routes for each climber. Attempts to produce graded lists have thrown up countless anomalies which at times highlight the inadequacies of our current grading system. Perhaps the next guidebook will reveal a solution, and like limestone itself the grading will need extensive gardening and cleaning to reveal the perfect solution.

In eighty years limestone climbing has come a long way, from the ascent of High Tor Gully with the aid of an ice-axe to an athlete hanging from his finger-tips high on the great airy Prow of Raven Tor, chalk-dipping casually while his sticky-boots cling neatly to the smooth white rock. Between these two extremes there is a whole spectrum of experience for the lifetime of an average climber, from the quiet pinnacles of Dovedale, and epics in the still-loose quarries, to the superb faces of High Tor, Chee Tor and Stoney Middleton where future generations will make their mark on the history of limestone which will provide the next chapters in the story.

Geoff Milburn (November 1986)

ACKNOWLEDGEMENTS

*"Have you checked that horrible smelly thing?" [i.e. the
Stoney new route book.]*

Anon

It is 25 years since the first Derbyshire limestone guide by
Graham West and a great debt is owed to early compilers and
editors such as Eric Byne, Paul Nunn, Doug Scott, Geoff Birtles,
Dave Gregory and Chris Jackson. Originally the aim of the current
team was to produce a single guidebook but this ambitious plan
was defeated partly as a result of the considerable output of new
routes but also by the decision to document as much of the Peak
climbing history as possible before records are lost. Mike Browell
started this off with some enthusiastic hard spadework to
produce First Ascent Lists for High Tor, Stoney Middleton, Chee
Tor, Raven Tor and Beeston – a long and complicated research
project. This in turn inspired others to seek out missing
information and to check dates. Much of the later work was done
by Geoff Milburn with the aid of Graham Hoey, Chris Hardy and
Brian Cropper's YHA first ascents log books. In fact Chris Hardy
spent so many days researching in the Editor's library that the
neighbours had begun to think that he was one of the family!
Inevitably there will be errors but it is hoped that these will be
corrected prior to the next edition of the limestone guide.
Much of the guidebook work has been organised by the Executive
under the Chairmanship of first Dave Dickson, secondly Dave
Gregory and more recently Ian Smith. Most of the Executive
meetings have been held in the Old Bull's Head at Little Hucklow
and the team has turned up through rain, hail and snow to keep
the project going. Thanks are due to the landlord, Mr D G
Hawketts, for his hospitality and also to the locals who eventually
got accustomed to reaching the bar through a crowd of climbers.
Inspiration was provided by Winkle Ales with countless pints of
Saxon and Ivanhoe!
The task of drawing limestone diagrams has always proved well-
nigh impossible and one can only marvel at the unique talent of
Phil Gibson who has spent countless days in building up a
comprehensive set of first-class drawings. Several of Sue Lawty's
drawings have also been used. Keith Sharples then took over the
task of arranging for all the routes to be marked on and
numbered, with help from Gary Gibson.

In addition to valuable help from Paul Mitchell and Nigel Slater we should also like to thank Tony Howard and Paul Seddon of Troll for sponsoring the photographic competition as well as the team of judges: Geoff Birtles, Dennis Gray, Dougie Hall, Chris Hardy and Mrs Seddon.

The national postal system has been thoroughly tested with myriad copies of computer printouts which have shuttled between Cartmel, Sheffield, Stoke and Glossop. At one stage, despite a prolonged search, one master-copy went astray and escaped to the great post-box in the sky. This caused a major panic but the team pulled out the stops to replace the material. When these three limestone volumes reach the public there will possibly be some criticism but it must be remembered that the workload involved for these three volumes would normally have produced a whole series of guidebooks. One member of the team casually commented that he had put in well over 100 hours of work solely on the First Ascents Lists.

The task of word-processing the script and updating it at intervals can only be described as a nightmare as editorial red pen often exceeded black print on each page. Jean and Les Ainsworth have put in months of work to keep the script as up to date as possible. In fact so great was the amount of material that long before the work was completed the pile of draft scripts topped the one metre mark.

The Editor would also like to thank his wife, Wendy, for patiently putting up with countless 'comings and goings' of little groups of climbers at odd hours. Few wives take kindly to having both the sitting room and dining room tables out of action at the same time owing to piles of scripts, to say nothing of the conversion of the spare bedroom into a climbing library, or being interrupted at 'tender moments' when the phone on the bedside table suddenly shatters the silence.

It has become customary to dedicate each of our Peak guides to a climber (or climbers) who is greatly liked or respected by the climbing world at large. Volume 1 is dedicated to Graham West and members of the Manchester Gritstone Club for spearheading modern limestone climbing and documenting the initial exploration so well in their 1961 guide. Volume 2 can only be dedicated to one person; throughout the Sixties he not only worked tirelessly to record much of our limestone history in 'New Climbs' and the national magazines, but also fought hard against financial strictures to create not one but two volumes to the Peak Limestone area. He remains one of the great Peak characters – Paul Nunn.

After working on BMC guide-books for many years Nat Allen,who is regarded with great affection by all climbers, has finally resigned from the Executive. As he was involved with the early exploration of the Manifold valley it is apt that Volume 3 should be 'for Nat'.

Finally thanks go to the intrepid pioneers who braved the horrors of loose limestone crags and also to subsequent climbers who had the vision to strive to maintain free-climbing standards and keep ironmongery to a minimum.

Thank God we've finished the job at last!

Geoff Milburn, Series Editor (January 1987)

THE CRAG ENVIRONMENT

by Adey Hubbard

As with the previous two guidebooks in this series we have included this section on the crag environment in the hope that its message will be accepted by those who have chosen to visit the limestone quarries and dales to seek their recreation. The very future of our sport depends upon a sympathetic understanding of the environment, an appreciation of the pressures placed upon it from a variety of sources and a genuine desire to preserve it. The urgency in our minds is clearly emphasised by the events at Staden Quarries and the amicable arrangements which have been achieved there by patient negotiation.

INCREASING POPULARITY

Unlike the gritstone edges, which have always been very popular, the limestone crags have seen an escalation in climbing activity on a quite extraordinary scale. In the late seventies it was still possible to have the whole of Ravensdale, or even High Tor, entirely to oneself. Now they have become popular to the point that routes are frequently queued for and the belay ledge on Debauchery often supports more climbers than there are good belay points. As a consequence of this massive increase in climbing activity we now find few crags that have not been extensively gardened and the nettle-covered tracks have, in many places, become paths that can be confidently tackled in a pair of shorts during the summer.

Limestone has, in the past, suffered from a reputation of general looseness and insecurity. While this is certainly still true in some places, climbers have learned how to treat the rock and, by climbing on it regularly, have turned many of the pitches that were once considered to be especially hazardous into classic trade routes.

GRADING IRREGULARITIES

It is interesting that much more downgrading has occurred on limestone than on any other rock type. Routes are no longer put up without considerable cleaning, a precedent set many years ago with the trundling of such horrors as the big flake on Sirplum. In a sense the limestone crags are now much more secure than they were ten or fifteen years ago yet caution is still advisable.

Flakes do break, blocks do fall off and the grades of some routes can change overnight in a manner that seldom happens on gritstone.

GEOLOGY

The geology of the White Peak has produced some dramatic gorges and buttresses, together with a host of pleasant dales, most of which contain their fair share of exposed rock. The emergence of Britain from its chalk sea about 60 million years ago produced, after erosion in the Peak District, a domelike core known as the Pennine Anticline, edged to the west and east by areas of gritstone and, to the north, by the shales and peat bogs of the Dark Peak. At this time, also, there began a sequence of erosion which continues to the present day. The limestone area extends from Rushup Edge in the north to Dovedale in the south. Altogether, a thickness of around 450 metres depth of limestone is exposed in the White Peak, which accounts for the variety of rock features and the differing qualities of the rock in each area. Three main areas of sedimentation can be identified. The central core of the White Peak extends from Castleton as far south as a line parallel to, and just east of, the River Dove. To the west are found sediments deposited in more shallow waters to give the reef limestones with their characteristic pocket holds. In the south-east another reef area has resulted in the exposure of reef knolls up to 30 metres thick at High Tor.

The climbing history of the limestone areas is closely related to the structure of the rock itself. The early routes mostly followed crack and groove lines provided by vertical jointing between blocks of limestone. Routes of this type include such classics as Highlight, Venery, Mortlock's Arête and Sin, a classic Very Severe route at Stoney that was originally graded Exceptionally Severe! Later, as protection improved and the emphasis shifted away from big aid routes, the compact faces of the reefs and of the thickly-bedded limestone in the centre of the area began to yield their secrets. This trend was heralded by the ascent of Debauchery, in concept way ahead of its time, and brought to maturity by routes such as Black Grub, Supersonic, Tequila Mockingbird and the impressive developments on the arm-pumping Raven Tor. Similarly developed are the pinnacles and towers, exemplified by Tissington Spires, which are such a characteristic feature of reef limestone.

Not all the climbing in this book owes its origins to the weathering and glacial processes of thousands of years. Some of the best routes contained in this area only exist as a result of quarrying, both ancient and some very recent. Of the quarry workers, many are long since dead but others are still very much alive. A good portion of Stoney Middleton is quarried and routes such as Bitter Fingers and all those in the quarry would not exist but for this past activity.

There is no doubt that, in recent times, the rate of erosion of the crags described in this book and the land around them has increased considerably. Although the action of frost, solution and vegetation play a part it is not very significant compared with the effect that man has had, and continues to have on the environment. In the White Peak a climber can encounter both quarried and natural rock on the same route, a feature not often found on gritstone. It is even possible to climb with one foot on limestone and the other on grit — a unique exercise in differential friction!

Another interesting oddity are the routes on the crags around Brassington. This rock is subject to selective weathering out of the magnesium-containing pockets from the calcium carbonate base. The result is a series of climbs on amazingly etched pockets and flutings, good for beginners and for developing the finger strength of experts too.

VEGETATION

With very few exceptions, and these are mainly quarries, all the crags described herein lie on the steep sides of valleys. Many of these still contain, albeit rather occasionally in the Manifold Valley, the rivers that have given them their shape. One of the consequences of a moist, calcareous landscape is an extraordinary variety of vegetation, together with the insect life and larger fauna that thrive upon it. Limestone supports a much more diverse range of plants than the harsh gritstone environment. Much of the limestone upland is now reduced to grass and scrub by the grazing sheep and cattle. Deep in the valleys, however, the situation is very different and the flora is dependent upon the wetness of the valley and the extent of grazing that it suffers.

In essentially dry valleys, a gradual colonization by grass and scrub has allowed more delicate plant life to thrive. Nowhere is this better illustrated than in Cressbrook Dale where climbing is discouraged. In the gritstone areas, a botanist would probably be hard-pressed to find more than twenty different plant species close to a crag. In Cressbrook Dale there could easily be more than two hundred, including a number of rare flowers, grasses and ferns. In the wet valleys, this richness is further enhanced by a wide variety of water-loving plants. It is not difficult to understand the great concern of conservationists when large numbers of climbers and walkers visit crags in force, making their own tracks through such diversity in total ignorance of its importance and vulnerability.

Many climbers are surprised by similar concern about vegetation on the crags themselves and in the quarries that appear as desolate as a lunar landscape. What the climbers do not realize is that the nooks and crannies of limestone crags hold nutrients that can be used by ferns and other species. On some of the vertical faces in the limestone area are plants that are found nowhere else in the Peak District. Ardent gardeners of new routes might reflect on this fact the next time they remove a 'weed' from its precarious existence. The situation in abandoned quarries can be even more important. Bare quarries can be colonized to an amazing diversity in just two or three decades, forming botanical oases in an upland biological desert. This occurs for one reason only — the colonization is not disturbed by man or by grazing animals. Priestcliffe Quarry, for example, is now reaching a high level of botanical diversity and hence the desire of Derbyshire Naturalists Trust to discourage climbers.

LANDSCAPE MANAGEMENT

Management of the limestone dales is often devised intentionally so as to improve the habitat for certain species of plant or animal. In Dovedale the National Trust has taken a very bold and far-sighted policy decision to create good rock scenery by felling major tracts of trees which have invaded since the traditional coppiced woodland management ceased last century. Now we see the spires and tors which made Dovedale a famous landmark for the Victorian tourists. At the same time, the opportunities for wildlife and soil erosion (!) have been greatly increased, both in the dead timber and also on the sunny bare rock and screes. Thus it is that the vegetation around all these crags and, indeed, the very rock itself is worthy of protection. It is not capable of sustaining the pressure of large numbers of climbers on its own and the work of the various conservation bodies and the Peak District National Park is to be encouraged. Climbers should be aware of this aspect of the environment and be prepared to accept footpath diversions and car-parking restrictions. Similarly, care should be taken when abseiling down highly vegetated parts of crags, especially in areas such as Dovedale. In a climatically poor year you could be destroying the only specimen of a particular plant which has managed to flower and form seeds.

BIRD LIFE

Quite apart from the flora, the fauna of these dales is also of interest to naturalists. The birds of prey and ravens which gave their name to many Peak District buttresses have now largely disappeared, harried to their deaths by egg collectors, shot by gamekeepers and poisoned by agricultural pesticides. In recent years, however, the breeding populations have been growing and spreading, returning to ancestral nesting sites, especially in the less frequented areas. A wide berth should be a matter of course, particularly during the nesting season from March to June, disturbing birds from a nest can cause eggs to chill or unattended chicks to die. The rarest species are protected by law, making it an offence to cause disturbance.

LITTER

Climbers should remember that while they are using the crags they are also acting as custodians for a generation; soon they will pass them on and, we hope, in a fit state. Increasingly the biological diversity is finding itself in competition with many undesirable bits and pieces including broken glass, tins, scrap food, plastics and human excrement. This is inexcusable. None has a place here, as those who have inadvertently fallen into the latter will agree. All rubbish should be removed from the crag and taken to the nearest litter bin, or taken home. The crags have already survived for several million years; surely we cannot break them in a century?

CONFLICT OF INTEREST

Other groups of people, as we have seen, are interested in the same areas of the landscape for different reasons. Naturalists and climbers share these dales with walkers and fishermen, who also enjoy the open space and freedom. All have an equal right to their recreation and it is good that we have reached the mid-eighties without a serious conflict of interests.

PROTECTION

Co-existence must continue to be the theme for the future. On the crags themselves conflicts have arisen and died down. It has long been accepted that peg protection is often required on limestone, although modern protection renders many of those placed a few years ago unnecessary. By and large, recent routes have shown a high ethical standard and the tendency is towards the elimination of as many as possible of the old aid routes. The big aid pitches of the sixties and seventies, such as those on

Raven Tor, have been climbed free using in-situ gear. Bolts have made possible some superb routes that would not otherwise have been attempted but we hope that the peculiar British tradition of 'sticking the neck out' (total commitment) is not to disappear altogether beneath a tonne of metal. The ugly sight of long coloured slings hanging from in-situ gear is another form of pollution which should be avoided.

LAND OWNERSHIP

Every piece of land covered in this guidebook has an owner. Some are private landowners which make their living from the land, some are public authorities which manage the land for a specific purpose, others are societies and groups of people who own the land to protect their own interests. Most of the crags described in this book are within the Peak District National Park. This designation gives a high priority to the conservation of the landscape, and to the provision of facilities and opportunities for public recreation. It does not in itself provide any rights of access to the countryside, but legislation does allow local authorities to negotiate access agreements to specific areas of land. The Peak Park have negotiated more access land than any other local authority in England and Wales. A number of crags are owned or managed by either the National Trust, the Nature Conservancy Council or the Derbyshire Naturalists Trust. While it is true that, in some ways, these bodies see things differently to climbers it is equally true that they have shown a very enlightened attitude to climbing and have been willing to agree access to a number of botanically sensitive areas.

Where access agreements exist there are provisions for suspension of the right to go on the land when periods of drought result in a high fire risk. Fires can spread rapidly and cause severe long term damage. It is essential that every care is taken to avoid the possibility of starting a fire — cigarettes and camping stoves are the most obvious dangers. The argument has been successfully made that climbers who spend all day on a particular section of cliff are very effective fire-watchers rather than fire-risks. The passing walker who leaves his fire to smoulder behind him is more likely to be the culprit. It is hoped that climbers as a whole will accept the responsibilities that negotiated access agreements place upon them with understanding.

Camping is NOT allowed at any of the crags within this guidebook; there is always an obligation to obtain the landowner's permission. There are, in any case, a number of camp-sites within the region.

ACCESS

There is no legal right of access to climb on any of the crags in this guidebook, but at most of them climbers have long enjoyed a traditional freedom to climb. On the others, unless a problem is indicated in the crag notes, a request for permission is usually granted. It is well to be aware that technically, unless there is a right of access, a climber is trespassing — a civil wrong against the ownership of property, not a criminal offence. Landowners are within their rights to request a trespasser to leave. As the number of climbers has increased in the past decade, so too has the concern of landowners who are often worried about liability, vandalism and protection of their livelihood. The Landowner's Liability Act, passed in 1984, has gone a long way to solving the former problem, but fears of the other problems are still real and, sadly, often justified. Simple things such as damaged walls, or gates left open, can lead to considerable problems for the farmer; time is wasted on rounding up strayed stock or making repairs and income is lost. It is vital for the present generation of climbers to recognize that climbing is only possible because of the continuing tolerance and goodwill of the landowner. Providing that we continue to show a responsible attitude to the land, and especially other users of the land, we shall probably continue to enjoy our freedom.

Occasionally, conflicts will arise. When this happens it is imperative that individual views and political allegiances should be put aside in the short-term, in the interests of the long-term security of our traditional climbing grounds. **Too many hours of patient negotiation have been put in jeopardy by the selfishness and bad manners of a few climbers**. Major confrontations should be avoided at all costs. If there is an access problem to any crag in this volume, then it affects climbers nationally, and the British Mountaineering Council should be advised. Many minor access problems have been amicably settled by the anonymous work of guidebook writers and local club members, but the major issues are best tackled at national level. Whatever the size of the problem, the guiding rule should be not to assume right of access. Details of any particular access agreements are given before each crag description but THE INCLUSION OF A CRAG OR THE ROUTES UPON IT IN THIS GUIDEBOOK DOES NOT MEAN THAT ANY MEMBER OF THE PUBLIC HAS THE RIGHT OF ACCESS TO THE CRAG OR THE RIGHT TO CLIMB UPON IT.

TECHNICAL NOTES

'Mechanical aids are now completely accepted by modern climbers if used correctly and if precedence is given to the man who can do the route free.'

B Webb. S.U.M.C. Journal 1960-61

CLASSIFICATION

Adjectival Grades

These are subjective assessments of the overall difficulty of a route and the seriousness involved in doing it. They take into consideration the quality of the rock, the exposure, quantity of protection, technical difficulty, strenuousness and sustained nature of the route. They assume that climbers carry a comprehensive range of modern protection devices.

The grades are: Moderate, Difficult, Very Difficult, Hard Very Difficult, Severe, Hard Severe, Very Severe, Hard Very Severe, Extremely Severe. The Extremely Severe grade is open-ended and is indicated by E1, E2, E3, E4, E5, E6, E7, etc.

Technical Grades

The technical grade is an objective assessment of the cumulative difficulty of a pitch and, as such, considers the strenuousness and sustained nature of the climbing up to and after the hardest move. There is no definite relationship between the technical grade and the adjectival grade although climbs of a given adjectival grade are likely to cover a limited range of technical grades. Technical grades have mostly been given to climbs in or above the Very Severe category. The grades used are 4a, 4b, 4c, 5a, 5b, 5c, 6a, 6b, 6c, 7a etc.; the system being open ended.

The climbs are graded for on-sight leads but some of the harder routes have not been led without some prior knowledge. The symbol † has been used after the technical grade to indicate routes where the grade is in doubt, either because the first ascent has not been authenticated or the climb has had insufficient ascents to arrive at a consensus grade.

Protection

As we are now firmly in an era of free-climbing on limestone wherever the words 'peg', 'bolt' and 'thread' appear in this text it means that they are only for protection. The only exceptions are a few old aid routes (which will have an A1, A2, A3 etc grade) and a few free routes which still have a stated aid point. The placing of bolts on Peak limestone is still a highly controversial issue. The majority of climbers who are to be found on the lower grade routes, where bolts are never going to be placed are very clearly against this practice although they will seldom refuse to clip one if they find one on a route. In recent years in particular, a relatively large number of new routes have utilized one or two bolts for protection. The majority of these are on routes which are still quite serious propositions with longer run-outs and harder climbing than ever before seen on Derbyshire limestone. However some are neither desirable nor necessary and will undoubtedly soon be chopped. The placing of bolts is therefore a delicate act and climbers must think carefully before drilling, bearing in mind the unique nature of climbing in Britain.

Style of Ascent

Climbing standards have increased dramatically since the advent of the seven day climber and intensive training methods. At the present upper limits the state of the art seems to have arrived at a point where it is unlikely that a climber will complete the hardest new pitches in one push without first practising the moves. There is an opinion amongst the top climbers that for pitches around E6 6c and above a new code, that will allow the practising of the hardest moves prior to a normal lead (frogging), ought to apply. It is important to realize that various underhand practising methods have gone on during countless first ascents — and these have promptly been 'forgotten' or ignored later. Perhaps it is better to practise moves openly, aiming for an eventually flawless lead of each of the hardest routes of the day. An open-minded attitude in this direction may help the sport to develop along healthy lines in the years to come. One thing is certain though, there will be far more problems in the future when it comes to reporting how the new climbs have been done and it will be of paramount importance to discover the first ascent tactics for those wishing to repeat new routes.

Route Quality

A system of stars is used to indicate the quality of the routes; only the most outstanding climbs are given three stars.

First Ascent Lists

This volume sees the beginning of an attempt to chronicle the history of the limestone crags in the Peak District. It is perhaps necessary to stress that this is a first attempt to unravel what is a very complex story and at times conflicting evidence and opinion have given many problems. Nevertheless an attempt has been made to give the year of first ascent of each route and where two dates are stated the second is usually the year of first free ascent. In some cases the second date is that for a variation. At the end of each crag is a First Ascent List and where grades are given these are the original aid-climbing grades or grades of routes now abandoned. All other routes are free although for various reasons grades may have changed over the years. Each chronological list is as accurate as possible, but the Guidebook Executive welcomes further information which will be included in future editions. Please contact Geoff Milburn with any amendments at 25 Cliffe Road, Whitfield, GLOSSOP, Derbyshire, SK13 8NY.

New Routes
Descriptions of all new routes should be sent direct to B.M.C., (New Routes), Crawford House, Precinct Centre, Booth Street East, Manchester, M13 9RZ. Second-hand information from the magazines is often insufficient.

MOUNTAIN RESCUE and FIRST AID

Dial 999 or Ripley 43551 and ask for POLICE OPERATIONS ROOM. Rescue equipment is kept at: 1) the Ranger Briefing Centre at Stoney Middleton — telephone Hope Valley 30541, 2) the Centre at Brunts Barn, Nether Padley which is manned from 9.00a.m. to 5.30p.m., 3) White Hall Outdoor Pursuits Centre, Long Hill, Buxton — telephone Buxton 3260, 4) the Mountain Rescue Post at The Mill, Upper Hulme.

FIRST AID in case of ACCIDENT

1. IF SPINAL INJURIES or HEAD INJURIES are suspected DO NOT MOVE THE PATIENT without skilled help, except to maintain breathing.

2. IF BREATHING HAS STOPPED, clear airways and commence artificial respiration. Do not stop until expert opinion diagnoses death.

3. STOP BLEEDING by applying direct pressure.

4. SUMMON HELP.

Reports of accidents should be sent to the Secretary of the Mountain Rescue Committee, R.J. Davies, 18 Tarnside Fold, Simmondley, Glossop, Derbyshire.

GENERAL NOTES

BRITISH MOUNTAINEERING COUNCIL

The B.M.C., Crawford House, Precinct Centre, Booth Street East, Manchester, M13 9RZ is the official body representing the interests of climbers. Clubs and individuals may, on application, become members.

COUNCIL FOR THE PRESERVATION OF RURAL ENGLAND

The Sheffield and Peak District branch has a fine record of defending the Peak District from the various threats to it. Contact Lt. Col. G. Haythornthwaite, 22 Endcliffe Crescent, Sheffield 10.

STONEY MIDDLETON DALE

STONEY MIDDLETON   O.S. ref. SK 218 758 to SK 227 757

Neil Foster and Mark Pretty

---

*'From the thirties till the early fifties the crag's history is
shrouded in mystery, then Joe Brown and others,
members of the old Valkyrie Club, visited the crag a
number of times and put up some fine routes. Apart
from this very little serious work seems to have been
attempted before 1957 . . .*
*The cliff had an almost evil reputation, forbidding
appearance and bad rock being the major
complaints . . . Childs and Johnson were struck by the
unsuspected free possibilities of this cliff. Subsequent
outings saw "peculiar upward thrutchings" being
made, which in some cases even resulted in a man
reaching the top. This was termed, we believed,
climbing "free". An armed invasion of the rocks
followed. Ice-axes, shovels, choppers, coal rakes, yard
brushes, pruning shears, pokers – even a saw and a
butchers' knife were used to penetrate the jungles.'*

Dave Johnson. 1961 Guide

SITUATION and CHARACTER

These impressive cliffs, over 1km in length, flank the north side of
the A623 road west of Stoney Middleton village. They are about
14km south-west of Sheffield and 9km north of Bakewell.
The crags mostly face south and being low down in a valley they
tend to be much more sheltered than the nearby gritstone
outcrops such as Froggatt and Curbar. The rock dries very quickly
after short rain showers but after prolonged rain much of the crag
gets soaked by seepage and the presence of trees below most
sections propagates dampness.
The quality of the limestone varies a great deal from section to
section, with the spectrum ranging from very solid to downright
lethal. Sadly some of the routes are now highly polished.No
description of the character of Stoney Middleton would be
complete without mention of its role in Peak District climbing
history. This crag lies at the heart of many climbers. It provides a

focal point, a meeting place, and eventually, somewhere to shun when the jaded climber is bored with too many visits. Stoney Middleton shares a love-hate relationship with climbers, but there is always life after death. For Stoney, it is the famous cafe . . . The cafe (caf!) in Stoney Middleton has for many years been one of the great meeting places of the climbing fraternity, where one can eat, drink and argue the toss about routes, grades and affairs in general. Cars can (but shouldn't) be parked outside the cafe or, better, in the lay-by on the other side of the road a short way up the dale.

APPROACHES and ACCESS

The T208 bus service from Sheffield to Buxton and Hanley passes through the dale and the Sheffield to Bakewell bus stops at Calver Sough 1.5km from Stoney Middleton. From Chesterfield, buses go to Baslow. There is a local connection from there. One can also stroll over the hill to Stoney Middleton church from Grindleford Station (three quarters of an hour). From Manchester the most practical route is the regular bus service to Bakewell via Buxton. There are various connections from Bakewell to Calver or Stoney Middleton.

Apart from near the cafe and in the layby, parking is also possible at various points under the crag, however, the rutted tracks have claimed many victims. Beware!

To the south and east of Windy Buttress the crag is owned by Sir Charles Denman who has no objection to climbers using the rocks providing that their activities cause no danger or affront to other members of the public. NO CLIMBING MUST TAKE PLACE ON ROCKS NEAR TO OR ABOVE THE GARAGE OR THE HOUSES IN THE VILLAGE.

The section to the north and west of Windy Buttress is owned by the Trustees of the Chatsworth Estate and leased by them to a local quarry company. There has been no objection to climbing taking place.

West Stoney Middleton belongs to the owner of The Hall, Eyam. He is willing to allow climbing provided that no damage is done to the land and walls above the cliff (a plague on those who do not adhere to this!).

HISTORY
by Mike F. Browell
Over the centuries the rock at Stoney Middleton has been carved away by quarrymen to give the present configuration. Like some

Garage Buttress with climbers on Pendulum, Stoney Middleton.
Photo: Riche Brooks.

new route protagonists these quarrymen had no inhibitions about removing loose and sound rock alike and in so doing created a unique series of rock features of varying quality. These met the tastes of each successive climbing generation which passed through this forcing ground since 1950.

Along the way the quarry workers probably climbed the easier lines and although accounts of the early exploits are not readily available, we can however be fairly sure that lead miners climbed *Mineshaft* and *Fingal's Flue* but left them ungraded until J.W. Puttrell came along in 1918 exploring for caves.

The early Peak pioneers who normally operated on gritstone found nothing much to their taste at Stoney and passed by leaving the crag undisturbed until Frank Elliott climbed *Aurora* in 1933. This remarkable ascent probably took today's top pitch only, but was of mind-boggling boldness, and featured in the Sheffield Telegraph.

Eric Byne and Clifford Moyer also climbed with Frank Elliott and they recorded ascents of *Fingal's Cave* and *The White Knight*. Their real interest was however gritstone and they also didn't linger long at Stoney.

Another lull occurred, until the Valkyrie arrived in 1950 spearheaded by Joe Brown, Ron Moseley, Slim Sorrell, Nat Allen and Don Chapman. They found a profusion of unclimbed cracks and being well versed in jamming and aid climbing, attacked virtually every obvious line on the main crag (except Windy Buttress) with varying degrees of success. Their period of exploration began with *Morning Crack* and *How the Hell*, the first Triglyph crack to be climbed. Brown and Moseley then attacked *Kink*, a fairly hairy exercise and graded A3. This was as far as they went onto the gripping Windy Buttress.

The Tower of Babel also came in for some attention, initially by Brown and Moseley on *Glory Road* and then in February 1952 when Moseley created *Sin* and labelled it Exceptionally Severe. He might well have been nervous about the security of the entire tower!

Whillans came to Stoney in 1952 and left a minor legacy; *Thrutch* and *Frisco Bay*.

By 1952 the Valkyrie had transformed into the Rock and Ice and the legend had spread across the country. Stoney Middleton's intimidating reputation was further enhanced by the Brown and Whillans mythology, and for three years climbers progressed warily.

Four Minute Tiler, Stoney Middleton.
Photo: Chris Craggs.

It took the disrespectful attitude of young Sheffield University climbers to break down the myths. Armed with ice axes, shovels, choppers, rakes, yard brushes, pruning shears and pokers, not to mention saws and knives, they set about hacking away the impenetrable jungle and exposing the rock below. Spearheading the attack were Dave Johnson and Dave Mellor with an army of others, some of whom are mentioned in recorded ascents. Amongst them were Jack Soper and Neville Crowther, Trevor Brooks, Jack Wade, John Childs and Ron and Brenda Salt.

As well as discovering *Minestrone, Gabriel, The Pearly Gates* and *Minus Ten*, this team plucked up courage and attacked Windy Buttress. Roy Leeming had already pegged *Scoop Wall* and Dave Mellor and Dave Johnson put up *Kingdom Come* and *Windhover* and in so doing established Stoney's best known route.

Windhover was a terrific breakthrough, giving the first ascensionists a very spacey feeling overhanging the road for 200 feet'.

As well as discovering new routes the SUMC teams rediscovered much that had been forgotten and as the Rock and Ice were less than careful about recording their ascents there was some confusion. So much so that when Graham West produced Rock Climbs on the Mountain Limestone of Derbyshire in 1961 there was a bit of double counting!

University climbers come and go and Dave Johnson and Dave Mellor both disappeared from the Stoney scene in 1959 after three exceptional years in which the Rock and Ice myths were exploded and the crag was laid bare for exploitation.

This began in earnest in 1961 when Barry Webb arrived. All his routes were climbed that year and all have become classics. *Compositae Grooves, Padme, Mortuary Steps* and *Brown Corner*. He had little regard for tradition and climbed as free as he could but nevertheless some aid was used, mainly due to loose rock and dirt.

Medusa fell at last in 1961 to Len Millsom, after numerous failures. It retained its aura of difficulty which was further enhanced in 1963 when a local climber fell from the top and narrowly missed the deck.

By 1963 the Cioch Club had arrived and encamped in a hut at the end of Eric's Cafe. Amongst them were Jack Street, Chris Jackson, John Atkinson, Brian Moore and their apprentice Geoff Birtles. Geoff was a colourful character of the group and had several monster falls and lucky escapes. For aspiring hard men, Windhover was the route to attempt and gradually its pitons were eliminated. However the total number of active climbers at

Stoney was very few and a typical weekend might see only a half dozen. Climbing on limestone had nevertheless arrived.

The Cioch held sway for four years and produced some top quality routes at an incredible standard. The Stoney cafe and pub scene had arrived. John Atkinson was a fine technician and *Om* was his best climb. Jack Street dominated the scene however, and his routes were probably the hardest in the country at the time; *Jasper, John Peel, Sycamore Crack, Dead Banana Crack* and *Boat Pusher's Wall*; one of the most serious leads around which still stops climbers in their tracks.

Jack Street really took Stoney Quarry to task, having the vision to see climbs where others saw rubbish.

While the Cioch members were busy free-climbing, Bob Dearman was hammering his way up *Circe, Dies Irae, Damocles* and others. When he set out to climb Alcasan he used quite a lot of aid, cleaning as he went. On his first foray he reached Kingdom Come. Chris Jackson was waiting in the wings and when Dearman abandoned his efforts Chris attempted the crossing with Jim Ballard and eliminated much of the aid. He then teamed up with Brian Moore who had accompanied Dearman on the first attempt and pushed another two pitches. The first complete traverse of this mega-route was finally strung together by Chris Jackson and Geoff Birtles in December 1964.

Jackson was quite prepared to try his hand at anything as his five-day ascent of *Little Plum* proves. Twice he and Birtles had to descend to buy more pegs and return to their high point by lowering a rope and a wooden rung caving ladder.

Despite Little Plum, Jackson held a healthy contempt for aid climbing and after Dearman had pegged and wedged his way up *The Flakes* he made a second ascent with only one point of aid. Quite an achievement to climb an aid route free within weeks of its first ascent!

Ivy-covered walls were stripped of their cover and routes were forced up the cleaned rock. *Augean* was discovered and when the ivy on Dead Banana Wall was dragged away by Ian Conway's six-cylinder Vauxhall they found *Fe Fi Fo Fum* lurking underneath.

Street's last desperates were climbed in 1966 and from then on for almost fourteen unbroken years the crag became the domain of Tom Proctor. Tom was a gentle giant with a very open and easy going temperament, immensely strong and totally committed to the one crag. He did of course climb elsewhere but always returned to the forcing ground of Stoney Middleton. At any single time it was possible to find the highest standard routes at Stoney and they were always Proctor's.

Geoff Birtles flitted in and out of the scene; he was both advisor and confidante and as a team they formed a dynamic and determined partnership; sometimes ruthless.

Proctor's first route was the bold *Lucy Simmons*. Birtles was very impressed; having just failed to lead it. Tom took the lead and cruised to the top. He later confided that he had practised it on an abseil rope the previous weekend. This type of forethought appealed to Birtles and the bond was formed.

Proctor then followed with five phenomenal routes; *Pickpocket*, *Our Father*, *Dies Irae*, *Scoop Wall* and *Wee Doris*. Proctor had arrived and was exploding the existing grading system. His routes didn't fit the top category and normal XS climbers reeled in awe. Some of Proctor's free-climbs were taking lines up virtually unpeggable rock!

For several years hopefuls came and paid homage, the bolder ones trying *Our Father* but few succeeded. One of Proctor's party pieces was to solo up the first few moves of *Our Father* in Hush Puppies and fix protection for aspirants who then struggled to leave the ground.

When the Northern Limestone Area guidebook was published in 1969 it failed to acknowledge Proctor's ascents in the history, having been written a couple of years earlier. In retrospect it is difficult to imagine a more significant collection of routes than Proctor's pre-1970 efforts.

The early seventies saw a new crop of Proctor desperates including *Special K*, *Hercules* and *Bubbles Wall*. Al Evans was muscling in on the action and manoeuvred his way up *Menopause* with aid, and *Cool Hand Luke*.

The intense young men managed to put their noses in and John Allen, Steve Bancroft and Neil Stokes climbed a couple of lesser routes, *Belinda* and *Syntax Error*. Allen and Bancroft had the gritstone scene well and truly sewn up but were seldom active on limestone.

Gabriel Regan was far more forceful. He snapped up the brilliant *Bitter Fingers* from Proctor's empire and then grabbed the incredibly fierce *Scarab* using two aid points and two rope manipulating teams. Proctor was not going to let this go unchallenged and in 1979 succeeded in free-climbing *Scarab* by a left variation. Since then the route has lost many key holds and been subjected to regular top-roping, becoming very much harder on the way.

For some years the Quarry had been neglected. A momentous achievement in 1976 gave Geoff Birtles *The Millionaire Touch*. Today this daunting route scares off most people but with the elm tree a mere bridging distance away in 1976 it was at least possible to escape for a rest at half-height even though the crux had first to be climbed.

Bob Dearman returned to Stoney in 1977 after a long absence, once again with his bag of aid tricks. He added *Speed Kills* and *The Morgue*, each mixed with some aid, to the Mortuary Steps area. It was again left for Proctor to clean them up.

From 1977 to 1979 Proctor's total domination of the crag continued unchallenged. He put up a series of routes ranging from the desperate *Traffic Jam* to the dangerous *Flycatcher*. Some were definitely scraping the bottom of the barrel and others were somewhat man-made . . .

In 1979 however, the pressure was on and some last minute fillers-in before the Northern Limestone guidebook fell to others. Geoff Birtles was in on the action and eventually freed the magnificent wall left of The Millionaire Touch. *Oliver* was named after his son. Proctor's coup of the year was the long-awaited free-ascent of *Circe* soon to become the replacement route for aspirant hard men after Our Father and Bitter Fingers.

His parting shot came in 1980 when he went over the roof of *Four Minute Tiler*, which was undoubtedly one of the hardest routes. At the end of the Proctor era one needs to picture the scene in 1980: the new guidebook published and a list of unrepeated desperates laid down as a gauntlet to the new generation, in exactly the same way as he had done a decade earlier with the old Northern Limestone guidebook.

Just after the guide came out Chris Hamper freed Menopause, a route which had previously defeated Proctor. He then repeated Circe which was the trigger for a flood of subsequent ascents. It was not long before Jerry Moffatt, a young up and coming star who had an early reputation for dubious tactics, picked up the gauntlet – yet to go into Proctor's domain and snatch the line of *Helmut Schmitt* was unbelievable. A couple of years later and Moffatt had completed *Little Plum*, spread over 1981 and 1982. As Moffatt said "there exists no other pitch that is more out there". 1980 was the start of fierce competition amongst the new wave. By the year end many Proctor desperates were reduced to trade routes; Kink, Circe, Scarab and Four Minute Tiler.

An unlikely guest appearance by Steve Bancroft resulted in *Emotional Rescue*, an obvious challenge needing Steve's mature hand.

Paul Mitchell had already made several minor additions to the crag, including the final freeing of Kingdom Come with John Kirk. In 1980 he produced *Breathing Underwater*, an instant classic.

The pace slackened as Jerry Moffatt moved on to greater things.
A new dynamism was needed and this arrived in the form of Andy
Pollitt. He spent weeks working on Little Plum and spotted the line
of *Easy Skanking* in 1984. *Virgin on the Loose* came later.
Protection bolts were placed; one of them which unfortunately
protected the previously unprotected crux of Flycatcher was a
retrograde step.

1984 gave Paul Mitchell three additions in the form of *You're Only
Mortal*, *Swine Vesicular* and *Scurvy Knave*.

Mark Pretty took over new route pioneering activities in 1985
having previously accompanied Neil Foster and Andy Pollitt on
their exploits. His additions include *The Disillusioned Brew
Machine*, *Stay Hungry* and *Jam Sandwich*; obviously a man pre-
occupied with food. Other hard routes done by pretty included
Big Nose, *Dead on Arrival* and *Hart Attack*.

In the middle of 1985 Quentin Fisher finally succeeded on the
original line of Scarab, often top-roped for practice not least by
Quentin. His phenomenally long reach must have played its part
in *All Systems Go*.

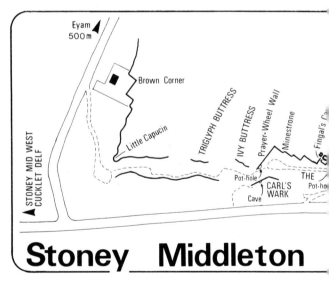

Stoney   Middleton

Early in 1986 Pretty managed to squeeze in another route on Garage Buttress – *La Belle et la Bete* and later in that year he added two more routes – *My Personal Pleasure*, which was subsequently straightened out by Craig Smith, and *Flavour of the Month*. All three routes are, at least, partly bolt-protected and it will be interesting to see if they survive the lifespan of this guidebook.

At the end of 1986 it takes a very clinical mind to classify the remaining rock into potential new routes or pointless variations. The gaps between routes grow smaller but larger in number as each new crop is harvested. Experienced Stoney watchers shake their heads in disbelief at what the future holds.

THE CLIMBS are described from RIGHT to LEFT as most people approach the cliffs from the village or cafe. A short way up the road on the right is a filling station. Just beyond this lurks Garage Buttress which houses the first routes.

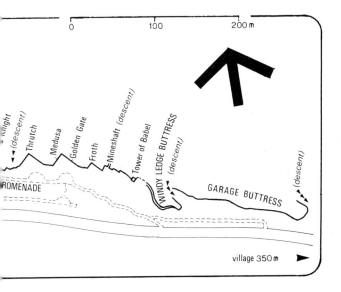

GARAGE BUTTRESS

There is a very obvious horizontal break running along its full
length at 20m height. This gives the first route, a classic of the
crag, which can be approached either from the easy gully on the
right of the buttress, or via the first pitch of Aquiline.

1   The Pendulum   90m   HVS   4c,4c,5a   ***
1. 36m. From the belay follow the break past several pegs and
threads, to a stance beneath an impressive jutting roof (Little
Plum).
2. 24m. Continue pleasantly along the break to a corner. Swing
left around a prow to an uncomfortable stance – The Saddle.
3. 30m. Traverse the break, with some difficulty in the central
section, to a point above a large yew tree. Reverse awkwardly to
the tree to finish (don't forget to protect the second!). Abseil
descent. Masochistic purists may continue the traverse, but this is
not recommended.   (1963)

*The next route starts up the first of two ribs on the right-hand side
of the buttress.*

2   Aquiline   48m   HVS   4b,5b   *
1. 36m. The rib is climbed for 7m until a rising traverse rightwards
leads to a short wall which is climbed to a tree. Move left and go
up to belay at the start of The Pendulum. Care is needed with the
rock.
2. 12m. Climb the wall on the left to a peg, then move steeply left
and go up into the finishing groove.   (1965)

Variation. 1a. 36m. 5a. The rib may be followed direct instead of
traversing right.

*The next route starts below the hanging bay just left of Aquiline.
Only those who have done everything else need apply!*

3   Ployed   36m   E4   6a
Climb steep grass to below a groove in the back of the bay. Hard
moves up this lead to a peg, and a treacherous exit left onto grass
and ivy. Climb the wall above to the break. Step right and pull
over the overhang at a rightward leaning arch, crux, peg. Finish
up the wall above past a sapling.   (1977)

The second rib gives the start of:

4 Evasor   45m   VS   4b,4c   ★★
One of the best lower grade routes at Stoney; well worth doing.
1. 18m. Climb slightly leftwards up ledges for 9m. Continue up the rib
to a tree belay. The rock is now mainly sound.
2. 27m. Climb up to the rake. Traverse left to the base of a steep
groove which is climbed to an overhang. Pull over this, then move
right in a fine position, to finish at a small tree.   (1965)

5 Atropos   60m   HVS   4b,5a,5a   ★
1. 18m. As for Evasor pitch one.
2. 30m. A traverse line leads out leftwards. Follow this at hand level
for 3m, then foot-traverse it for 10m to a small ledge (on Little Plum).
A swinging hand-traverse leads left to a stance below a groove, if
fate allows!
3. 12m. Traverse left round the arête to meet Rippemoff beneath its
crux bulge. Neatly, though illogically, avoid this by descending to a
grass ledge and peg belay.   (1967)

Variation 3a. A better finish is to climb the groove above the stance to
The Saddle (4b) and then finish up the top pitch of Rippemoff (5a).

*Round to the left is a large overhanging wall above a narrow ledge
system at about 12m. The left-hand end of the ledge is reached by
dirty scrambling and pull-ups on tree branches. The following route
starts from the right-hand end of the ledge. A peg belay exists at the
right end of the ledge which is the belay for the next two routes*

6 Flycatcher   45m   E4   5c   ★
Climb slightly rightwards from the ledge for 2m. Move up and then
left (bold) to below a groove. Pull awkwardly into the groove which
leads to a ledge. Step right and climb the tricky black flake to
Pendulum. Move 2m right and make unusual moves through the
overhang to reach the easier finishing groove. The bolt on 'Virgin' (or
not so virgin!) now protects the crux of the route.   (1977)

*The steep wall to the left sports two bolts, the line of a sustained
pitch. Start 2m left.*

7 Virgin on the Loose   18m   E6   6b
Gibber up the steep wall to a bolt. Make difficult and bold moves up
left to the second bolt. Pass this awkwardly to a peg. Abseil off.
                                                                    (1984)

19
18
16
15 13 11
10 8

Garage Buttress

Phillip Gibson

6   4   3   2

*Above the middle of the narrow ledge are two bolts at 6m. These
are frequently masked by an in situ climber (who will insist that he
is not resting) but, when visible, indicate the crux of the next
climb.*

8   Little Plum   30m   E6   6c,6b   ★★
A tremendous route with a desperate first pitch and an
exhilarating second pitch.
1. 18m. Make awkward moves up the shallow groove, to a bolt
equipped with an in-situ krab. Very hard moves right of this lead
to easier climbing above and a belay at the break.
2. 12m. Step left, then launch rightwards across the wild roof
hopefully to reach a niche on the lip. (Several pegs). Resist posing
unless still fresh, swing left and crawl up easier rock to finish.
                                                        (1963/1982)

9   Big Nose   15m   E4   6a   †
An exciting pitch through the bulge right of Little Plum's roof.
Belay as for Little Plum. Move right to a small groove just left of
Evasor, peg. Climb the left arête of the groove to a large sloping
hold. Move up and left to a small niche, cross a bulge to an easy
groove, then step left to finish as for Little Plum.   (1985)

10   Easy Skanking   36m   E6   6b,6a   ★★
The shallow groove left of Little Plum proves easier to gain than
Little Plum, but is then frightening above.
1. 19m. As for Little Plum to the bolts. Move out left with difficulty,
then boldly climb the shallow groove above. Easier climbing
reaches the break. Step left to a peg belay.
2. 17m. Go back right then straight up to the break then traverse
left and cross the roof just right of Gerremdown, peg, to finish
rightwards up an easier corner and loose wall.   (1984)

*The next seven routes all start from a grassy ledge 10m left of
Little Plum reached by a steep, well-worn scramble past trees and
rock steps. Peg belays.*

11   Gerremdown   27m   E3   4c,5b   ★★
A slightly devious approach – the original aided start is not yet
free – leads to an exciting roof on pitch 2. Start at the right-hand
end of the ledge.
1. 12m. Climb the groove to below the overhang, traverse right
(soportA) to belay on a large flake below a groove.

2. 15m. Climb the awkward groove to the break. Step right and attack the daunting roof to huge holds above. Cut loose (obligatory) and pull over to an easier groove. Wild.

(1960s/1970s)

12 Chewemoff 29m E3 5c,6a   *
The airy second pitch provides a fine finish.
1. 17m. Climb the groove as for Gerremdown but continue making a difficult exit left around the overhang to the break. Traverse 6m right to belay on The Saddle.
2. 12m. From a point just left of the arête move up, then right with difficulty, peg, to finish up an easier groove and wall.

(1968/1979)

A better finish is provided by:

13 Rippemoff 34m E1 5c,5a   **
An excellent route, low in its grade.
1. 17m. As for Chewemoff.
2. 17m. Move 2m left. Climb over the bulge onto the headwall where a thin crack leads to a finish up the groove on the right.

(1965/1971)

14 Pullemdown 24m E5 6a   †
A precarious and dangerous eliminate. Friends useful (in both senses of the word!). Do the first move of Gerremdown then swing right and climb the creaking flake to Gerremdown's traverse. Pull directly through the bulge above to Pendulum. Recompose, then pull onto the steep headwall which is climbed just left of a thin crack. Where this ends step left to a thin flake (crux) and finish direct.   (1983)

15 Helicon 22m E2 5c   *
Follow Chewemoff to the break. The right-hand of two obvious corners has a difficult start and a tricky finish on the top wall. (2 pegs).   (1963/1970)

16 Colonel Bogey 24m E4 6a   **
A good pitch following the wall and groove left of Helicon. Start from the ledge 5m left of Gerremdown. Climb the scary wall with a move rightwards to a flake. From the narrow ledge above step right, 2 pegs, and up into a shallow scoop which is gained with difficulty and followed to the break. Make a hard pull up to gain

the left-hand groove and climb it to its termination. Follow the
blunt rib just left to the top (or more easily move right to finish as
for Helicon).   (1979)

Variation
Two alternative starts are possible, though of somewhat different
standards.
a). (5a). Gain the narrow ledge by following Four Minute Tiler and
then traverse right to the pegs. 5a.
b). (6a). Start 2m right and reach blindly up right to good holds.
Boldly go up and left to the pegs. 6a.

17   La Belle et la Bete   28m   E5   6b   *
As for Colonel Bogey to the pegs. Move up and leftwards to gain
the break. Step right and pull through the bulge (bolt) to gain a
short hanging groove. Pull into this, crux, bolt, and then swing left
into Four Minute Tiler. Finish up this.   (1985/1986)

18   Four Minute Tiler   25m   E5   6b   **
An enjoyable (?) route up the bulging wall left of La Belle et la
Bete. Start 2m left of Colonel Bogey. Climb the shallow groove
and flake to the break. Step right and pull forcefully (or lunge)
through the bulge then go up to a thin break. Swing merrily right
for 3m and before strength fades pull up to good but poorly
'grouted' flakes. Continue direct up the awkward headwall, 2
pegs, to finish.   (1980)

19   Matrix   42m   E3   4a,5b
Start from the track about 25m left of the Gerremdown approach.
1. 21m. Climb steep grassy rock rightwards to a tree belay.
2. 21m. Traverse right along the ledge to a left-leaning groove
which leads to the break. Move up to an overlap, undercut right
and pull over on good holds, to a short groove. Traverse back left
into a short groove; climb this and finish direct up the precarious
headwall. A direct finish from the first short groove is possible but
not recommended.   (1970s)

*Left of Garage Buttress is a tower displaying a prominent groove.
To its right is a large yew tree at half-height and an unpleasant-
looking wall above. This gives three suitably unpleasant routes
which are impossible to grade (Scottish VS).*

20 Happy Wanderer 38m Choss E1
1. 21m. An unhappy start up chossy rock leads to the yew tree and belay.
2. 17m. Climb the wall just right of the tree, but left of the obvious leaning flakes above the break. Climb these flakes and pull over the small overhang onto the upper wall which is traversed left to finish.   (1970s)

21 Grotty Totty 40m Grot E1
1. 21m. As for Happy Wanderer.
2. 19m. Climb the wall left of the tree to the overhang. Pull over using the flakes above to an arête which is followed, passing a tree, to the top. Aptly named.   (1970s)

22 Ernie 38m Tot E1
1. 21m. As for Happy Wanderer.
2. 17m. Climb the back of the bay to the break. Move left, then pull over the bulge to finish up the slabby wall on the right.   (1970s)

The next two routes climb the aforementioned tower.

23 Compositae Groove 45m HVS 4a,5a   *
1. 27m. Climb grassy rock direct to a tree belay below the groove in the tower.
2. 18m. Step left into the base of the groove and climb it, 2 pegs, to a small overhang. Swing out left to the arête and go up to a tree belay. Escape by abseil.   (1961)

Variation
2a. (5b). It is possible to finish direct over the overhang (5b).

24 Ticket to the Underworld 45m E4 4a,5c
1. 28m. As for Compositae Groove, but belay on a tree just left.
2. 17m. Climb the wall via an awkward, slight groove just left of Compositae Groove, to a ledge on the right. Make difficult moves over the overhang, peg. Bold moves leftwards up the horrific hanging flakes above and a tricky exit right lead to a tree belay and an abseil escape.   (1979)

As well as Pendulum, Garage Buttress also has the following left to right high-level girdle. Most parties find the approach the most taxing part of the route. Either traverse right into the gully right of Compositae Groove, or, perhaps more easily, abseil into the start of the break if one is familiar with the topography of the buttress.

25   My Girdle is Killing Me   66m   E4   6a,5b
1. 33m. Traverse right on poor rock, past an old tree. Step down
into a faint groove then continue via an intricate hand-traverse to
a belay in the groove of Helicon. Several pegs. An enjoyable pitch.
2. 33m. Move up and make an exciting (especially for the second)
traverse right, with the break at foot-level, into Rippemoff. Move
down and continue round the arête to a yew tree. Traverse right
on poor rock to follow the final easy wall of Little Plum.

(1967/1979)

*To the left of the tower containing Compositae Groove are several
poor buttresses and towers which give several esoteric
nightmares and which may prove attractive practice grounds for
aspirant explorers of The Lost World.*

26   Leprosy   42m   VS   4c
1. 27m. Climb steep choss to a tree belay 9m left of Compositae
Groove.
2. 15m. Climb the wall and groove above the tree. Move right and
then go up past two pegs to the tree belay of Compositae. Well
named as something is always dropping off!   (1968)

*Left again is another tower just before a very poor buttress which
flanks the gully separating Garage Buttress and Windy Buttress.*

27   Blue Banana   24m   HVS   5a   †
Gain and climb a crack right of an obvious groove to an overhang
which is climbed on the right. Climb straight up a crack then finish
rightwards across the final wall.   (1964)

28   Pineapple   24m   HVS   5a   †
Climb the groove mentioned above, to an overhang. Follow this
and a crack above. Traverse right and again finish by moving
diagonally right.   (1960s)

The last buttress before Windy Buttress has two poor routes.

29   Elsanity   24m   HVS   5a   †
An effluent route for those round the bend with time to kill. On the
front face of the buttress, at the lowest level, is a corner which is
climbed by a crack to the overhang. Move right and climb the wall
and crack in the arête to finish.   (1978)

30 Scrubber 14m   HVS   5a   †
On the gully side of the buttress climb up to an arch which is
followed rightwards to finish up a groove. Needs a good clean
up.   (1978)

31 The Fluff Pirate 12m   HVS   5a   †
The obvious groove right of the descent gully. Move right at a
bulge to the finishing crack.   (1985)

WINDY BUTTRESS

*An excellent buttress giving some of the best and certainly the
most popular routes at Stoney, if not in the Peak. Above a steep
grassy bank is the obvious Windy Ledge, which is most easily
gained at the left-hand end. Below the right-hand end of the ledge
is a large corner. The first routes start on the left-hand side of the
easy descent gully, flanking the right-hand side of the buttress
above a small cave. This, the back entrance to Keyhole Cave, is
probably the least pleasant approach to Windy Ledge.*

32 King Kong 21m   HVS   5b
Start just left of the entrance to Keyhole Cave, about half-way up
the gully. Climb up a corner and crack over the bulge. Traverse
left into a finishing corner. An alternative finish takes a crack on
the right.   (1960s)

*A corner groove left of the cave is the next obvious feature. 2m
right of the groove is:*

33 Melting Pot 21m   E3   5c
Climb the crack to ledges. Move right, peg, and pull over the
overhang past a frightening hanging block. Follow a groove,
move right and then back leftwards to finish.   (1978)

34 Tiger Trot 9m   VD
This short traverse links the ledge below the large groove, with
Windy Ledge itself. Easy climbing in a very exciting position.
                                                      (pre-1960)

*On the right-hand side of Windy Buttress is a prominent arête
leading to an obvious groove at the right-hand end of the upper
buttress.*

35   Aurora   51m   VS   4c,4c   ★★★
A fine classic route – 'to the dawn it is dedicated'.
1. 30m. Just left of the base of the gully is a steep wall leading to the
right arête of a huge corner taken by Memnon. Climb this wall, past a
tricky move at 6m, onto a good ledge. Step left onto the arête and
climb this then move right and climb a wall to the top, belaying
below the groove. An exposed pitch with poor protection.
2. 21m. Bridge and jam the large groove to a point 6m from the top.
Move out left onto the exposed arête (The Altar) and continue airily
to the top. An inferior variation continues up the groove.   (1933

36   Aurora Arête   51m   HVS   4c,5a   ★
1. 30m. As for Aurora.
2. 21m. Step left onto the front face of the ridge. Climb the groove,
pegs, to an overhang which is passed awkwardly on the right.
Continue direct to The Altar and finish as for Aurora.   (1963

Left of the first pitch of Aurora a large corner rises from a grassy bay.

37   Racial Harmony   27m   E4   5c   ★
Climb the centre of the right wall to a peg then move up and right to a
second peg. Pause for a while then climb diagonally left to a small
overhang. Pull over this rightwards (crux) and finish up the cracked
upper wall to Tiger Trot.   (1978

38   Memnon   51m   E2   5b,5c   ★
1. 30m. Climb the large corner, peg, escape left and continue up
grass and rocks to Windy Ledge. A pleasant pitch in its own right.
2. 21m. At the extreme right-hand end of Windy Ledge is a groove.
Climb to an overhang and go over this with difficulty, pegs, then
move right to a finishing groove.   (1963

Aga   Variation 2a. 21m E3, 5c From the base of the groove on pitch 2
climb the wall on the right and the disgusting crack through the
rotten bulge, which leads to The Altar. Finish as for Aurora.
Appalling.

Variation. 2b. E3 5c. From the overhang on the normal climb step left
and climb a thin crack and wall.

39 Breathing Underwater   30m   E4   5c
From the left-hand end of the grassy ledge below Memnon, climb
an awkward shallow corner, finishing left past a poor peg and flail
up the grassy bank to Windy Ledge.   (1980)

40 You Are Only Mortal   33m   E4   6b
The cleaned wall left of Breathing Underwater gives good
climbing for a short distance then much grass to finish.   (1984)

*Round to the left of the Memnon bay is a slabby wall, almost
directly below the arête of Windhover.*

41 Orrid   36m   HS
1. 18m. Climb the slabby wall to a ledge and belay.
2. 18m. Traverse left and climb the wall and groove to Windy
Ledge. A contender for the worst route at Stoney but combined
with Choss it provides a limestone classic of its type!   (1960s)

42 Alcasan   135m   E2   4c,5b,5a,5c,5c,5b   ***
One of Derbyshire's classic expeditions giving interesting,
sustained climbing in a fine position.
1. 30m. 4c. As for pitch one of Aurora.
2. 30m. 5b. Climb the second pitch of Aurora as far as The Altar.
(Possible belay). Traverse left to a peg. Move down and make
some tricky moves, particularly for the second, left to the cave of
Our Father.
3. 14m. 5a. Traverse left into the corner and descend awkwardly
for 2m. Continue traversing left to belay round the arête on
Windhover.
4. 15m. 5c. Traverse left as for Armageddon then swing round
under the roofs to follow The Flakes to its belay.
5. 11m. 5c. Traverse left with difficulty, peg, and then make a
difficult sequence of moves down into the groove of Kellogg, past
2 pegs. Traverse across the wall into Kink. Belay.
6. 35m. 5b. Move left into the groove of Circe. Climb this for 3m
then move left around the arête. Continue across the wall in a
superb position to finish up the groove of Inquisitor.
                                                       (1964/1970s)

*The remainder of the routes on Windy Buttress start from Windy
Ledge itself and although they are approached from the left they
are described from RIGHT to LEFT.*

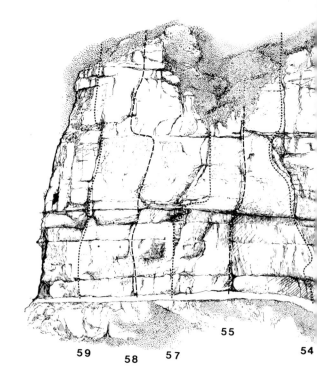

59   58   57   55   54

Windy Buttress

Philip Gibson

43   **Menopause**   24m   E5   6a,6b   ***
A fine route of some character which has already gone through the 'change of life'.
1. 15m. Just left of the second pitch of Memnon is an obvious hanging flake above a bulge. Climb the bulge and flake with difficulty to a break. Step left into Our Father and follow this to belay in the cave.
2. 9m. From the left-hand side of the cave make a series of powerful moves into the sadly short-lived hanging groove. This soon eases and leads to the top.   (1971/1980)

44   **Hysterectomy**   9m   E5   6c   *
A short technical test-piece starting from the cave. Pull out of the right-hand side of the cave and make hard moves to clip a peg. Technical climbing past this reaches better holds and the top. Normally protected by the first nut on Menopause pitch 2.
(1981)

The wall left of Menopause pitch one has a rightward slanting flake guarded by a roof – the line of the next route.

45   **Our Father**   24m   E4   6a,5a   ***
A celebrated route from the 1960s, which for some time gave the ultimate in difficulty and which still sees the odd quick pull on a sling!
1. 14m. Pull painfully round the overhang, with a prayer, and then precariously layback the flake to a peg. Traverse right to a second peg and gain the seemingly distant undercut above. Pull round the bulge and belay in the cave.
2. 10m. Step right, peg, and finish up a pleasant groove.   (1967)

Just left of Our Father is a niche 3m off the ground.

46   **Scoop Wall**   27m   E2   5c   ***
A superb route in a fine position – Stoney's classic route of this grade.
Climb to the niche, continue to a bulge, peg, then pull round it with difficulty. Climb the steep crack above to join the traverse line of Alcasan. Move up, peg, and step left across the wall (crux) to gain a wide finishing crack. A direct finish is possible at the same grade. It is also possible to split the pitch by belaying in the cave of Our Father.   (1955/1967)

Four metres left of Scoop Wall is a bottomless and well-named groove:

47 Choss 23m HVS 5b
Climb the steep wall to the groove which is followed to the overhang, peg. Traverse left then climb the wall to finish in the top groove of Windhover.   (1964)

48 Windhover 24m E2 5c   ★★★
An exhilarating climb up the exposed central arête of the buttress; which regularly used to repel VS leaders or push them beyond their limit. After the initial loose start the route is a sustained HVS, 5a.
Pull carefully round the oft-changing bulge, (peg sometimes in place), to a ledge. Step left and go up to another peg. Traverse right to the arête which is climbed on either side to a ledge, pegs (possible belay). Finish up the awkward crack above. The original, but inferior finish follows a corner right of the arête.
                                                   (1958/c 1960)

49 Armageddon 27m E2 5c   ★★★
Originally the 'living end' for VS leaders! Follow Windhover to the base of the final crack (possible belay), then traverse left to a short corner. Awkward moves up, 2 pegs, lead to a further traverse left in a superb position to a finishing crack. (Armageddon near the top!). The initial bulge of Windhover is still the crux.   (1964)

50 The Flakes 36m E2 5c,4c   ★★★
A superb outing with the distinct feel of being on a big crag.
1. 26m. Follow Windhover to the ledge at 5m. Move up then traverse left under the large overhangs. Make a couple of polished moves (a bit of fore-thought avoids an awkward hand change) to reach a belay on Kingdom Come.
2. 10m. Finish up the corner crack on the left or attempt:
                                                  (1964/1970s)

51 Flakes Direct 10m E2 5c   ★★★
A far superior finish. Just before the Kingdom Come belay climb the bulge above with difficulty, peg, to finish up the fine flake and crack above.   (1964)

52 Special K 26m E4 6a   ★★
Start about 4m left of Windhover. Make scary moves past a 'funny farm' nut runner through the initial bulge (crux) to a flake. Follow

the wall and short groove to the overhang which is crossed with abandon at its widest point on huge holds to reach Armageddon. Move left then up and back right to finish in a small groove.

(19

About 9m left is the front entrance to Keyhole Cave. Just left is the start of:

53   Kingdom Come   26m   E4   6a
The steep black wall and hanging groove are climbed boldly to a good hold and peg. Traverse right and gain an overhanging black flake groove which is followed to a cleaner corner and the top. Flakes Direct gives a much better finish. Harder for the short.

(1959/19

Left of Kingdom Come is a prominent hanging groove at 10m. This is taken by:

54   Kellogg   21m   E4   6b
Climb the hard wall above a painful landing (several variations) to a peg. A catching team is useful! Move up to below the roof, peg, go left to gain the groove with difficulty and follow it more easily to the top.

(1969/1974/19

Just left is a blind and smelly cave entrance below a crack.

55   Kink   15m   E5   6b
Climb the crack to the roof. Pull over the roof (threads) on painful jams and continue (crux) to the easier upper crack. Altogether a desperate affair.

(1951/19

To the left are two rightward-leaning grooves in the lower wall. The right-hand one gives:

56   Swine Vesicular   18m   E5   6b
Climb the right-hand groove to the top. Make hard moves up and left to join and finish up Circe. A wire linked to the peg on Circe provides protection for the crux.

(198

57   Circe   19m   E5   6a   *
A brilliant pitch to lure aspiring hardmen. (Circe transformed men into swine by a magic beverage. Beware The Moon!). Gain the left-hand groove by a difficult move and continue to 2 old bolts.

Dominic Lee on Kink, Stoney Middleton.
Photo: Keith Sharples.

Move right then up and right to a hanging block (crux). Pull up
and undercut strenuously rightwards to exit round the bulge.
Follow the easier groove above to finish. Easier for the tall.
(1963/1977)

Just left of Circe is a niche in the middle of the wall. This is:

58   Dies Irae   24m   E2   5c   ★★
Excellent climbing up an impressive bulging wall to the left of
Circe. Climb a steep crack and bulge to gain the niche. Move up to
a peg, move left, then climb the awkward brittle upper wall
finishing slightly rightwards. A wimpish finish is to traverse left
along Alcasan to join the top moves of Inquisitor.   (1963/1967)

Farther left is an obvious rightward facing groove high up.

59   Inquisitor   21m   E1   5c   ★
Make awkward moves up to a horizontal break. Pull up and
rightwards over the bulge, with difficulty, peg, to gain the groove.
Follow this escaping left at the top.   (1967)

60   Black Teddy   30m   E2   5c
As for Inquisitor to the roof, step right then use undercuts to gain
a blank wall leading to Alcasan. Traverse 4m right to a flake, and
climb this until it fades then step left to finish up a hairline crack.
(1979)

61   Do Nothing   18m   E3   5c   †
Follow Inquisitor to the roof. Pull round and follow the slim
groove to finish.   (1980)

62   Chantrelle   18m   E1   5a
Starting from the left-hand end of the ledge, climb the wall and
bulge to gain the left-facing groove. Finish up this.   (1960s)

BOULDERING
Apart from the classic routes on Windy Buttress there is also a fair
amount of bouldering. There is a long low-level traverse which
gives easy climbing from Circe to Windhover, then increasing
difficulty to Scoop Wall. The section of rock beneath Choss sports
many difficult problems. The roof just right of Our Father has a
few hideous problems including a nightmarish, tendon-snapping
one-finger deadhang (or pull-up!).

Neil Foster climbing Dies Irae, Stoney Middleton.
Photo: Foster Collection.

The next buttress left of Windy Buttress is the obvious semi-detached pinnacle known as **THE TOWER OF BABEL**. *On the right-hand side of the pinnacle is a rather dirty corner capped by an overhang. Right again is a loose vegetated arête containing a groove. This gives the next route.*

63   Truffle   15m   VS   4c
Climb the groove passing a small overhang. Continue up the crack above, peg.   (1965)

64   Revulva   21m   HVS   5b
The dirty corner just left guarded by a prickly bush is climbed after a difficult start. Pull over the overhang either on the right or left, to gain an easier corner and the top.   (1963/1976)

Last Stand, HVS 5a is a poor route just to the right of Revulva.

The next five routes start from the base of the tower's front face.

65   The Tower of Babel   33m   E1   5b
Climb the front face of the tower for 7m. Move right with difficulty into the obvious groove and follow this to the top.   (1957/1963)

66   Lucy Simmons   30m   E2   -,5b   ★★
A Stoney classic in a fine open position.
1. 7m. Climb the easy chimney on the left-hand side of the tower.
2. 23m. Move to the base of the right-hand of two grooves (Sin) and climb this to an obvious horizontal break at half-height. Swing right onto the exposed face and, without pulling too hard, climb it to the top. Becomes more overhanging each year!
                                                                (1967)

67   Sin   30m   VS   -,4c   ★★
A delightful jamming crack with a fine finish.
1. 7m. As for Lucy Simmons.
2. 23m. Move right to the foot of the right-hand groove. Climb this to the top by a mixture of bridging and jamming techniques.
                                                                (1952)

68   Glory Road   28m   VS   -,4b   ★★
1. 7m. As for Lucy Simmons.
2. 21m. Move up to and climb the awkward and highly polished left-hand groove.   (1951)

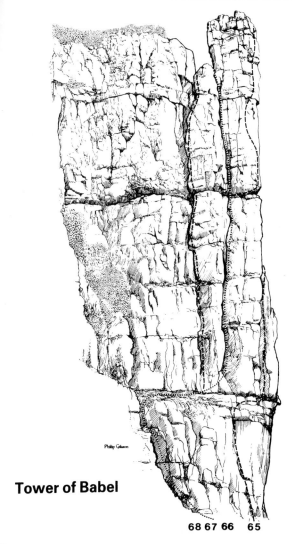

Philip Gibson

Tower of Babel

68 67 66   65

69 Babylon By-Pass   27m   HVS   4b
Climb the chimney and continue direct to a steep landing onto
grass. Finish up the corner above. A route well worth by-passing.
(pre-1961)

A rather trivial girdle traverse can be made along the horizontal
break.

There are several descents from the top of The Tower of Babel.
Either:-
i) Follow the path back into the jungle, and then traverse left
*(facing in) along a path to the top of **Mineshaft** which is an*
obvious easy gully leading to a Difficult chimney.
ii) Follow the path rightwards to the Windy Buttress descent
gully.
iii) By abseil from trees in the bay left of the tower (facing in).

THE PROMENADE

Below Windy Buttress a deeply-rutted cart track leaves the road
and passes through trees to a clearing. On leaving the trees, the
deep chimney of Mineshaft is seen back on the right. To the left of
this landmark is a series of right-angled bays finishing at the clean
Prayer Wheel Wall. Cars with armoured sumps may be driven to
that point.
Nine metres right of Mineshaft is a small cave entrance at 6m up.

70 Tantalus   35m   HS   4b
1. 15m. Climb to the cave. Traverse right to a groove which is
followed to a ledge and tree belay.
2. 20m. Traverse right to a clean groove. Climb this and finish up a
short chimney.

Variations
1a. A direct start is possible 9m right of the cave.
2a. It is also possible to finish directly above the tree. Harder.

71 Shellfish Shuffle   24m   S
Climb the slabby wall right of Mineshaft trending left at the top to
finish at the winding room.   (pre-1961)

72 A.N. Other   12m   E1   5c
The groove just right of Mineshaft is climbed direct.   (1970s)

*Immediately right of Mineshaft lurks the legendary Tom's Roof,
home of many of the Peak District's hardest boulder problems,
most based around a now very polished flake, araldited back to
the roof when it broke off many years ago. To sample the delights
of* **The Womb, Swing Thing** *and* **Power Allowance** *just follow the
billowing chalk amidst distant sounds from ghetto blasters.*

73   Mineshaft   24m   D
The obvious chimney is climbed by a combination of bridging
and chimneying to an easy gully finish. A popular descent,
though care is needed.   (pre-1900)
A variation follows the outer edge of the chimney at Severe.

74   Anything Corner   18m   VS   4b
The clean corner on the left edge of Mineshaft gives a pleasant
pitch.

75   Slab and Arête   19m   HVS   5a
Left again is an obvious sharp arête high up. Climb the slab left of
Mineshaft to a ledge. Move up a scoop then traverse right onto
the arête which is followed to the top.   (1970s)

76   From Here to There   36m   E1   5b
A fairly pointless girdle at the obvious half-height break leading
into the corner of Froth. Climb the large corner of Ivy Grotto Direct
for 4m. Make an awkward traverse left to a ledge and continue to
the arête. Swing round on a horizontal break which leads to a
poor resting ledge on Bitter Fingers. Continue traversing to
Mottled Wall which is followed to a ledge and iron stake belay.
Abseil descent or continue up Froth or Wallop.   (1975)

77   Ivy Grotto Direct   20m   HVS   5a
Follow the obvious steep corner direct to the top.   (pre-1961)

78   Hercules   17m   E4   5c   *
Start just left of Ivy Grotto Direct with difficult moves to stand on a
ledge. Boldly climb the wall above to pockets, then move
leftwards to a crack. Follow this to a difficult exit. A Stoney special
which gets the visitors gripped.   (1971)

79   Augean   21m   VS   4c   *
Left of Ivy Grotto Direct and just before the arête is a crack. Climb
the crack and niche to a ledge on the arête. Finish up a crack just
left of the arête.   (1964)

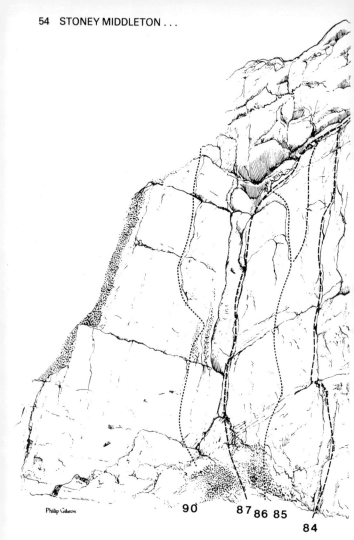

Dead Banana Bay

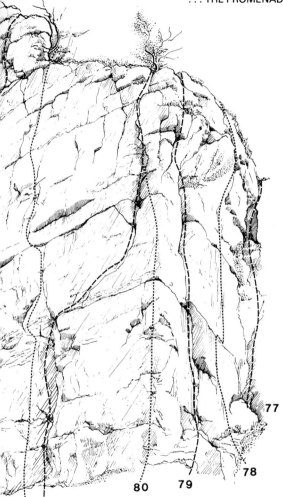

77

78

80 79

83 81

To the left is **DEAD BANANA BAY**

80   Beanstalk   18m   E3   5c
Climb the arête left of Augean on its left side with difficult but
reasonably protected moves at half-height. Finish as for Fe Fi Fo
Fum.   (1971)

81   Fe Fi Fo Fum   18m   HVS   5a   ★★
3m left of the arête of Beanstalk is a flake crack. Follow this
rightwards to a wide crack finish. Good steep climbing.   (1964)

82   Okra   20m   E4   5c
From the Fe Fi Fo Fum traverse move left and go up to the break
on Bitterfingers. Move slightly right and boldly finish up the wall.
                                                                                        (1980s)

*To the left of Fe Fi Fo Fum is an indefinite crack with a peg runner
at 7m. This is:*

83   Bitter Fingers   22m   E4   6a   ★★★
A Stoney test-piece. Climb the wall to an obvious undercut. Make
tricky moves right to the thin crack and pass the peg with difficulty
(crux). Swing left along the break, have one yourself, then follow
a flake to an overlap. Pass this with difficulty to an easier finish
through a small roof.   (1976)

84   Dead Banana Crack   24m   E1   5c   ★★★
A fine route up the steep wall. Climb the wall just left of Bitter
Fingers to a break. Make difficult, though safe, moves left and go
up to the crackline. Follow this direct to the big break above and
then traverse rightwards to finish as for Bitter Fingers.
                                                                                   (1965/1968)
Variations
1a. The Flakes on the right are an easier alternative.
1b. The original finish traverses the break left to a small tree.
Stand gingerly on this and climb the headwall leftwards into a
corner which leads to the top.

85   Mingtled Wall   9m   E2   5c
The short, thin crack left of Dead Banana Crack can be approached
from that route or, perhaps more logically, from Mottled Wall. At
the overhang traverse right to finish as for Dead Banana Crack.
                                                                                        (1983)

86 Mottled Wall 18m E4 5c
Climb the wall 3m right of the large corner with difficult,
unprotected moves past the horizontal break. Follow the easier
groove above to the belay ledge on Froth. Side runners in Dead
Banana give fewer 'E' points but greater peace of mind.   (1976)

87 Froth 33m VS 4b,4c   ★★
A vintage classic with an exciting traverse high above the big
wall.
1. 18m. Climb the large corner direct to the ledge.
2. 15m. Traverse right along the quartz frieze, passing the small
tree, to a niche and peg. Gain and climb the worrying wall above
to a tree belay or continue rightwards at 4b. Easy ground leads to
the top.   (1959)

88 Wallop 24m HS 4b   ★
Follow Froth to the ledge then escape left to finish.   (1959)

89 The Rainbow Woman 20m E3 6a
For some curious reason the thin, horizontal break in the wall left
of Froth is hand-traversed past a peg from right to left.   (1984)

90 Belinda 18m E4 6a   ★
Follow the thin crack 2m left of Froth to a break. The shallow
groove above leads to a break and the top. Traditionally climbed
with side runners at an easier grade (E3).   (1974)

91 My Personal Pleasure 19m E5 6c
2m left again. Gain a thin crack, past a bolt, then go up to a break
(2 pegs). Move up and right to a good hold (bolt). Pull straight up
above this by one of a variety of subterfuges to a faint break. Step
left onto the arête and finish up this. An easier and more obvious
6b variation is to move onto the arête lower down.   (1986)

92 Flavour of the Month 9m E4 6b
Climb the pocketed wall and thin crack just to the left of My
Personal Pleasure, with one bolt.   (1986)

93 Bluefinger 27m VS 4c
The groove in the arête is followed to a large ledge. Grovel up a
vegetated corner to finish.   (1968)

Left of the arête is a large sycamore close to the wall.

94 Stheno 30m VS 4c,4a
1. 15m. Climb the wall behind the tree into a rightward facing groove. Climb the groove to a ledge then follow the corner above to a large ledge and tree belay on the left.
2. 15m. Follow the large crack above to the top.   (1968)

95 The Year of Living Dangerously 30m E4 5c
Round to the left of Stheno is a slabby strip of rock. Grovel up to this. Climb a thin crack in the slab to a break, then climb the slab above to the final scary moves.   (1986)

Just left is a steep wall with an obvious undercut 'eye' at 6m.

96 Kelly's Eye 15m E4 6a   ★
Climb the wall to the flake. Pass this to a rounded ledge, swing left (taking care not to touch the chipped hold!) and gain the break. The thin crack just right gives an intricate finish. Low in the grade.
          (1979)

97 Mindblind 15m E5 6b   †
The shallow groove between Kelly's Eye and Bingo Wall, for many years a top-rope problem, has now been led.   (1984)

98 Bingo Wall 30m E2 5b,4c   ★★
1. 15m. Climb the crack just right of the chimney, to the eye and overhang. Rock left onto the ramp and reach the horizontal. Step right and climb the wall to a ledge and tree belay. Fine balance climbing.
2. 15m. Climb the wall behind the tree, pulling leftwards over a small overhang and finishing via the amazing knobbly wall.
          (1966)

99 Golden Gate 36m HVS 5a,4b   ★★★
A classic route which is one of the best easier routes on the crag.
1. 18m. Climb the deep chimney crack (tree runner) then make awkward, very polished moves up and right to the tree belay on Kelly's Eye.
2. 18m. Traverse left along the ledge to the main corner. Continue traversing left in a fine position, climb a slight pillar and finish up the exposed arête.   (1950)

100 Hinges 33m E1 5a,4b
A greasy and poor route.
1. 18m. Follow Golden Gate for 10m then traverse right onto the slab. Climb this a few feet left of Bingo Wall to the tree belay.

2. 15m. Move left, then follow the wide crack to the top. Now very mossy indeed!   (1976)

101   Bay of Pigs   30m   E1   5b
Climb the wall just right of the large corner to a tree, usually greasy and mossy. Follow the awkward crack above to the ledge of Golden Gate. Peg belay. Finish up Hinges.   (1976)

102   Frisco Bay   30m   VS   4c,4c   ★★
1. 18m. Climb to the tree as for Bay of Pigs, then step left into the main corner. Follow this with a difficult exit onto the ledge.
2. 12m. Finish direct up the open corner. The corner can be started direct, though this is harder and less pleasant.   (1952)

To the left is the steep **WEE DORIS WALL**.

103   Pickpocket   33m   E4   6a,4c   ★★★
Steep and fingery climbing leads to an easier finish.
1. 20m. Climb the wall and thin crack 4m left of the corner to a difficult exit onto a ramp. Gingerly climb it to a ledge using large pockets. (Possible belay). The thin crack on the left is followed, with difficulty, to Golden Gate.
2. 13m. Traverse right to the corner which is climbed for a couple of metres. Traverse left to a thin crack which is followed to the top.   (1967/1976)

104   Gesemini   30m   HVS   5a   ★★
Climb the obvious crack to a tree stump at 4m. Follow the crack above to a break, swing awkwardly right to the right-hand crack and follow this to the top. The direct start is E3, 6a.   (1964/1977)

105   Medusa   24m   HVS   5a   ★★★
A good old-fashioned crack which yields to traditional techniques. Climb the crack as for Gesemini then continue directly up the steep, wide crack. Finish slightly to the right.   (1961)

106   Wee Doris   18m   E4   5c   ★★★
A classic which is unfortunately becoming very polished. Follow the vague scoop in the wall 3m left of Medusa making an awkward step right onto a ledge. Follow the steep crack past the overlap, then go-for-it up the wall to a nose-grinding and dirty finish. Strenuous.   (1967)

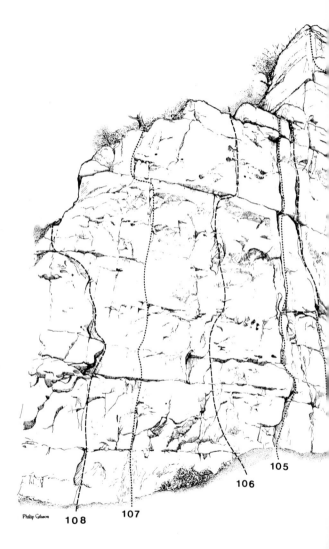

Philip Gibson **108** **107** **106** **105**

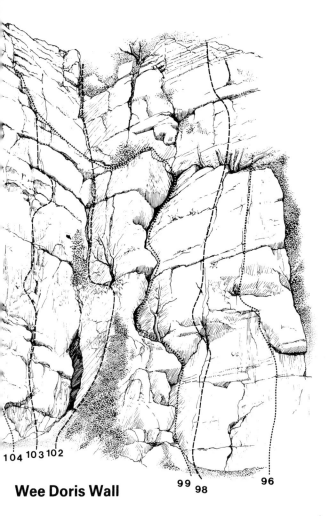

104 103 102

99 98   96

Wee Doris Wall

107   Boat Pusher's Wall   18m   E3   5c
Climb the wall just left of the start of Wee Doris to a ledge at mid-height. Intriguing moves gain the break. Step left then go up into a short finishing groove. Good climbing but very serious.

(1966)

108   Sickle   12m   E1   5a
Start just left and climb the wall onto a ramp. Move awkwardly left then go up to finish.

(1965)

The wall to the left is **Whet** E2, 5b, †, (1985)

109   Hammer   9m   HS   4b
Climb the wall 4m right of the arête, finishing up a shallow groove.

(1970s)

110   Syntax Error   42m   E2   5c,4c
1. 30m. Traverse the obvious horizontal break at half-height from left to right with difficult moves to gain Pickpocket.
2. 12m. Finish up the corner as for Frisco Bay.

(1974)

The wall also has a popular low-level girdle as well as many 'up' problems.

Descents from this wall are best made down a steep stepped path above Wee Doris. Care is needed, especially in wet weather as it would be all too easy to slide over the edge.

Just around the arête left of Hammer is a short bulging wall known as **GEORGE'S WALL**. *It has several difficult boulder problems.*

The next bay is the last of the three surrounded by trees.

The right wall of the bay was once taken by the classic **My Hovercraft is full of Eels** though the ivy has once more taken over. The legend, however, lives on.

111   Blisters   17m   HVS   5b
Climb the vegetated right wall of the bay.

(1976)

This wall is split by a ledge at half-height. Above Blisters is:

112 Crutch   E1   6a
Hobble up the short, tricky wall which is quickly being climbed by the ivy.

113 Thrutch   20m   HVS   5a
Climb the main corner of the bay to a ledge. Continue up until a nasty mantelshelf right can be made. Continue easily to the top.
(1952)

114 Pygmies Walk Tall   24m   HVS   5b   *
Follow Thrutch to the ledge. Traverse diagonally left across the wall to an overhang. Climb this and a second overhang to reach a horizontal break. Move right on this to a finishing groove.
(1967/1970s)

115 The Flashing Fisher   20m   E3   5c
The wall left of Pygmies Walk Tall is climbed on pockets, moving left past a peg. Worthwhile.
(1984)

116 Cointreau   20m   VS   4c
Climb the obvious steep jamming crack 5m left of Thrutch to a ledge. Continue up the corner, past ledges, to the top.   (1970s)

117 Double Scotch   18m   E2   5b
Climb the thin crack just left with spirit and some difficulty at first.
(1960s)

118 Traffic Jam   19m   E5   6a   **
A classic pumper. Follow the wall just left of Double Scotch to a prominent ledge. Continue up and right via a ramp to slots which lead left to a short thin crack. Fingery moves past this reach the break and an easier finish. The wall to the right of the crack can also be climbed at E5, 6b.
(1979)

119 Jam Sandwich   18m   E5   6b   *
The narrow wall left of Traffic Jam submits to a technical approach. Climb direct with escalating difficulty, two pegs, to a swing leftwards on large pockets just below the top.   (1985)

120 Minus Ten   15m   VS   4c   *
The fine jamming crack to the left is now somewhat the worse for wear. The scene of many exciting falls.
(1959)

121   Great Escape   15m   HVS   5b
A pointless traverse of the horizontal break from Minus Ten to
Cointreau.   (1976)

122   Minus Wall   14m   HVS   5b
Start 3m left of Minus Ten and follow the thin crack and creaky
wall above.   (1960s)

The base of the Minus Ten Wall is probably Stoney's most
popular bouldering ground with various low-level traverses and
problems. The dedicated have been known to arrive armed with
blow torches to ensure all year round bouldering! A
reprehensible practice!

*To the left the trees finish and there is an easy descent before a
white tower with a large corner at its base* **PEARLY GATES
BUTTRESS**. *To the right of this is a second, smaller corner. The
next route starts at the arête right of the wall.*

123   Au Gratin   14m   HS   4a
Climb the arête with an awkward mantelshelf at 4m. Finish on the
right-hand side of the arête.   (pre-1960)

124   Roman Candle   14m   VS   4c
Climb the wall immediately left, direct to the arête which is
ascended on its left.   (1961)

125   Parachute   14m   HS   4a
A classic thrutch up the polished corner to the left.   (pre-1960)

126   St. Paul   14m   E3   5c
An eliminate line up the wall left of Parachute. Tricky at mid-
height.   (1982)

127   St. Peter   14m   E1   5c
The arête left of Parachute sports a perplexing overhang and a
glassy lustre. The crux can be tackled left or right of the arête.
                                                                              (1960s)

128   Solitaire   18m   E2   5b
The centre of Gabriel's right wall is poorly-protected. (HVS with a
side runner).   (1966)

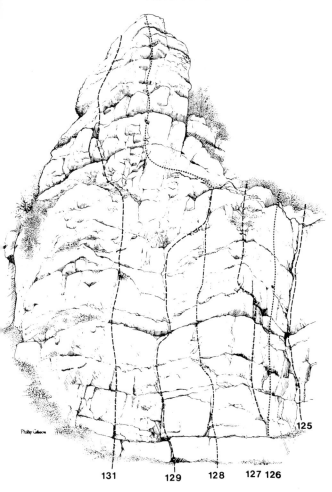

131   129   128   127 126   125

Pearly Gates Buttress

129 Gabriel   22m   VS   4c   ★★
The large corner is climbed direct to a ledge and peg. Traverse
delicately right towards the arête and finish just left of this. It is
better to continue straight up from the ledge on the right wall.
(1957)

130   The Pearly Gates   45m   VS   4c   ★★
1. 5m. Traverse easily left from the top of Gabriel to a ledge and
tree belay.
2. 18m. Climb a groove to a band of white rock. Move right to a
groove on the front arête of the tower, peg. Follow this in an
exposed position finishing left near the top. Originally called Cauli
Tower as a result of rank vegetation.   (1959)

Variations
1a. 4c. From the top of the corner of Gabriel climb the wall behind
the ledge to a traverse line which leads left into the groove on the
normal route.
2b. 4c. The wall right of the final groove may also be climbed.

131 Ben   30m   E2   5c
The centre of the left wall of Gabriel and the arête above are
climbed to join Pearly Gates at the white band. Traverse 3m left
and climb the wall above to the top (crux). A poor route.   (1970s)

132   The White Knight   30m   VD
1. 15m. Right of a large vertical shaft entrance (Fingal's Cave) is a
broken wall. Climb this moving right near the top to a ledge and
tree belay on the left.
2. 15m. Climb a groove in the centre of the face above to a
traverse left and an easy finish up a gully between two rock
towers.   (1933)

133   Scurvy Knave   9m   HVS   5b
Start up White Knight but continue straight up the wall just left of
a hanging bush. Bold.   (1984)

134   The Groper   27m   VS   4c,4b
1. 14m. Just right of the entrance to Fingal's Cave climb to a
blocky overhang which is passed on the right to a ledge and
belay.
2. 13m. Ascend the left-hand tower starting at the left corner and
finishing diagonally right.   (1960s)

Variation
1a. A harder variant is to move left at the block overhang.

*The next two routes take lines inside the large cave on the left and
the walls contain good traverses in dry conditions.*

135   Fingal's Cave   29m   VS   5a
1. 17m. Bridge up the inside of the cave close to the entrance to
gain the hole in the roof and belay.
2. 12m. Continue up the easy chimney.   (1933)

136   Fingal's Flue   29m   VS   4c
1. 17m. Climb the back of the cave to enter a black hole. Emerge
into another dimension. Often dangerously greasy.
2. 12m. Continue up the easy chimney as for Fingal's Cave.
                                                            (pre-1900)

137   The Crux   24m   HVS   5c
The thin crack just left of the entrance to Fingal's Cave.
                                                    (Traditional.)

138   Aux Bicyclettes   24m   VD
1. 14m. Climb the arête just left of the cave to a ledge and tree
belay.
2. 10m. Pedal up the crack above to finish.   (pre-1960)

139   Lost Horizon   24m   VD
Just left of Aux Bicyclettes climb the wall to a ledge. Move left and
mantelshelf into a corner. Traverse diagonally left to finish at the
top of Horizon.   (1957)

140   Juggernaut   30m   VS   5a
Start just left of Aux Bicyclettes and climb easy rock to a corner
which is followed to a peg. Move left with difficulty to a band of
white rock then move right to finish up a groove.   (1965)

141   Horizon   21m   VD
The right wall of the corner left of Juggernaut is climbed by the
line of least resistance finishing at the top of the corner.
Alternatively, though harder, the corner can be followed direct.
                                                            (1957)

142   Pollyanna   12m   E1   5b
The overhanging crack on the left wall of the corner gives a stiff
but worthwhile little climb.   (1960s)

Prayer Wheel Wall

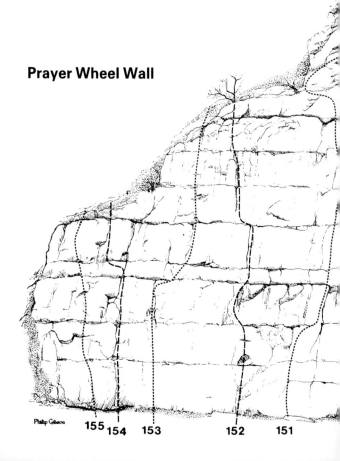

Philip Gibson

155 154 153 152 151

150 149   **148**   **145**

143   Jungle Arête   9m   VD
The loose left arête of Pollyanna is unattractive.   (1960s)

Left again is a further corner just where the crag re-emerges from the trees.

144   The Thorn   11m   VS   4c
On the right wall of the corner is a shallow groove. Climb this for 5m, move left onto the wall and climb to the top.   (1960s)

145   Rosehip Wine   18m   HS   4a
Go easily up to the base of the corner and climb this to a ledge. Step left and finish up another corner. Pleasant.   (1961)

The final bay comprises a steep clean back wall, Prayer Wheel Wall, with a hole in the ground, the refuge of numerous small troglodytes. The right-hand wall is more broken.

146   Minestrone   27m   HVS   5a
On the right-hand side of the right-hand wall is a steep little groove. Climb this (polished) to a small overhang. Step left to ledges which lead leftwards to the large corner of Asparagus. Finish up this.   (1957)

147   Vinegar Fly   18m   VS   5a
Climb the tricky wall between Cock-a-Leekie Wall and Minestrone. Step right and climb the arête right of Cock-a-Leekie finishing up the corner above.   (1979)

148   Cock-a-Leekie Wall   21m   E2   6a
Start just left of Vinegar Fly and climb the awkward wall to easier ledges. From the break above climb the short blank wall rightwards to easier ground. A must for Italian mountaineers. Variation finish, E4 6a †.   (1960s)

Robin E2, 5b Climb the wall and faint rib a couple of metres left of Cock-a-Leekie Wall.

149   Asparagus   21m   VS   4b
Climb the angle of the bay direct pausing only to view one's reflection in the holds. From a ledge move right and climb a short wall to a tree belay.   (pre-1960)

150 Looking Through Gary Gibson's Eyes 27m HVS 5a
Start up Asparagus but where that route goes right climb the
awkward wall trending left. Follow the groove above to finish
over an overhang. Better than it looks. (1979)

PRAYER WHEEL WALL

151 Padme 28m HVS 5a,4c ★★
1. 16m. Climb the shallow depression just left of Asparagus,
awkward, peg. Step left to a ledge and tree belay at the top. Most
people lose interest here but the top pitch is quite pleasant.
2. 12m. Move right from the ledge and climb a corner and
overhang to finish up a groove on the right. (1961)

A very poor eliminate has been squeezed in between Padme and
Mani.

152 Mani 15m E1 5b ★
Start just left of Padme at a hole. Climb direct passing an awkward
overlap. Move left and continue with interest to a tree belay.
(pre-1960)

153 This Wall! 12m E2 5b
Climb the wall between Mani and Om passing a thread. Loose
towards the top. (1979)

154 Om 9m HVS 5b
Climb the strenuous crack just left with one difficult move to
swing left just below the top. A test-piece at the grade.
(pre-1960/1963)

155 Omelette 9m E3 6a
Climb the wall above the hole just left with obvious trepidation.
Scrambling (!) remains. Side runners reduce a potential fall of
twice the height of the route. (1976)

156 Brassiere Strap 45m S
A real twangeroo and well worth (un-)doing! From the top of the
first pitch of Padme traverse right to large ledges just below the
top of Asparagus. Continue to Rosehip Wine at the same level.
Move up a few feet then go right to the top of Horizon. Descend
Lost Horizon for 6m then traverse right to Aux Bicyclettes.
Continue along a ledge and across to the top of Gabriel to finish.
Perseverance with the frustrating route-finding reveals hidden
delights. (1964)

CARL'S WARK

*Beneath the end of the Promenade and near road level is an area
known as Carl's Wark. This is approached either from the road,
via a steep track beneath Prayer Wheel Wall, or, for those of
speleological bent, via the aforementioned hole in the ground.
The climbs are described from RIGHT to LEFT.*

157 Shaky Crack 12m VD
On the right-hand end of the right wall is a flake. Follow this and
the wall above.   (1960s)

158 Soapsuds 12m E3 6a   *
Start in the centre of the wall 3m right of Green Crack. Move up to
a crack and pass the break. Continue direct via whatever holds
remain, passing a further break just below the top.   (1979)

159 Green Crack 14m VS 4c   *
The obvious corner crack gives an enjoyable pitch when dry. An
alternative finish, blinkers required, takes the crack just left at 5b.
                                                                   (1970s)

160 All Systems Go 14m E6 6c   *
The blank wall right of Scarab gives intricate climbing coupled
with a terrifying run-out. Follow Scarab to the break. Move up to a
thread, then climb the weakness above, ensuring all mistakes are
confined to the lower section. The thin crack above leads direct to
a darkened room! A bolt exists (without a hanger). This was not
used on the first ascent which was pre-practised on a top-rope.
                                                                   (1985)

161 Scarab 15m E6 6b   **
A very sustained and oft-changing test-piece. Start at a thin crack
or the flake just left of Green Crack. Climb the crack to a break and
swing strenuously left on this to a niche. Pull up and right to a
short thin crack, hastily arrange protection and sprint direct to the
break. Finish direct or via the crack to the right. Carl's Wark Crack
is out of bounds!   (1976/1979)

162 Carl's Wark Crack 14m E2 5c   **
The crack directly above the cave entrance gives sustained
climbing after a muddy start.   (1960s/1970s)

The Tower of Babel with climbers beginning Lucy Simmons, Stoney Middleton.
Photo: Chris Craggs.

163 Black Kabul 15m E5 6a
The wall left of Carl's Wark Crack leads boldly to the break. Step
right then climb the wall to a hole (large Friend). A long reach
gains a good fingerhold. Bold moves lead to the next break. Finish
direct with interest. Eminently more sensible with side-runners.
(1981)

164 Bubbles Wall 15m E3 6a ***
An excellent steep climb, the start providing the crux. Follow
Black Kabul to the break. Pull up past the niche then left to a
thread runner. Step left and climb the wall on pockets to the
break. Finish rightwards. A much easier start traverses in from
Flake and Pillar.
(1975)

Au Revoir Monodoigt E5, 6c, † – a finger-ripping problem up the
short wall left of Bubbles Wall, finishing at the break. (1986)

165 Flake and Pillar 14m E1 5b
The obvious line left again has a puzzling move at half-height.
Finish direct with trepidation.
(1970s)

166 Little Crack 6m VS 5a
The awkward thin crack just left of Flake and Pillar. (1970s)

167 Aerospace 24m HVS 4c *
An enjoyable and sustained high level girdle hand-traversing the
break from Little Crack to Shaky Crack.
(1979)

An excellent low-level traverse – **"The Jerry Traverse"** from Little
Crack to Bubbles Wall is possible.

*150m left of Carl's Wark is a small wall directly below the path to
the quarry. At the right-hand end of this is a cracked groove,*
Liquid Dream, *HVS, 5a (1986).*

*About 50m further left is a little tree-shrouded wall, home of the
esoteric:*

168 Costa Brava 7m HVS 5b
Follow the thin crack past old pegs.
(1980)

169 Just What the Doctor Ordered 7m E1 5b †
Climb the wall left of the ivy direct to the top finishing to the left of
the tree.
(1986)

Nigel Slater starting the "run out" on Wee Doris, Stoney Middleton.
Photo: Keith Sharples.

165

164 163

162

Carl's Wark

Philip Gibson

158

161   159

Returning to the same level as The Promenade a path skirts the hillside to the Quarry. Two buttresses overlook this path. The right-hand one is Ivy Buttress.

IVY BUTTRESS

The first route is on the front of the buttress.

170   Emanon   20m   HS
Start just right of the arête. Climb over the bulge via a crack and continue up a shallow corner to the top. Poor.   (1960s)

171   Child's Arête   20m   HVS   5a
Climb the obvious arête direct.   (1960s)

172   Marasmus   20m   E3   5c
The excellent-looking wall left of Child's Arête proves disappointing on closer acquaintance.   (1970s)

173   Naze   20m   VD
Start just left again. Climb the wall to a corner which is followed, finishing up a second corner.   (1957)

THE TRIGLYPH

The left-hand buttress, sporting several fine crack and groove lines.

174   Morning Crack   20m   S   *
Follow the right-hand crack direct to the top.   (1950)

175   What the Hell   26m   VS   4b   **
The central crack gives a fine route approached via a short wall.
                                                                        (1957)

176   How the Hell   26m   VS   4c   **
Start as for What the Hell but move into the left-hand crack.
Follow this exiting right at the top. Alternatively finish up the crack on the left or directly over the overhang.   (1950)

177   To Hell and Back   18m   E3   5b   †
A poor route up the arête between Who the Hell and How the Hell.
Climb the blunt rib to a break, step right almost into How the Hell, then swing back left to gain a dangerously loose flake. Stand on

this with trepidation, then make awkward moves right to a foot-ledge. Move up and trend left to finish. (1985)

178 Who the Hell   26m   E1   5c
Start on the grass bank 6m left of How the Hell. Climb the overhanging wall for 5m, move 3m right and climb a loose bulging wall to finish on the left side of the buttress. (1971)

To the left of The Triglyph is the prominent **MORTUARY STEPS BUTTRESS** *where the track swings right. This overlooks the junction of the main road with that of the Eyam road (B6521). The buttress has two faces, one overlooking the Eyam road while the other overlooks the main dale. Just before the main buttress is a smaller buttress with a tree covering its front.*

Diamonds and Rust, 11m, E2 5c follows the crack behind the tree. The wall is then climbed past a break, peg, to a scary finish. (1987)

To the left is the start of the main buttress.

179 Midi   30m   HVS   5a,5a
1. 18m. Climb the centre of the front face to a belay in the break below the main face.
2. 12m. Climb the short corner on the right and trend left to finish near the top of Little Capucin. Slightly loose. (1970s)

180 Little Capucin   30m   HVS   5a,5b
1. 18m. As for Midi, pitch one.
2. 12m. Follow the thin crack in the centre of the wall. Pleasant.
(pre-1960/1961/1975)

181 Cardiac Arrest   30m   E4   4a,6a   *
1. 18m. Climb to a large tree on the left arête of the buttress. Step left and go up an easy groove to belay in the break below an overhanging crack.
2. 12m. Step right to below a groove in the arête. Pull into this awkwardly and follow it leftwards to a break. Make a heart-stopping swing right, in an exciting position to finish up a thin crack. (1979)

Variation
Hart Attack 6b †. From where the route goes right continue direct through the bulges passing two pegs. (1985)

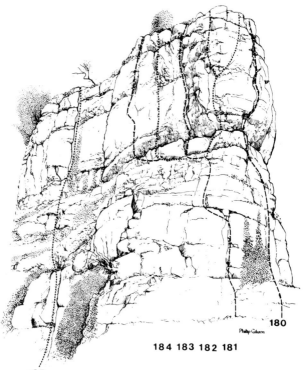

184 183 182 181

187

Mortuary Steps Buttress

182 Mortuary Steps 30m HVS 4a,5b   ★★
1. 18m. As for Cardiac Arrest pitch 1.
2. 12m. Climb the bulge to gain the prominent groove above.
Follow this, peg, to the top. Not a place for the faint hearted.
(1961)

183 The Morgue 30m E3 4a,5c   ★
1. 18m. Follow Cardiac Arrest pitch 1 but belay in the break 5m
left.

2. 12m. Pull round the bulge (scary) above the belay to gain a short layback crack. Follow this, peg, then step right to the continuation crack which is followed to the top. A stiff problem.
(1977/1981)

184   Speed Kills   30m   E4   4a,6a   ★★
1. 18m. As for The Morgue pitch 1.
2. 12m. To the left, a shallow, clean groove sports a peg tantalisingly out of reach. Gain this from the left and race past it with difficulty. Follow the groove to the top. A fine little problem.
(1977/1979)

185   Dome's Groove   30m   VS   4c,-
1. 18m. To the left is an obvious groove-cum-chimney in the upper wall. Climb the wall, crack and loose rock to belay below this.
2. 12m. Thrash up the appalling groove above (or don't, probably better).   (1963)

186   Dead on Arrival   30m   E4   5c   ★ †
A high-level girdle of the Mortuary Steps buttress gives enjoyable, airy climbing. Follow Dome's Groove to a rose bush 6m up the second pitch. Move up right, then traverse the break rightwards to Mortuary Steps. Step down and swing right on an obvious jug into Cardiac Arrest. Follow this out right to finish via Little Capucin. Care needed to prevent rope drag.   (1985)

187   Drainpipe Groove   30m   VS   4b,4c   ★
1. 18m. Left again is a corner. Climb this first on the right and then the left to a peg belay.
2. 12m. Climb loose rock to gain a cracked, leaking groove. Follow this to the top.   (1960s)

188   The Real Thing   30m   HVS   5a   ★
To the left is a rib between two ivy fields. Climb this to a white overhanging wall. Follow cracks through the overhangs and finish up a groove to an obvious tree.   (1979)

189   Ivy Groove   30m   VS   4c
1. 18m. Climb the grassy groove left of The Real Thing to a peg belay right of a blind groove.
2. 12m. Move left and climb the groove and crack above past a peg.   (1960s)

190   Gripple   27m   VS   4c
Left again is a shallow groove in the upper wall. This is reached
awkwardly via the wall below and right (peg on the right). Exit left
near the top of the groove to finish.   (1960s)

191   Aspirant Desperado   30m   S   4a
Just left are two corners. Climb the right-hand one to an overhang
which is passed on the right. Continue to a hawthorn tree then
traverse rightwards to the final wall. Never makes the grade.
                                                                   (1979)

192   The Slurper   30m   E1   5c,5b   **
1. 15m. Left again is a huge right-angled corner taken by Acrophobia.
Near the right edge of the right wall is a thin crack. Follow this,
rapidly easing, to a good ledge with peg belays.
2. 15m. Move left and climb a thin crack to a niche. Step left and
follow more broken rock to the top. Belay well back. A good route.
                                                              (1965/1970)

193   Easy Action   30m   E1   5b   *
A good sustained pitch more in keeping with the upper pitch of The
Slurper. Climb the centre of the steep right wall to a thin crack on the
right. Climb this strenuously with a tricky exit left to gain the ledge.
The Slurper crack gives a fitting finish.   (1976)

194   The Disillusioned Brew Machine   35m   E3   5c   †
Start from the belay above pitch one of The Slurper. Climb the
shallow scoop directly above to a small bulge. Move right and pull
over the bulge to finish up a dirty groove.   (1985)

195   J. Arthur   30m   E1   5b
Climb the groove right of the corner, then a thin crack before making
a rising traverse to belay on The Slurper. Finish as for that route.
Rank!   (1963)

196   Fallout   30m   HVS   5b
Start as for the previous route but continue direct passing a loose
bulge. Continue up easier ground.   (1970s)

197   Acrophobia   30m   HVS   5a   *
A satisfying route – but DON'T look down!
1. 21m. Climb the main corner passing a tricky bulge near the top.
Tree belays.
2. 9m. The clean groove on the left to finish.   (1963)

Philip Gibson

197 195   193 192

Slurper Wall

198   Prolapse   30m   S
Climb the corner in Acrophobia's left wall to the bulge. Finish by
traversing left as for Predator.   (1963)

199   Thirty-Four Candles   21m   HVS   5a
Climb shallow grooves behind a tree to gain an overhanging wall.
A rising traverse right to finish at an ash tree. An illuminating
problem.   (1970s)

200   Predator   30m   VD
Start right of a clean groove on the arête. Climb directly to a bulge
then traverse left passing trees to an easier finish.   (1963)

201   Pastoral Corner   24m   VS   4c
Climb the groove on the arête and continue through the bulge to
finish.   (1963)

202   Rubbish   24m   VS   4c
This aptly-named route takes the filthy groove left of the arête
where the ground drops to a lower level. Easier climbing to finish.
                                                                   (1963)

To the left is **THE QUARRY** *which has a sub-station in situ.* **The
sub-station is not to be used as a climbing wall.** *Since the last
guide the huge elm has been removed by an obliging feller to
leave one of the finest walls at Stoney. Just left of a fence in the
Lower Quarry is a corner. Starting immediately left is*:

203   Gollyberry   24m   E2   5c   ★
Climb the thin crack to the overhang. Pull round this then
scramble off left or abseil.   (1964/1970s)

204   Psychopath   24m   E1   5b
Follow the corner direct. Awkward at mid-height.   (1960s)

Just left is what is left of **Psycho** and the arête left again which
was once **Stupid Cupid**. Go to it new-routers!

205   Icarus   57m   E1   4a,5b,5a
1. 15m. Climb a wide crack 3m left of the arête to a ledge and tree
belay on the right.
2. 24m. Move left on easy rock then traverse a break across
deteriorating rock, peg, to Damocles. Continue left to belay in

Brown Corner. (Jumping into the large missing tree is no longer recommended!).

3. 18m. Continue along the break in a fine position to finish via Jasper.   (1964)

206   John Peel   30m   E2   5b   *
Start 6m left of Icarus. Climb the steep crack passing an awkward overhang. Step left and climb excitingly loose flakes and a short left-facing corner to the top.   (1965)

207   Emotional Rescue   35m   E5   6a   **
Climb the thin crack 5m left to a break. Move right and climb a further thin crack boldly to a peg, swing left and pass the bulge with difficulty until easier climbing leads to Icarus. Follow the corners leftwards to a ledge. Perplexing moves above this reach a break. Step right and finish up thin, twin cracks. An excellent, big pitch, low in the grade. The rescue may well be required on the upper section of this pitch.   (1980)

208   Damocles   30m   E3   5b   *
To the left is an imposing hanging crack. Gain this with trepidation and follow it passing an awkward overhang at 18m. Continue up the loose corner to a small tree belay near the edge.
                                                                (1963/1970s)

209   Brown Corner   26m   HVS   5a   ***
Superb when dry otherwise dreadful. Ascend the huge corner starting via a crack 3m right of the main corner.   (1961)

210   The Millionaire Touch   27m   E4   6b   ***
A brilliant pitch with a sustained lower section where a rapid approach pays dividends. 3m left of the corner is a tree stump. Climb the thin crack behind this to the overlap and step left to pull past a peg with difficulty then continue to the break. Move left to a further bulge which is passed by moving rightwards. Finish direct.   (1976/1980)

211   Oliver   24m   E4   6a   ***
A bold and strenuous pitch of high quality. Climb the black groove left of Millionaire Touch to a bulge. Move left and boldly climb the scary, awkward wall to a break. Step right and stand in the break, crux, to reach the traverse line of Icarus. Move left and up on quartz nodules finishing direct.   (1979)

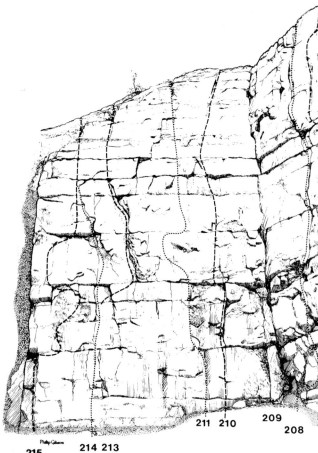

Philip Gibson

215   **214 213**   **211 210**   **209**
                                                        208

The Quarry

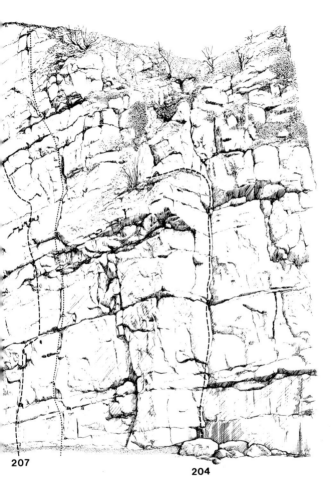

207   204

212   The Heat   22m   E5   6a   † †
To the left is a blank wall with a faint groove on its left side. Climb
this boldly to the break. Move left and do the crux of Jasper.
Swing out right then go direct up the right-facing corner to finish
as for Twist!   (1980)

213   Jasper   21m   E3   5c   ★★
Climb the awkward wall 5m right of the arête to an overhang, peg.
Swing right and make a hard move into the groove above. Climb
this finishing more easily up the wall above. An alternative direct
start follows the groove left of The Heat with a difficult start, 6a.
                                                                (1963/1975/1980)

214   Cabbage Crack   21m   E4   6a   ★★
Follow Jasper to the overhang and pull round this via a thin crack
to pass a further overhang with difficulty. Finish leftwards more
easily or better, go direct to join Jasper. A strenuous pitch.
                                                              (pre-1960/1979)

215   Helmut Schmitt   21m   E6   6b   ★★
Climb a tiny groove in the arête then swing right on the break. Go
up left, then back right to a prominent jug, peg. Move up to a
break, step left and pull round the overlap at a tiny corner. Gain
the final roof and round this with difficulty to finish as for
Cabbage Crack. Very sustained and strenuous. A direct start is 6c.
                                                                        (1980)

216   Roraima   21m   HVS   5b
Climb the left arête swinging left at 6m to finish on the left side.
                                                                       (1960s)

A long low-level traverse exists from the start of Oliver across to
Helmut Schmitt.

45m left is another bay.

217   Orang Utang   12m   HS
Climb two successive corners. A must for swingers.   (1970s)

*The remaining routes at Stoney Middleton are located on several
smaller buttresses beyond the Eyam junction. 50m past the
junction on the right (travelling towards Litton) is a small side
valley, hidden behind trees parallel to the Eyam road. This is:*

CUCKLET DELF

*The dale contains several rather poor buttresses. The first crags
are on the right looking in. There are two buttresses, the first of
which has two very obvious cracks.*

1 Right-Hand Crack 18m VS 4c   *
(1965)

2 Left-Hand Crack 18m S
(1965)

The second buttress is to the left.
On the right side of this buttress are hanging flakes.

Just Another Tricky Day, 16m, E3 6a †, starts left of Allergy at a
groove. Climb the groove to a roof and move round on to the wall.
Climb this and move right near the top to finish as for Allergy.
(1987)

3 Allergy 15m VS 4c
Climb the flakes, then oscillate right, go up and back left. Finish to
the right.   (1965)

4 The Trundler 18m VD
Follow the crack left of Allergy moving left to a tree. Move left and
climb a groove to finish.   (1965)

5 Snerp 14m VS 4c
Start at a groove 3m left of The Trundler. Climb the groove to a
niche and finish up the wall above trending left.   (1965)

On the left-hand side of the dale is an obvious buttress.

6 Tomarwa Groove 20m E1 5c
An obvious pinkish groove up the front face of the buttress leads
to an overhang finish. Two pegs. Worthwhile.   (1966)

7 Cucklet Delf Eliminate 21m HVS 5a
To the left of the previous route, climb directly up the
overhanging front face of the buttress to finish up a short crack.
Peg and thread.   (1977)

8   Candy Store Rock   21m   HVS   4c
On the left-hand side of the buttress is a groove. Climb it to a
bulge, step left and move up to a horizontal break. Move right and
climb up to a peg in the top bulge. Step left, and bridge onto a
convenient tree branch to finish over the bulge.   (1977)

*Returning to the main dale, the next climbs are found
immediately past the entrance to Cucklet Delf. This area is known
as Stoney West.*

STONEY WEST

History
by Geoff Milburn
In the Fifties the Rock and Ice climbers had plenty to think about
when they tackled the big lines on the main cliff at Stoney. Later,
in the Fifties, climbers such as Dave Johnson, Dave Mellor, Jack
Soper and friends spread farther along the crag but did not need
to look higher up the dale. It was only in 1961 when the
Manchester Gritstone Climbing Club visited Stoney that after two
or three minor routes they discovered the smaller cliffs at Stoney
West. Graham West led *Cave Crack* while the Baxter brothers
accounted for *Flaky Pastry* (long before Malc's baking days) and
Bay Rum. All the seven routes done at that time were written up
for the 1961 guide by Neil Parker who had led *Bayliff* during the
first onslaught.
Geoff Birtles visited the crag for *Patience* in 1964 and the same
year Bob Dearman climbed the fine route of Spiron. A year later
Paul Nunn and Oliver Woolcock found the line of *Swansong* as
well as *Devil's Eye*. Also in 1965 Brian Moore and Jim Ballard
climbed the only recorded artifical route on the crag, *Twang* an
A2. When work on the Northern Limestone guide was under way
in December 1965 and early 1966 the writers, Dave Nichol and
Brian Moore accounted for *Muscle Cock Crack*, *90cm Diédre*, *Cray
Pas* and *Ben Stirer*.
Over the next ten years nothing of any importance was done until
Tom Proctor freed Twang, and it was not until the 1980s that a
spate of hard routes was done. Paul Mitchell had the crag almost
to himself and in 1981 he climbed three hard routes – *Southerners
Can't Climb*, the fine *Northerners Can't Climb* and the slightly
confusingly named *Elective Affinities*. Mitchell departed for other
interests but returned in 1984 for *Prison Flower* and the difficult
Arbeit Macht Frei.

Finally in 1985 the crag was brought into the modern bouldering era when Quentin Fisher sieged the extremely difficult *Tequila Tory*. Undoubtedly other routes remain to be discovered.

The crag can be approached via a path up the bank just left of the entrance to Cucklet Delf. This leads to an obvious chimney/crack at the right-hand end of the cliffs

1 Flaky Pastry 14m S
Climb the shallow corner just right of the cave to the top. (1961)

2 Cave Crack 14m S
Ascend the outside edge of the cave direct. (1961)

3 Pot Full 17m VS 4c
The shallow groove in the cave's left rib. (1961)

4 Running Over 17m VS 4c
Just left of the overhang is a corner. Climb this, move right and up a crack, trending left to a chossy finish. Alternatively climb the arête left of Pot Full to join and finish up it. (1970s)

5 Bay Rum 18m VS 4c
Start in a shallow groove just left. Climb diagonally right to a thin crack. Continue up this to easier ground above. (1961)

6 Bayliff 18m VS 4b
The obvious clean straight crack left of Bay Rum is followed direct. (1961)

7 Swansong 21m HVS 4c ★
To the left is an obvious line of flakes running diagonally left to right. Move up and left to the flakes and follow them to a step onto the arête. Climb the arête and the groove above to finish. Pleasant. The crack just left can be taken as a direct start. (1965)

8 Horrorscope 21m E2 5c
Climb the thin crack just left to an overhang. Traverse 3m left to a further crack which is followed, past a hole, to a groove finish.
(1970s)

9 Fred 15m HVS 5a
The crack-line 6m right of the obvious flake crack is followed direct to the top past several 'Freds'. (1960s)

10   Postman's Meander   23m   D
Gain the obvious flake from the wall below. Follow it to a tree,
then traverse left to a corner which gives the finish.   (1961)

*To the left is an obvious tree at the top of the crag. Just below and
right of the tree is a prominent crack. Start beneath this.*

11   Rainsong   12m   HVS   5a
Climb a short groove and then move right to gain a right-facing
corner. Follow this and the crack over a bulge to finish.   (1977)

12   Elective Affinities   21m   E2   5c
Start 5m right of Southerners Can't Climb. Follow a short groove
and wall to a break. Traverse left to the arête and follow this to the
top.   (1981)

13   Southerners Can't Climb   21m   E2   5c   *
Start below and right of the prominent roof. Climb the wall with
tricky moves at 3m. Continue up to the roof. Swing left around it
to a strenuous pull onto a short blunt arête. Ascend this to finish.
A good pitch.   (1981)

14   Northerners Can't Climb   21m   E5   6a   **
Excellent climbing and quite bold. Start 3m left at a crack. From
this climb the interesting steep slab above to the roof. A difficult
move over this leads to blind climbing, crux, first left then back
right over a second bulge. Finish easily but with care.   (1981)

15   Spiron   27m   HVS   4c   *
Start to the left of Northerners Can't Climb. Move up a few feet
then follow a rising traverse rightwards to a ledge. Move left onto
the arête to finish. Worthwhile.   (1964)

*30m left is another buttress with an undercut base. A third of the
way up it on the right is a crack.*

16   Devil's Eye   18m   VS   4c
Traverse left from the grassy bank to gain and climb the crack.
                                                               (1965)

17   Arbeit Macht Frei   18m   E4   6b
Climb direct up the groove leading to the end of the Twang
traverse past 2 pegs. Finish up Devil's Eye.   (1984)

18 Tequila Tory   20m   E5   6c   ★ †
The blank wall bisecting the traverse of Twang has a fierce
boulder problem start and a sustained upper section. Start 3m
right of Twang. Crimp optimistically up the blank wall. Should the
traverse be reached, celebrate briefly, recompose and attack the
wall above to a difficult finish. For socialists only.   (1985)

19 Twang   21m   E3   5c   ★
On the front face of the buttress move up a large flake until an
awkward 5m traverse right is possible, thread. Difficult moves
lead to an overhang which is passed to a ledge. Step onto the
right arête and follow it to the top.   (1965/1976)

20 Turkey-Vulture Crack   21m   HVS   5b
A worthwhile route. Just left is an obvious crack and groove. This
is gained from the flake below and followed past an awkward
bulge to a ledge. Finish up the right arête or thrash left through
jungle.   (1960s)
A direct start is possible at 5c. (1987)

The horizontal break of the buttress can be traversed at HVS, 5b,
(1976).

*There are several buttresses on the hillside farther left. The first
worthwhile one has very prominent cracked blocks in its upper
half.*

21 Crazzled Cracks   14m   S
Climb the wall to gain the cracks which are followed to the top.
                                                              (1960s)

22 Muscle-Cock Crack   9m   S
This takes the weakness in the right-hand side of the next
buttress.   (1966)

23 Clean Crack   9m   S
Just left is this well-named crack.

24 90 Centimetre Diédre   9m   VS   4c
On the next buttress, climb a corner just right of ivy and finish up
a flake crack.   (1966)

25   Obvious Crack   12m   VS   4c
Takes the obvious line right of the chimney-crack in the well-positioned buttress to the left.   (1970s)

26   Cray-Pas   12m   VD
Climb the chimney-crack just left, finishing leftwards.   (1966)

27   Patience   9m   S
Climb the crack left of the ivy direct to the top.   (1964)

Left of a shallow gully is the final buttress.

28   The Grauncher   11m   VS   4c
The right-hand crack is followed direct.   (1960s)

29   Lefrack   14m   VS   4c
The left-hand crack.   (1960s)

30   Benstirer   15m   VD
An obvious crack-line left of Lefrack.   (1966)

Before the obvious right-hand bend on the main road is a wall at road level.

31   Poison Flowers   15m   E1   5b
Climb the centre of the wall.   (1984)

32   Black Bryony   15m   E1   5b
Ascend just left of Poison Flower.   (1984)

On the left of the main dale immediately after the right-hand bend is **Hidden Quarry**. *This houses two esoteric horrors.*

1   Sniffer Clarke   39m   HVS   5a   †
Climb the right-hand of two cracks on the big white buttress on the right of the quarry.   (1973)

2   Big Chiv   39m   E2   5b   †
Gain the hanging chimney-crack via a groove. Follow the crack to a finishing bay.   (1973)

STONEY MIDDLETON LIST OF FIRST ASCENTS

by Mike F Browell and Geoff Milburn

Pre-1900 **Mineshaft & Fingal's Flue**
Lead miners climbed these routes centuries ago but didn't grade or record them.
Re-ascended circa 1918 by J W Puttrell, H Bishop, D Yeomans, while exploring for caves. Fingal's Flue was recorded as Very Difficult, with 3 matches. 'Back and footwork well inside the cave leads with increasing difficulty to a comfortable dozing position in the roof.'

1933 **Aurora** F Elliott
An incredibly bold achievement, showing the vast potential for limestone climbing. The ascent of The Great Ridge was pictured in the Sheffield Telegraph. It was probably the top pitch only.
Three young men from the Nottingham area later fell from the climb; one was killed and the others badly injured — casting a dismal shadow over the crag.

1933 **Fingal's Cave** E Byne, C Moyer, F Elliott

1933 **The White Knight** E Byne, C Moyer, F Elliott
Various tentative explorations from these great gritstone pioneers, other lines not recorded. As was later to become common practice they bivouacked on Windy Ledge.

1950 Oct. **The Golden Gate** J Brown, S Sorrell, N Allen, D Chapman
Via a grassy finish — probably improved by J Soper in 1958. First of the recorded Valkyrie/early Rock & Ice routes.
'The position is hair-raising, out above the overhanging face with the rope swinging away across the gulf just like the cable of the famous bridge.'

1950s *Various other fine lines by J Brown and Valkyrie members. Not recorded; some around the Tower of Babel.*

1950   **Morning Crack**   J Brown, D Chapman
            The first of the stunningly obvious (to a gritstoner)
            Triglyph cracks.

1950   **How the Hell**   J Brown

1951   **Brown's Overhang/Kink** (A3)   J Brown, R Moseley
            A tough exercise in exposed aerobatics — their only
            excursion onto Windy Buttress.

            Pitons were an obvious resource and gave the
            necessary key to the next fifteen years' development
            at Stoney. Free-climbing potential also existed
            however while other limestone crags were the
            exclusive domain of peggers, Stoney retained a
            strongly competitive free tradition.

1951   **The Glory Road**   J Brown, R Moseley
            The first attack on the Tower of Babel. A route
            destined to be claimed and reclaimed by successive
            generations.

1952 Feb.   **Sin**   R Moseley
            Exceptionally Severe!
            'It is now apparent that the entire top spire of the
            Tower of Babel is detached and balances only on a
            fine point . . . '
            Rediscovered by D Mellor 1959.

1952   **Thrutch**   D Whillans

1952   **Frisco Bay**   D Whillans
            'Pursue a line of mantelshelves in the upper part of
            the angle. These are five acrobatic specimens,
            especially climbed so as to be too high for short men
            to reach and too narrow for big men to stand up on.'

            'The cliff had an almost evil reputation, forbidding
            appearance and bad rock being the major
            complaints'.
            No doubt this reputation was compounded by the
            Valkyrie/Rock & Ice mythology.

1952   **Little Capucin** (A1)   D Gray, J Ramsden
            Dennis had borrowed Arthur Dolphin's pegs and
            hammer and at the age of 15 he was making his first
            visit to the crag. 10-15 pitons were used.
            First free ascent by T Howard, P Fearnehough in
            1961.

1955   **Scoop Wall** (A1)   R Leeming
An attack on the scooped wall of Windy Buttress,
which used 12-15 pitons.
First free ascent by T Proctor, G Birtles in 1967.

1957   **The Tower of Babel** (A2)   J Childs, D Johnson
Sheffield University MC members beginning a three
year term of exploration, virtually ignorant of
previous climbs.
Reduced to 3 pegs by P Nunn, March 1961.
Free, B Moore circa 1963.

During the next three years, 40 new routes were
recorded; many had been ascended by the Valkyrie.
An armed invasion of the rocks took place. Ice axes,
shovels, choppers, coal rakes, yard brushes, pruning
shears, pokers — even a saw and butchers' knife
were used to penetrate the jungle.

1957   **Minestrone**   D Johnson, T Brooks, J Wade, J
Childs.
'Vegetation abounds — every conceivable plant —
even a Brussels sprout once grew from the head of
Minestrone'.

1957   **Horizon**   R Salt, Brenda Salt
Part of D Johnson's army, climbed on same day as
Minestrone.
Lost Horizon nearby was recorded but since
abandoned.

1957   **Child's Play** MS   J Child
Now abandoned, somewhere up on Ivy Buttress.

1957   **What the Hell**   J Soper, N Crowther, D Johnson,
ANO
More SUMC members, gritstone-trained.

1957   **Gabriel**   J Soper, N Crowther, D Johnson, ANO
'All horrible layaway things'.

This group climbed 'several other routes of fine
character', but not fine enough to record them.
Most other routes were climbed by D Mellor, D
Johnson with occasional shanghaied SUMC
members. Mellor was the first British climber
trained
solely on limestone.

1958 Dec.   **Windhover** (VS & A2)   D Mellor, D Johnson
*Climbed 'with the generous co-operation of the
Stockport potholers' — a splendid climax to the
year.
Several pegs were used.
'This route almost overhangs the road for 200
feet . . . '
More or less free by B Webb in 1960.*

1959 Feb.   **Kingdom Come** (A3)   D Mellor, D Johnson
*Pegging where no peggage existed.
First free ascent by J Kirk, P Kirk on 22 April 1978.*

1959 Spring   **Froth**   D Mellor, D Johnson

1959   **Wallop**   D Mellor, D Johnson

1959   **The Pearly Gates**   D Mellor, D Johnson
*This was Johnson's last route. He completed his
University studies and returned to Northumberland
leaving Stoney for posterity (and Eric's tea).*

1959   **Minus Ten**   D Mellor, D Johnson
*G Birtles created a variation finish by traversing
horizontally right,* **The Great Escape,** *1976.*

Other routes pre-1960, no first ascent details.

Cabbage Crack
*Written up but no grade – a futuristic eye for a line?
Later A2.
Aid reduced to 1 pt. by A Rouse in 1971.
First free ascent by T Proctor, J Kirk in 1979.*

Dandruff VD
*Avoids Little Capucin Tower – now abandoned.
'Dandruff, half a mile, Very Difficult . . . Under the
overhang traverse right along an obvious weakness
leading to exposed vertical scree, which showers
down like scurf. Press on diligently . . . '*

Evening Wall E   Abandoned

Valkyrie VS
*This may have been a variant on Golden Gate, also
climbed by Valkyrie members.*

Vegetation Wall S   Abandoned

Naze

Om (A1)
'A beginner's exercise in piton work. It gives few of the elementary limestone delights, blind cracks, a pastoral finish, a bit of loose rock etc.'

Mani (Aid)
'VS + one or two pegs'. Doubtful understatement – a fully-blown peg route!
'It is usual to climb the lower section with the first piton between one's teeth, as great difficulty may be found in trying to bring it to hand when it is needed!'

Padme
Written up but not climbed. Eventually done by B Webb in 1961
'Anyone who takes some ironmongery onto the climb will find sufficient cracks and will be rewarded with a fine new route of considerable length'.

Hum
A traverse of no great character – no grade!

Asparagus

Aux Bicyclette

The Groper VD with three matches
'On gaining a footing in the false roof, strike match number two to locate holds; this flame will blow out in the draught'.

Kaysor Bondor VD
A link pitch from Gabriel to The White Knight, now abandoned.

Parachute

Au Gratin

Cointreau HS
'A double hangover. The total overhang amounts to eighty feet'(!!) Has since suffered two big rockfalls, one when Pete Fieldsend fell with a monster block from the top. Fortunately he let go! The block stayed for years – 'Pete's Block'.'

Martin Atkinson starting Our Father, Stoney Middleton.
Photo: Bernard Newman.

Medusa
Written up but not climbed.
'There is no reason why it shouldn't be . . . .'

Ivy Grotto Direct

Shellfish Shuffle

Cutty
Variation on Shellfish Shuffle now abandoned.

Babylon-By-Pass

Tigertrot

Handy Groove
A mystery pitch – somewhere around Aurora and below Windy Ledge. This was the first pitch of what is now Memnon.

1961 July	**Rosehip Wine**	Manchester Gritstone Climbing Club

1961 July · **After Effects**   Manchester Gritstone Climbing Club
Near Rosehip Wine, now abandoned.

1961 July · **Roman Candle**   Manchester Gritstone Climbing Club

1961 · *These were all recorded in Graham West's guide in 1961 – 'Rock Climbs on the Mountain Limestone of Derbyshire'.*

1961 · *A visit by Graham West, Neil Parker and the Manchester Gritstone Club produced several climbs on West Stoney Middleton.*

1961 Sept. · **Flaky Pastry**   G Baxter

1961 Sept. · **Cave Crack**   G West, M Baxter

1961 Sept. · **Pot Full**   C 'The Praying Mantis' Phillpot, N Parker

1961 Sept. · **Bay Rum**   M Baxter, J 'Thin Jim' Hayes

1961 Sept. · **Bayliff**   N Parker, C Phillpot

1961 Sept. · **Postman's Meander**
Named after Jack Mason who was sent to the cottage at Glen Brittle to see if the boatman would ferry the lads round to Scavaig.

961 Sept.   **Ting-a-Ling Crack**
             (The latter is on the isolated buttress 100 yards west
             of the main crag.)

961   **Compositae Grooves**   B Webb, C Curtis
             The start of a brilliant series of additions by the new
             wave – post Mellor/Johnson.
             Free routes on limestone were exceptional at the
             time – Webb's foresight and brash disregard for
             tradition opened the door.

961   **Pology Wall/Padme**   B Webb, N Crowther, M Wild
             Sheffield & SUMC domination of development
             continued.

961   **Mortuary Steps**   B Webb, C Curtis
             Loose and precarious.

961   **Brown Corner** (2 pts.)   B Webb, C Curtis
             After a liberal intake of good beer. Two pegs used –
             the crack was choked with loose blocks and mud.

961   **Little Capucin** (1 pt.)   T Howard, P Fearnehough
             Nearly free, but not the present bottom pitch –
             cleaned and climbed in 1975 by C Jackson.

961   **Medusa**   L Millsom, M Rainey
             A long-standing problem.
             Attempting a repeat in 1964, G Birtles fell from the
             top and just missed the bottom.

962   *The Cioch Club had become established in Eric's*
             Cafe and in a hut at the end of the building –
             amongst them were Jack Street, Chris Jackson, John
             Atkinson, Brian Moore and Geoff Birtles.
             Street, fiercely competitive, dominated the Cioch but
             Jackson was the club's adventuring spirit and has
             sustained his enthusiasm over a twenty-five year
             span. Birtles the apprentice had a short life
             expectancy but miraculously escaped several hair-
             raising falls. 'Ackers' was the best technician.

963   *By 1963 Sin, Glory Road, Aurora, Froth and the*
             Triglyph cracks were accepted classics. Windhover
             became a top route for aspiring climbers to attempt
             free; other pitons were being eliminated. A typical
             weekend would find half a dozen climbers at Stoney
             – limestone climbing had definitely arrived!

1963 Jan. **Helicon** (A2)   R Dearman, G Hawker
Dearman was an SUMC member and committed to hard aid-climbing. A multi-day ascent.
Reputed to be 'the beginning of the last great phase of development' – thereafter the routes began to fall thick and fast.
First free ascent by J Street, P Nunn in 1970.

1963 **Om**   J Atkinson
Free but less intimidating – the cave wasn't there. It was opened up one day in the early Seventies by potholers.

Domes' Groove   C Crookes

1963 Spring **Damocles** (A2)   B Dearman, J Street, C Jackson
Reduced to one point by Birtles; freed by R Fawcett by 1976.

1963 **Rubbish**   J Street

1963 **J Arthur**   J Street

Several other climbs were put up in the quarry by this team and also some by Dave Nichols and Gerry Langsley, revealing the merits of climbing in a superficially unattractive place.

1963 Spring **Memnon** (2 pts.)   G Birtles, C Jackson

1963 Spring **Circe** (A2)   R Dearman, G Hawker
First free ascent by T Proctor, S Bancroft on 13 August 1977.

1963 Spring **Dies Irae** (A2)   R Dearman, G Hawker
First free ascent by T Proctor, M Peters in 1967.

1963 Sept. **Jasper** (3 pts.)   J Street, G Birtles
Three pegs – Street was beginning to establish a very effective technique.
Free, T Proctor 1975.
A massive flake fell off in 1980; climbed again by T Proctor, harder.

1963 Sept. **Aurora Arête** (2 pts.)   R Dearman
Crumbling but spectacular.

1963 Sept. **The Pendulum** (Aid) B Moore, P Fieldsend
Named because of the peels on the first ascent. A lot of aid used; climbed free by Street and Jackson. The first ascentionists couldn't have made more than a token attempt at free-climbing – they carried so much aid gear.

1963 **Revulva** (A1) B Moore
Free by G Regan, Spring 1976.

1963 Oct. **Little Plum** (A3) C Jackson, G Birtles
A five-day ascent, hampered by twice having to buy more pegs and lowering a rope and wooden-rung caving ladder to return to the high point.
First free ascent by J Moffatt in 1981-1982.

1964 Feb. **Icarus** J Street, G Birtles
Traverses were very much in vogue – this one involved a jump into a tree, a tea-break, and a jump back onto the rock.

1964 **Gollyberry** (A1) B Roe
Reduced to 1 rest point in mid-seventies, then freed by A Parkin.

1964 **The Flakes** (Aid) R Dearman, M Battersby
Aided, carrying an enormous amount of gear. Within weeks reduced to one peg by C Jackson; free in early Seventies. Pundits thought the flake would fall off. Direct Finish, one point of aid, added by G Birtles.

1964 **Brassiere Strap** C Jackson, J Atkinson

1964 Sept. **Fe Fi Fo Fum** B Moore, G Birtles
Hidden beneath the colossal ivy growth covering Dead Banana Wall – Ian Conway's six cylinder Vauxhall was used to drag it off!

1964 Sept. **Augean** B Moore, G Birtles
Also found beneath the ivy, choked with grot.

1964 Sept. **Gesemini** G Birtles, C Jackson
Direct start by Mark Stokes and Dave Humphries 6 March 1976; high side runner used.
After unsuccessfully trying to prove that the spelling should be 'Gethsemane' the Editor finally found 'Gesemini – the name of this route is Latin for the big toe on the right foot of a Chelsea Pensioner.'(!) 1966 Stoney Middleton Dale guide.

1964 **Alcasan** (5 pts.)   R Dearman, B Moore, C Jackson, J Ballard, G Birtles: various combinations
Dearman & Moore reached Kingdom Come with much loose rock and aid, largely dispensed with by Jackson and Ballard. Jackson and Moore extended by two pitches; final complete crossing by Jackson and Birtles, December 1964. Four pegs, three used in sequence to gain Kellogg. Freed in early Seventies, traditional.

1964 Autumn **Armageddon**   C Jackson, B Starkey
G Birtles' secret line – he's still weeping . . .

1964 **Choss**   J Street, C Jackson
Two routes at the opposite end of the pleasantness spectrum.

1964 **Blue Banana**   C Smith, B Moore, J Street

1964 **Patience**   G Birtles

1964 **Spiron**   R Dearman, M White

1964 **Devil's Eye**   P Nunn, O Woolcock

1964 Dec. **Swan Song**   P Nunn, O Woolcock

1965 Jan. **The Slurper** (2 pts.)   J Street, B Moore
First free ascent by the early Seventies.

1965 Jan. **Juggernaut**   B Moore

1965 Jan. 8 **Evasor** (5 pts.)   P Nunn, M Richardson
Nunn did the left-hand start with Janet Cox on 2 February 1965.

Cucklet Delf was discovered and a few routes were climbed.

1965 April **The Hex** (6 pts.)   J Street
The pitch was also started from the tree which has now gone.

1965 April **Sickle**   J Street

1965 April **John Peel**   J Street, John ??
So called because of the second's efforts to lead the climb.

1965 April **Rippemoff** (2 pts.)   C Jackson, G Birtles
Peg and nut for aid, free K Myhill 1971.

1965	**Left-Hand Crack** I Conway, D Nichols
1965	**Right-Hand Crack** I Conway, D Nichols
1965	**The Trundler** I Conway, D Nichols

1965 May **Sycamore Crack**   J Street
A good effort but poor tree-spotting – not a sycamore! It died of dutch elm disease in 1983.

1965 May **Dead Banana Crack**   J Street, C Jackson
One nut for aid eliminated by T Proctor in 1968. G Birtles and C Jackson found a bold direct finish by standing on the tree.

More very hard routes from Street. Almost certainly these were Derbyshire's hardest limestone climbs for the time.

1965 July **Aquiline** (1 pt.)   R Dearman, R Brown

1965 **Truffle**   C Jackson

1965 Dec. **Twang** (A2)   B Moore, J Ballard
First free ascent T Proctor in 1976.

1966 Jan. **Musclecock Crack**   D Nichols, R Bellamy

1966 Jan. **90cm Diédre**   D Nichols, R Bellamy

1966 Jan. **Cray Pas**   B Moore, L Arnold

1966 Jan. **Benstirer**   D Nichols

Stoney Middleton had by the mid-sixties become the focus of the Peak climbing scene, a position it still holds. Evening festivities were part of the myth; clubs active were the Parnassus, Cioch, Ripley, Black & Tans, Manchester Gritstone and Nottingham MC.

Geoff Birtles produced an Interim guide at the end of 1966 as the Northern Limestone volume was delayed.

1966 Aug. **Boat Pusher's Wall**   J Street
One of the hardest routes around – a very serious lead. A tied-off peg was later replaced by a hex which fitted the shot-hole precisely, but still serious.

1966 Aug. **Bingo Wall**   J Street

1966 Aug.   **Solitaire**   J Street
Solo!.
These were Street's final contributions before handing over to T Proctor.

1966   **Allergy**   C Jackson, R Conway

1966   **Snerp**   C Jackson, R Conway

1966   **Tomarwa Groove**   C Jackson, R Conway

1967   **Lucy Simmons**   T Proctor, G Birtles
The girl on the Pirelli calender.
Secretly practised on an abseil rope the previous weekend – Birtles was impressed!

1967   **Pickpocket** (2 pts.)   T Proctor, G Birtles
Peg and nut for aid; peg eliminated by A Parkin, Spring 1976.
First free ascent by R Fawcett, Spring 1977.
The route was soloed by M Stokes in the late Seventies.

1967   **Our Father**   T Proctor, G Birtles
A breakthrough in hard climbing – probably the hardest route in Britain at the time. Top climbers rushed to try it and many failed.
Four years before a repeat – Proctor's party-piece was to solo up in Hush Puppies and place the first protection for aspirants!
Eventually soloed by N Plishko and also by P Burke. The route has even been done at night with headtorches.

1967   **Dies Irae**   T Proctor, M Peters
Free.

1967   **Scoop Wall**   T Proctor, G Birtles
Free.

1967   **Pygmies Walk Tall** (1 pt.)   T Proctor, G Birtles
First free ascent in the early Seventies.

1967   **Wee Doris** (2 pts.)   T Proctor, C Winfield
Doris was a climber's wife who held the ropes. The route was practised on abseil. Two rests used.
'Rouse made the second ascent of Proctor's Wee Doris which is widely regarded as the most difficult problem on the crag.' Mountain 1971.

S Bancroft soloed the route in Summer 1975.

Proctor had arrived and was exploding the existing grading system. He free-climbed several hard aid-routes and developed audacious routes up un-peggable rock.
Climbers reeled in awe.
By constant vigilance and mid-week rehearsal, Proctor was to keep the crag within his personal control from 1966 to 1980.

1967	**Inquisitor** (Aid) G Birtles *First free ascent R Fawcett c1976.*	
1967	**Atropos** C Jackson, I Conway	
1967	**Upper Girdle of Garage Buttress/My Girdle is Killing Me** Originally aided by an unknown party *Led with four points of aid by K Myhill, T Proctor in 1969 then led free by T Proctor, G Birtles ten years later and eventually called My Girdle is Killing Me.*	
1968	**Chewemoff** (1 pt.) G Birtles, T Proctor *First free ascent T Proctor 1979.*	
1968 Feb.	**Stheno** N Elliott, C Winfield, P Newall	
1968 Feb.	**Bluefinger** N Elliott, C Winfield, P Newall	
1968 Feb.	**Bluetof** N Elliott, C Winfield, P Newall	
1968 April	**Leprosy** P Shine, R Cole	

Other routes climbed between 1960 – 1969, no first ascent details

Psycho

Psychopath
Both became harder when the transformer pen was built (?)

Pastoral Corner

Predator

Prolapse

Acrophobia

Gripple

Ivy Groove

Drainpipe Groove
The majority of these are probably the result of B Dearman, J Street, C Jackson, G Langsley and D Nichols exploitation in 1963.

Carl's Wark Crack (Aid)
First free ascent by 1969.

Green Crack

Shaky Crack

Autumn Leaves   R Dearman

The Thorn

Jungle Arête
Jungle Groove. A block came out.

Pollyanna   G Birtles

St Peter

Minus Wall

Double Scotch   M Barnicott
'Mouse' after a session in the pub.

Bluetof Direct

Kellogg (A2)

King Kong   T Proctor

Pineapple

Gerremdown (VS & A2)
10 pitons, 5 bolts and a sling.
First free ascent in the 1970s.

120 routes were included in The Northern Limestone Area guidebook, edited by Paul Nunn and published in 1969. The incredibly significant ascents by Tom Proctor were not mentioned in the history, however, due to a long delay in publication.

1969   **Kellogg**   T Proctor, G Birtles
Almost free. Originally an A2 ascended by unknown climbers. The route lost holds to peggers and was climbed with one rest by J Allen and S Bancroft, in August 1974.
First free ascent by 1978.

1970   **Helicon**   J Street, P Nunn
First free ascent.

1971   **Special K**   T Proctor, A Dawson
Repeated within three days by T King.

1971   **Cabbage Crack**   A Rouse
Reduced to one peg but ignored due to proximity to Jasper. Free 1979 by T Proctor shortly after Jasper's flake fell off making it independent.

1971   **Hercules**   T Proctor, T Rogers.

1971   **Beanstalk Arête**   T Proctor, G Birtles
In-situ runner removed.

1971   **Menopause** (Aid)   A Evans
With rope-climbers Z Dyslewicz, B Chisholm and a few more.
Some aid, freed on-sight by C Hamper 1980, beating Tom Proctor on his home ground.
After this route Tom went underground, making only occasional appearances until 1977.

1971   **Who the Hell**   K Myhill

1973   **Sniffer Clark**   T Proctor, G Birtles

1973   **Big Chiv**   T Proctor, G Birtles
'A particularly impressive lead by Proctor with a forty-foot overhanging chimney that makes Elder Crack look pathetic. The route has only minimal protection.'
Both Sniffer Clark and Big Chiv look hideous. Situated in Hidden Quarry these two routes must rank with the most serious on Peak Limestone.

1974 April 13   **Belinda**   J Allen, S Bancroft, N Stokes
More logical Direct Start by A Bailey, summer 1984.

1974 April   **Syntax Error** (2 pts.)   J Allen, S Bancroft, N Stokes
Two rests, freed by P O'Donovan.

1975   **Bubbles Wall**   T Proctor
Rapidly acclaimed as a classic.
Originally started left; Direct Start by T Proctor.

1976 Spring   **From Here to There**   G Regan, J Moran

1976   **Twang** T Proctor
                    First free ascent.

1976 April 19   **Omelette** S Bancroft
                    *J Reading also claimed the route in May.
                    A popular top-roped problem.*

1976 May   **Cool Hand Luke** A Evans, G Birtles, T Proctor, E
                    Marshall, M Taylor
                    An eliminate on Minus Wall – now abandoned.

1976 May   **Stupid Cupid** N Colton, J Tout
                    Fell down 2 weeks later.

1976 July   **The Millionaire Touch** G Birtles, T Proctor
                    *Peg used for rest, and a rest and belay in the tree
                    were possible. Climbed free by N Colton 1980. Now
                    an altogether different proposition with the massive
                    elm tree missing.*

1976 Aug. 12   **Bitter Fingers** G Regan, G Birtles
                    *A masterstroke, rapidly becoming a Peak District
                    testpiece.
                    An earlier attempt ended in a 30-foot crater.*

1976 Aug.   **Mottled Wall** G Regan
                    Runners were placed in Dead Banana Crack.

1976 Summer   **Scarab** (2 pts.) G Regan
                    *Two aid points used and two support teams
                    manipulating the ropes.
                    Freed via a left-hand variation by T Proctor in March
                    1979.
                    Standard has increased due to lost holds – a too
                    popular top-rope problem.*

1976 Aug. 16   **Blisters** A Evans
                    Roped solo.

1976 Aug. 16   **Hinges** A Evans
                    Roped solo.

1976   **Ben** M Taylor

1976   **The Great Escape** G Birtles, E Marshall, A Evans

1976   **Bluetof Super-Direct** J Regan, J Kirk

1976 Aug. 27   **Bay of Pigs** S Donnelly, J Tout, J Moran

1976 Autumn   **Easy Action**   D Knighton, A Bonnett

*Tales from this era are legion and it was a common
occurrence for large teams to bivvy on Windy Ledge.
On one memorable night Gabe Regan rolled over in
his sleeping bag and nearly dropped off the edge of
the ledge. Phil Burke on another occasion did just
that while stepping back to take a photograph.
Neither of these events however compares with the
day when Keith Myhill raced another climber to
reach Our Father. Rounding the corner near
Windhover Myhill overshot the ledge and
plummeted to the ground. A climber found him lying
on his back and urged him to stay put while he went
for help. Myhill quickly came round, stood up,
brushed himself down and limped off to The Moon
where he downed a drink and started a game of
arrows. Soon after, an ambulance raced past with
sirens blaring. Myhill paused, thoughtfully, and
commented "I wonder what's happened?" The
driver was not too pleased to discover that 'the body'
had gone.*

1977   **Speed Kills** (3 pts.)   R Dearman
Three pegs; freed by T Proctor 1979.

1977 April   **The Morgue**   R Dearman, A Evans
Freed by T Proctor in 1979.

1977   **Ployed**   T Proctor

1977 May 1   **Rain Song**   D Knighton
Aided and abetted by Janet Ault.

1977 May 22   **Cucklet Delf Eliminate**   C Carey, J Tout, D Knighton,
M Thompson

1977 May 22   **Candy Store Rock**   D Knighton, C Carey, J Tout
*Both routes on this day were top-roped prior to
leading.*

1977 Aug. 13   **Circe**   T Proctor, S Bancroft
*Free; an amazing ascent.
Birtles set a precedent when he placed a new bolt to
protect his own intended ascent. Proctor's own
attitude to placing permanent protection was
incredibly altruistic; he is renowned for returning to*

routes to replace pegs, threads or bolts as a public spirited gesture.

1977 Aug. 29	**Kink** T Proctor	

Some dubious tactics were needed to place gear while leading. The route was led clean shortly after by J Kirk.

1978   **Elsanity**   T Proctor, A Bailey

1978 July 23   **Flycatcher**   T Proctor, N Stokes, S Bancroft
Unrepeated until 1983 – too dangerous!

1978   **Scrubber**   T Proctor, A Bailey
Two poor routes.

1978   **Melting Pot**   T Proctor

1978 April 22   **Kingdom Come**   J Kirk, P Kirk
Free at last after many whittlings.

1978 April 22   **Racial Harmony**   T Proctor
Led placing pegs on the way, then abseiled down and put better ones in!
Retaliation on the Kirk brothers who 'stole' Kingdom Come ten minutes earlier.

A succession of desperates from Proctor – total domination of the crag!

1979   **Ticket to the Underworld**   T Proctor, E Marshall, J Kirk
Named after a footledge which collapsed while Kirk was seconding.

1979   **Kelly's Eye**   T Proctor, J Kirk
Tom wasn't averse to wielding a nifty hammer.

1979 March   **Traffic Jam**   T Proctor
Despite a big team of hopefuls, no-one could second it!

1979 Spring   **Colonel Bogey**   T Proctor

1979 Spring   **Oliver**   G Birtles
Practised for months. Blatant 'prised flake' in the middle of a blank wall.
Instant classic, often failed on. Now considerably harder, with several holds missing.

1979 Spring	**My Girdle is Killing Me** T Proctor, G Birtles *First free ascent of the High Level Girdle of Garage Buttress.*	
1979	**Cardiac Arrest** T Proctor, E Marshall *Direct finish added by M Pretty, J Hart, C Plant in 1985.*	
1979	**This Wall** J Regan, P Mitchell *(Route name censored.)*	
1979	**The Real Thing** C Jackson	
1979	**Aspirant Desperado** C Jackson	
1979 Autumn	**Black Teddy** G Birtles, T Proctor	
1979 Oct. 1	**Vinegar Fly** A Evans	
1979 Oct. 6	**Aerospace** A Evans, C Jackson, N Siddiqui	
1979 Oct. 13	**Looking Through Gary Gibson's Eyes** S Bancroft, A Evans, N Siddiqui, A Phizacklea and a cast of thousands *Evans used to have a retinue of groupies.*	
1979 Oct. 14	**Soapsuds** A Evans, S Bancroft, N Siddiqui, A Phizacklea, E Jones, C Gore, A Bailey, S Gascoyne, P Booth and others *First free ascent of Green Wall.*	
1980	**Four Minute Tiler** T Proctor *Said to be the state of the art at the time. Received high acclaim, repeated by the Lee brothers and rated 6c. Holds fell off; now back to 6b!*	
1980	*Northern Limestone guidebook published, encouraging a fresh spate of interest.*	

Other routes climbed between 1969 – 1980, first ascent details not known:

Happy Wanderer

Grotty Totty

Ernie E Marshall

Orrid

Chantrelle T Proctor

A N Other   T Proctor

Slab and Arête

Green Crack

Flake and Pillar   T Proctor

Little Crack

Child's Arête

Midi

Fallout

Thirty-Four Candles   R Conway

Sword   K Myhill

Roraima   T Proctor

Orang-Utang   J Cooper

1980   **Emotional Rescue**   S Bancroft, J Stevenson
Side runner in John Peel.
An old aid route now free.

1980   **Costa Brava**   A Barker, J Kirk

1980   **The Heat**   R Fawcett
An enigma, seldom if ever repeated.

1980   **Helmut Schmitt**   J Moffat
The beginning of Jerry Moffat's glittering career and
the finest of this crop.

1980 saw many of Stoney's most recent desperates
repeated. The pace was feverishly competitive with
so many Proctor myths to explode.

1980   **Breathing Underwater**   P Mitchell
Another instant classic.

1980   **Do Nothing**   G Jewson, T Sawbridge

1981   **Southerners Can't Climb**   P Mitchell, I Jones

1981   **Northerners Can't Climb**   P Mitchell (unseconded)

1981   **Elective Affinities**   P Mitchell, I Jones
A most confusing route name which has also been
known as Effective Affirmities. Selective Infirmities

has also been suggested as well as various combinations of the above words.

981	**Black Kabul**	J Moffat

981   **Hysterectomy**   J Moffat
Dubious tactics – a long in-situ sling clipped on first ascent was changed for a short one!

981/82   **Little Plum**   J Moffat, N Molnar
A leisurely free ascent, spread over two years. 'There exists no other pitch that is more out there'. Pitch 1 done with 1 pt. aid by G Birtles, J Kirk on 6 October 1979.

982 Spring   **Blinkers**   J Taylor

982 Aug. 24   **St. Paul**   P Cropper, N Siddiqui, D Campbell

983 May 8   **Mingtled Wall**   A Barker

983 Nov.   **Pullemdown**   N Foster, M Pretty

984 Feb. 18   **Arbeit Macht Frei**   P Mitchell
The route name means 'Work makes free'.

984 Spring   **Easy Skanking**   A Pollitt
Spotted and climbed during weeks of attempting Little Plum.

984 May 6   **Mindblind**   M A Mitchell, D Fernig

984 May 23   **You Are Only Mortal**   P Mitchell

984 June 7   **Poison Flowers**   P Mitchell (roped solo)

984 June 21   **Scurvy Knave**   P Mitchell

984 June 28   **Swine Vesicular**   P Mitchell, K Jones
Complicated runners.

984 Aug. 24   **The Flashing Fisher**   P Mitchell (unseconded)
Quent "accidentally" exposed himself outside the cafe.

984 Aug. 31   **Black Bryony**   C Plant, M Pretty

984 Nov. 5   **Virgin on the Loose**   A Pollitt, M Pretty
Controversial placing of two protection bolts – one now protects the previously unprotected crux of Flycatcher.

1985 Jan. 2	**The Rainbow Woman**	P Mitchell
1985 March 3	**The Disillusioned Brew Machine**	M Pretty, C Plant
1985 March 5	**The Fluff Pirate**	P Mitchell, J Hart
1985 March 7	**Dead on Arrival**	M Pretty, I Jones

High girdle around Mortuary Steps. Describes the state of the second.

1985 March 16 **Big Nose** M Pretty, C Plant

1985 April 17 **Hart Attack** M Pretty, C Plant, J Hart
Also known initially as Ventricular Fibrillation. Direct finish to Cardiac Arrest.

1985 April 20 **Jam Sandwich** M Pretty, B Moon, T Ryan

1985 June **All Systems Go** Q Fisher
Original line of Scarab, first top-roped by Jerry Moffat 1983.

1985 **To Hell and Back** R Conway

1985 **Tequila Tory** Q Fisher
A typical Quentin seige.

1986 Jan. 26 **Just What the Doctor Ordered** S Cundy (solo)

1986 March **Robin** (Unknown)

1986 May 27 **La Belle et la Bete** M Pretty
Supersedes Stay Hungry.

1981 June 1 **Au Revoir Monodoigt** D Cope
'Powerful and painful.'

1986 Oct. 26 **My Personal Pleasure** M Pretty, A Goring

1986 Oct. 29 **Flavour of the Month** M Pretty, A Goring, G Gibson

1986 Nov. 2 **The Year of Living Dangerously** M Pretty, A Goring, I French, C Wright

1987 Jan. 18 **Diamonds and Rust** S Cundy (unseconded)

1987 Jan. 20 **Just Another Tricky Day** S Cundy, A Shaw

1987 Jan. 20 **Turkey-Vulture Direct** S Cundy

STONEY MIDDLETON GRADED LIST

E6
Little Plum (6c,6b)
All Systems Go (6c)
Scarab (6b)
Easy Skanking (6b,6a)
Virgin on the Loose (6b)
Helmut Schmitt (6b)

E5
Tequila Tory (6c)
Au Revoir Monodoigt (6c)
Hysterectomy (6c)
My Personal Pleasure (6c)
Menopause (6a,6b)
Swine Vesicular (6b)
Kink (6b)
La Belle et la Bete (6b)
Jam Sandwich (6b)
Four Minute Tiler (6b)
Pullemdown (6a)
Black Kabul (6a)
Traffic Jam (6a)
Circe (6a)
Emotional Rescue (6a)

E4
Kellogg (6b)
Arbeit Macht Frei (6b)
Hart Attack (6b)
Flavour of the Month (6b)
You are Only Mortal (6b)
Kingdom Come (6a)
Oliver (6a)
Millionaire Touch (6a)
Speed Kills (6a)
Bitter Fingers (6a)
Ployed (5c)
Hercules (5c)
Flycatcher (5c)
Colonel Bogey (6a)

Our Father (6a)
Mottled Wall (5c)
Cabbage Crack (6a)
Big Nose (6a)
Kelly's Eye (6a)
Cardiac Arrest (6a)
Belinda (6a)
My Girdle (6a,5b)
Wee Doris (5c)
Pickpocket (6a)
Ticket to the Underworld (5c)
Racial Harmony (5c)
Dead on Arrival (5c)
Breathing Underwater (5c)
Special K (6a)

E3
Bubbles Wall (6a)
Soapsuds (6a)
Chewemoff (5c,6a)
The Rainbow Woman (6a)
Omlette (6a)
The Morgue (5c)
Jasper (5c)
Damocles (5b)
Gerremdown (5b)
To Hell and Back (5b)
Boat Pusher's Wall (5c)
The Flashing Fisher (5c)
Twang (5c)
Marasmus (5c)
Beanstalk (5c)
The Disillusioned Brew
Machine (5c)

E2
Cock-a-Leekie Wall (6a)
Syntax Error (5c)
Gollyberry (5c)
Scoop Wall (5c)

E2 (cont . . .)
Memnon (5b,5c)
Alcassan (5b,5c,5c,5b)
Dies Irae (5c)
Helicon (5c)
Flakes Direct (5c)
Black Teddy (5c)
The Flakes (5c)
Armageddon (5c)
Windhover (5c)
Mingtled Wall (5c)
Lucy Simmons (5b)
Carl's Wark Crack (5c)
Bingo Wall (5b)
Solitaire (5b)

E1
Crutch (6a)

Inquisitor (5c)
Dead Banana Crack (5c)
Who the Hell (5c)
Rippemoff 5c,5a
St Peter (5c)
John Peel (5b)
Psychopath (5b)
Easy Action (5b)
Flake and Pillar (5b)
From Here to There (5b)
Pollyanna (5b)
Mani (5b)
The Slurper 5c,5b
Double Scotch (5b)
J Arthur (5b)
The Tower of Babel (5b)
Chantrelle (5a)

HORSE-THIEF QUARRY

The small quarry on the right of the bend on the way to Horseshoe Quarry. The wall is well-brushed and has a tree on its right, and the routes are described from LEFT to RIGHT.

1   Golden Brown   10m   E3   6a
Climb the wall to a break, crux, then make a long reach for a hold. Go up leftwards to a peg belay. Abseil off.

2   Ghost in the Machine   10mE4   6b
Climb the wall right of Golden Brown to the break and finish up the wall to a peg belay.

3   Gothic Demarcation   10m   E4   6b
To the right climb the rib to loose rock and a move left to the peg belay of Ghost in the Machine.

HORSE-THIEF QUARRY LIST OF FIRST ASCENTS

1987 Jan. 2   **Ghost in the Machine**   T Coutts

1987 Jan. 2   **Golden Brown**   S Cundy

1987   **Gothic Demarcation**   T Coutts

All routes were top-roped first.

HORSESHOE QUARRY   O.S. ref. SK 205 761

by Mark Pretty and Dave Gregory

SITUATION and CHARACTER

This is the large quarry up the dale from Stoney West and it lies immediately north of the Stoney Middleton to Peak Forest road (the A 623). It is not marked on the 1:50,000 map but is clearly marked as Furness Quarry on the 1:25,000 White Peak map. It gives a unique environment for experienced climbers. The quarry has smooth rock faintly reminiscent of Avon's Main Wall. The Doodah Buttress and the right-hand section of The Upper Tier are composed of natural rock similar in character to parts of Stoney Middleton. The quarried sections are loose in varying degrees and while most routes have just the occasional loose hold some are terminally loose. These routes have been marked — **DO NOT CLIMB THEM!** The nature of the rock has dictated bolt protection on most of the routes, particularly on The Main Wall of The Lower Tier but even on these the occasional nut or Friend will be found useful. On a few of the routes the protection is completely natural.

APPROACHES and ACCESS

Driving from Stoney Middleton towards Peak Forest one should go past the Eyam turn off and past several minor rock bays on the right-hand side of the road, including one containing a caravan, until a drivable track cuts back on the right-hand side of the road. There is a small cave a little farther up on the right; this is Tom's Cave, where several problems exist, but it is best left for troglodytes. There is space to park about four cars on the side of this track without blocking it. Notices inform one of the presence of a deep quarry and the desirability of one's going no farther. In view of the owners' evident opposition to people using the quarry it is inviting complete exclusion to draw their antagonism by breaking open the gate which blocks the track. Follow the track past the gate; after 300m the track forks — The Upper Tier routes are approached by the right-hand fork, passing below the Doodah Buttress. The Lower Tier routes are approached via the left-hand fork across the huge quarry floor.

HISTORY

The earliest rumours of climbing in the quarry date back to the early Seventies when Tom Proctor and Geoff Birtles went looking for caves. Much later, in 1982, Chris Jackson, Bob Conway and Roy Small made a bizarre ascent of the classic mud route, *Chocolate Blancmange Gully*. Nothing then happened until Senan Hennessy set the ball rolling with his ascent of *Knight Rider* in September 1984. This was quickly followed by Chris Jackson's excellent *Legal Action* in the same year. There was then a slight lull until Mark Pretty repeated Legal Action and then produced several new routes: *Litany Against Fear, The Entropy Effect, Do Androids Dream of Electric Sheep?*, and *Hot Zipperty* (the first route not on the Main Wall). Ian Riddington climbed the unstable *School's Out* and then departed.

Several months later Ian French, Chris Wright and Steve France visited the crag after a tip-off from Ron Fawcett. They were impressed and in the winter months between them added many routes including *Rain Dance, Nice Face, Shame about the Ledge, Lost Monolith, The Esso Routes, Demolition Man, Into the Labyrinth, Private Prosecution, Megalithic Man, Smoke Gets in your Eyes, An Ancient Rhythm, The White Dove, Mr Blue Sky* and *Shot Yer Bolt*. Meanwhile others became interested, Malcolm Taylor and Darren Hawkins added a route each; *Cafe Bleu* and *Nijinski* respectively. Inspired by all the activity Pretty then returned and added *The Party Animal, Say It With Flowers* and *Rotund Rooley*. On the small Doodah Buttress, Steve Ralph gardened while leading (!) various easier but more esoteric delights. John Godding climbed *Conformist* and the difficult *Southern Man* and Steve France, while everyone was in France, added *While the Cat's Away*.

Next on the scene was Chris Jackson drawn back to see what was left; with Bob Conway he added *Like Ice, Like Fire, Dalkon Shield* and with Al Churcher *Order Number 59*. Other routes fell (often literally!) to other teams but nothing major was done apart from Nigel Slater adding *Dinky Toy* while Pretty returned and climbed *Heart to Heart*. Sadly since then many bolts have been stolen from the Main Wall so 'look before you leap'.

There seems to be little left but the crag will remain an interesting spot to climb for those who are esoterically minded and to be able to climb on warm, dry rock in winter is something not to be sneezed at!

THE CLIMBS

Chocolate Blancmange Gully   50m   Scottish IV   E4   or Jackson 1
This unique expedition takes the attractive mud slope at the extreme left-hand end of the quarry. Climb the mud slope until progress is blocked by a suspect boulder. Climb onto this, then transfer to the right wall of the gully. Follow a series of delectable mud bands and rock steps, trending right, until a final corner/flake can be gained to finish. A route which still stops many modern rock stars.

At the entrance to the quarry is an obvious white pinnacle on the left. This gives:

1   The White's Height   18m   VS   4c
Climb the crack in the left-hand side of the pinnacle to a death-defying finish.   (1986)

THE MAIN WALL OF THE LOWER TIER

This, the main location of the good climbing in the quarry, is the obvious south-facing wall on one's right as one enters the main quarry. Well left of this and facing in the opposite direction is a very overhanging wall containing some cracks. The left-hand one is:

2   Heart to Heart   13m   E4   6a
Climb the steep crack (wires!) to a bolt belay and descent.
                                                                         (1986)

Returning to the Main Wall the routes start at the arête at the left-hand end of the Main Wall just before it drops back into a broken corner, with broken, blocky cracks on its right wall. They work from LEFT to RIGHT.

3   Knight Rider   22m   HVS   5b   †
Climb loose blocks to gain the obvious crack in the arête. Follow this to the top. DO NOT CLIMB!   (1984)

4m right is a shattered ramp.

4   Rain Dance   25m   E4   6a   ★★
Climb the wall just left of the ramp direct past a peg and a bolt to
another peg. Difficult moves, crux, lead to a break. Move up and
right to another bolt then move up into School's Out to finish.

(1985)

5   Physical Fizz   21m   E4   6b
A direct finish to Rain Dance. Climb left of the last bolt on Rain
Dance to an overlap. Go over this to a bolt and then climb up and
left to a jug. Move right and up to finish.   (1986)

6   School's Out   23m   E3   5c
A terminal route which follows the wall about 5m right of the foot
of the shattered ramp. Climb the short wall, peg, to a tottering
ledge (the continuation of the ramp). Climb the thin crack with
trepidation, peg, to the top.   (1985)

7   Rotund Rooley   21m   E2   5c   ★
As for School's Out to the ledge. Climb the scoop just right of the
thin crack of School's Out finishing up the wall above, 3 bolts.

(1986)

6m right of the foot of the shattered ramp is a crack-line.

8   First Day of Winter   21m   HVS   5b
Follow the crack-line with slight deviations. The first 4m are the
crux. The rest is 5a. Natural protection.   (1986)

Not far right is a lead vein which runs the full height of the crag.

9   Wall of Jericho   23m   E3   6a
Start 2m left of the vein and climb through a slight bulge to a large
flake and Friends. Move up to a bolt. Some difficult moves past
this lead past two more bolts. Finish direct.   (1986)

10   Say it With Flowers   23m   E4   6a   ★
Start 2m right of the lead vein and climb up to a bolt then traverse
left to another bolt. Go up into a groove, crux, past a bolt to a
break, bolt and peg. Go up and left, bolt, to a jug then go up and
right to a peg. Step left and climb a thin crack in the headwall,
bolt, to finish.   (1986)

Neil Foster climbing towards Kingdom Come, Stoney Middleton.
Photo: Ian Smith.

11 Legal Action 22m E4 6a ★★
A direct line up the left-hand section of the Main Wall, giving bold, impressive climbing. Fortunately with the hardest moves next to the pegs. Start as for Say it With Flowers. Hard climbing leads to the second peg where moves right allow a rest to be taken. Move back left and make a series of mantelshelving moves past a peg until another peg is gained. Committing moves up lead to a bolt from which a swing right allows a break to be reached. Friends useful. Finish up a slight corner above. (1984)

12 Private Prosecution 22m E4 6b ★★★
An excellent and sustained pitch. Start 4m right of the lead vein below a large broken-off flake about 2m up and climb a small groove leading to a bulge, then make difficult moves above it, bolt. Continue direct up the wall past bolts and a peg.

(1985/1986)

13 Run For Your Wife 23m E4 6b
A variation finish to Private Prosecution. After the third bolt go straight up past 2 bolts to finish. (1987)

14 Litany Against Fear 25m E3 5c ★★
Start 3m right below a large hold at 2m height off a slab of broken concrete. Awkward moves up lead to two pegs. Go up and slightly right to a large juggy break. Swing left, 2 pegs, then make more awkward moves up and right to another peg. Move right to yet another peg. A difficult move up, crux, leads to a break (Friends 1 and 2). Step right then finish direct. An excellent pitch with an exciting finish. (1985)

15 Megalithic Man 22m E4 6a ★★
A few metres right is a large drill-hole fluting in the middle of the wall. Climb the wall past 2 bolts to a bolt just right of the fluting. Continue to the break then swing left to a bolt. Move rightwards with difficulty to a peg on An Ancient Rhythm, then follow this to finish. (1985)

16 An Ancient Rhythm 22m E4 6a ★★
An excellent pitch. Start midway between the Megalithic fluting and the next, more definite one, which is Shot Yer Bolt. Climb the wall right of a thin crack past a peg to a bolt. Climb slightly left then go up and right, bolt on the left. Pull straight up to a ledge. Move left and go up to a break. Climb the thin crack to the top passing a peg and with a heart stopping mantel near the top. Wires up to Rock 8 useful in the top crack. (1985)

Martin Veale finishing the crux sequence of Bitterfingers, Stoney Middleton.
Photo: Ian Smith.

17   Demolition Man   22m   E4   6b   *
2m left of the Shot Yer Bolt fluting is another bolt ladder. Follow
this direct with hard moves past the first bolt to gain a large ledge.
Step slightly left and make some difficult moves up and right to
finish. One of the hardest and most scary routes on the crag.
(1986)

18   Shot Yer Bolt   22m   E3   5c   **
To the right is a shallow groove with the definite drill-hole fluting
in the back of it. Climb the groove direct, bolts, to a ledge. Move
left up a ramp to a ledge, bolt. Step right and go up past a bolt and
peg to finish. Sustained.   (1986)

19   Southern Man   22m   E4   6b   *
Start below a brown scar 3m right of Shot Yer Bolt. This is
difficult, particularly for the short, and leads to a peg. Easier
climbing up the wall leads to a ledge (bolt runner on Shot Yer
Bolt). Step right and go up to a small overlap, pegs. Go over this
to a bolt then climb straight up the wall above with difficulty.
(1986)

20   Nice Face, Shame about the Ledge   22m   E3   6a   *
Start 6m right of Shot Yer Bolt below the centre of the ledge at
6m. This pleasant pitch first follows a shallow groove to a small
bulge, peg. Swing right then go up to a large ledge. Climb past a
bolt (crux, and probably 6b for the short) to a break, bolt. Climb
the flake above past another bolt finishing slightly right.   (1985)

21   Lost Monolith   20m   E3   6a
Start just right of Nice Face . . . and directly below a crack splitting
a large perched block. Climb up easy ledges to the perched block.
Bolt above. Ascend the crack, wires, to a bulge, bolt. Difficult
moves, crux, bring good holds and the top.   (1986)

22   Screwy Driver   21m   E1   5b
Follow Lost Monolith to the last bolt, step right, and climb a
shallow groove via its left wall to a peg. Move up to a bolt then go
up to a ledge using a crack on the right. Continue to finish up a
slight groove.   (1987)

23   Sunday Sport   15m   E3   5c
To the left of the Main Wall is a disgusting corner with a sapling at
its foot. 3m left is another cleaner corner. Climb this to jugs and a
double bolt belay. Abseil off.   (1987)

There are two routes on The Main Wall which are almost girdle traverses, both going from right to left.

24 Conformist 30m E2 6a   *
Start up Lost Monolith then go left to the bolt on Nice Face. Step left then go up awkwardly to a break, Friends. Traverse left into Shot Yer Bolt and climb this to a ledge. Go straight up, past a bolt, crux, right of Demolition man to finish.   (1986)

25 The French Connection 46m E4 6a   *
1. 25m. As for Conformist to the ledge. Bolt belay.
2. 35m 6a. Traverse left into An Ancient Rhythm, peg, then make difficult moves to a bolt, crux (Megalithic Man in reverse). Step down and hand-traverse into Litany Against Fear, 2 pegs. Move up and left into Private Prosecution, bolt, then make an awkward traverse into Legal Action, peg. Step left and finish up Say it with Flowers.   (1986)

The Main Wall of the Lower Tier is ended by a hanging rib just to the right. The crack and corner on its left are:

26 Spring Awakening 21m HVS 5a   *
Ethical protection.   (1986)

The next routes are on the less striking face which runs to the right from the Main Wall and which can be called:

THE RIGHT WING of THE LOWER TIER

27 Spectrophotometry 21m E1 5b
About 10m right is a slight groove leading to a more definite one about 8m up. This has a black right-hand wall with an old peg runner in a crack at its foot. Follow the two grooves. The lower section still has some doubtful rock.   (1986)

28 Like Ice, Like Fire 21m E1 5b   **
Start 2m right of Spectrophotometry behind some shrapnel battered elder bushes. Climb a flaky groove past two bolt runners and two sections of layaway moves on good but doubtful-looking flakes. Finish, with difficulty, over a small overhang.   (1986)

Immediately right is a groove, facing right, with a rusty-looking crack, containing streaks of lead ore in its corner.

29   Galening Crack   21m   E1   5b   *
The crack is followed direct.   (1986)

*About 12m right, approximately opposite the last of the concrete
structures, is a badly shattered rib with a small pinnacle at its
bottom left-hand side.*

30   Order Number 59   21m   E2   5c
Climb easy ledges to the pinnacle and then twin cracks above it to
a small roof. Cross this, bolt, moving right and then come back
left to climb the yellow overhanging headwall on good holds.
                                                                       (1986)

*Just right of the shattered rib is a small ground level cave (for
dwarves only). Just right of the cave is:-*

31   Dalkon Shield   21m   E3   5c
Climb the wall past two bolts and two pegs finishing up the right-
hand side of the upper wall.   (1986)

*Further right is a corner with no right-hand side wall in its lower
section but with a fine black slab on its right in the upper wall.
This is* 'Do Androids Dream of Electric Sheep?'

32   Blade-runner   21m   E2   5b
In the wall left of 'Androids etc' is a bottomless sentry box at half-
height. Start directly under this. Climb to a bolt at 5m and into the
sentry box. Peg. Traverse 1m right and move up to a second bolt.
Move left into the finishing groove.   (1986)

33   Do Androids Dream of Electric Sheep?   20m   E3   5c   *
Climb the groove with care to a small bulge. Pull over the bulge
then traverse out right and ascend the black wall passing a peg.
                                                                       (1985)

34   Gritstone Transplant   20m   HVS   5a
Halfway between 'Androids etc' and the cave farther right, at half-
height, from which the soil fan debouches is a wide crack. Follow
it to a finishing iron spike.   (1986)

35   The Man From Delmonte – He Says "Yes".   20m   HVS   5b
Start from the bottom left extremity of the soil fan and climb a
thin crack to a small roof (thread). Finish over this.   (1986)

Just after the fork in the track and slightly right of the left-hand fork is a small concrete bunker, this gives three surprisingly good boulder problems. From left to right they are: **The Arête**, 6c, **The Rib**, 6b, *and* **The Wall Between**, 6b.

THE UPPER TIER — THE DOODAH BUTTRESS

This is the small natural buttress above and to the right of the track which breaks off that which leads to the main quarry and swings round, above the Lower Tier, and below the Upper Tier. The routes are much slighter. They all finish on slightly doubtful rock and a grass slope which adds to the seriousness of the grades given. About 10m back are two iron stanchions giving excellent belays. The climbs are all about 10m high and are described from left to right.

36   Slabbering Slab   9m   VS   4c
Go up the left corner of the slab to a break. Traverse right 2m to a crack which is followed to a finish left.   (1986)

Right of the slab is a chimney.

37   Shetland Chimney   10m   VD
Start just right of the nasty chimney and climb to and up the groove.   (1986)

38   Chicken   10m   VS   4b
Climb just left of a totty pinnacle below the overhang up to the overhang. Move left under it and back right above it to finish.
(1986)

39   Liquid Engineering   10m   E2   6a
From under the overhang reach over to a hold by a peg runner. Make a hard pull-up to better holds. Heavy leaders beware, the overhang has cracks all round it.   (1986)

40   Little Damocles   10m   VS   4c
Start just right of the totty pinnacle and climb the shallow corner to the left-hand of two V-grooves through the overhang.   (1986)

41   Cob   10m   VS   4b
Start just right and climb the flaky crack to the right-hand V-groove.   (1986)

42   Footprint   10m   VD
The wide twisting crack at the left-hand side of a narrow face.
(1986)

43   Golden Tights   10m   VS   4b
The straight crack above the elder stump.   (1986)

44   Pot-washer's Wall   10m   HVS   5b   ★
Start 2m right of the straight crack and climb direct to the top.
(1986)

45   Hot Zipperty   10m   HVS   5a   ★
Start 2m left of Bimbo etc and climb the twisting cracks to the
crozzly wall and the groove in the skyline.   (1986)

46   Bimbo Has His Head Examined   10m   VS   4b
An awkward start and then wide bridging up to the small
overhang. Finish up the right-hand crack and the crozzly jugs to a
tree belay.   (1986)

47   Grockle's Gully   10m   VD
Climb the short wall into the recessed gully/groove.   (1986)

48   Gold Label   10m   VS   4c
Start in Grockle's Gully and move out right onto the hanging rib.
(1986)

*At the far right-hand end of the buttress is a corner, then two
cracks and an arête.*

49   Bimbo on the Loose   9m   S
The left-hand crack with a rotting tree at the top and a crumbly
finish. Rather esoteric.   (1986)

50   Bimbo drops his Codpiece   9m   VS   4c
The first crack right of Bimbo on the Loose.   (1986)

51   Bimbo's Off-day Route   9m   VD
The second crack right of Bimbo on the Loose.   (1986)

52   Bimbo's Arête   6m   VD
The arête at the right-hand of the crag.   (1986)

Continuing leftwards along the track the main section of the Upper Tier is quickly reached.

THE UPPER TIER — THE MAIN FACE

This line of cliffs is above The Main Wall and is somewhat shorter and less appealing. However, towards the right-hand end and above some railway sleepers is an attractive looking slab of natural rock. The routes on it are described from RIGHT to LEFT.

53 Dinky Toy 10m E4 6a
The groove and hairline crack at the right-hand side of the slab. 2 pegs. Double bolt belay to rope off.   (1986)

54 Cafe Bleu 10m E3 6a   *
Climb faint cracks just to the left in the steep black slab to a double bolt belay or rope-off. Abseil descent. Good climbing but quite serious at the start (RPs essential).   (1985)

55 The Party Animal 10m E2 6a
Climb the left-hand arête of Cafe Bleu past two bolts and a peg to a difficult final move to the abseil bolt.   (1985)

56 Easy Interloper 13m HS
The wide crack between the two slabs can be followed to the top of the tier.   (1986)

57 Nijinski 9m E2 5b   *
Follow the slab just left with a bold start and a delicate traverse left. (Nut protection).   (1985)

10m left of Nijinski is an obvious brown corner facing left.
58 Bimbo Strikes Again 15m S
Climb the obvious corner to the top and a distant tree belay.

About 25m left of Nijinski is a definite arête. This is 'Smoke Gets In Your Eyes'. 4m right of this is a steep white wall.

59 Blue Sunday 15m E2 5c
Ascend the steep white wall past 3 bolts and a peg to a ledge below the top. The crux move is to reach the top from the ledge without using the tatt on the final bolt which is used to bale out.
                                                                        (1986)

60   Esso Extra   16m   E2   5c
Start on the immediate right of the arête of Smoke Gets in your Eyes
and gain the groove just right of the arête (crux). Follow it to a large
ledge. Move up and left and finish up a shallow groove with small
flake handholds. Bolt belay to rope off.   (1986

61   Smoke Gets in your Eyes   14m   E3   6a
Climb up just right of the arête until a swing left past a bolt onto a
good foothold is possible. Layback the arête facing right past a peg to
a ledge. Finish as for Esso Extra.   (1985

62   Esso Blue   13m   HVS   5b
Climb the crack just left of Smoke etc to the ledge at the top. Finish as
for Esso Extra.

63   Mr. Blue Sky   13m   E4   6b
3m left is a steep slab. Climb this direct past two bolts to the ledge.
Finish as for Esso Extra. A sustained and excellent little route.   (1986

20m left is a large overhang at 8m with a grotty corner at its right-han
side. Running up to the left-hand side of the overhang is a thin crack.

64   P.M.'s Question Time   16m   E3   5c
Climb the thin crack to the small pod in the bulge, peg. Move up and
right to a small overlap, bolt. Climb direct to finish, crux.
                                                            (1986

5m left of P.M.'s etc and opposite the first of a pair of circular piles of
stones used as belays for the Main Wall routes is a groove facing right
capped by two brown flakes.

65   Supplementary Question   18m   HVS   5a
Climb the broken wall below and slightly right of the groove and move
left into the groove. Follow it to the top.

66   White Dove   1m   E2   5c
About 7m left of P.M.'s etc is a prominent white buttress with a thin
crack leading to a blocky overlap. Follow the crack with nut protection
                                                            (1986

67   Into the Labyrinth   15m   E1   5b
7m left again and just right of a horrible clay-filled cave is a slight
arête. Climb the left-hand side of this past a peg to an easier
continuation.   (1986

8 Riser 16m HVS 5a
High up is an obvious cave. 2m right is an arête which gives the route.
(1986)

9 While the Cat's Away 15m E3 6b
At the left-hand end of the top tier is a wall with a ledge at 4m. Climb the wall direct in the centre via the ledge. 1 bolt. Finish up the cracks above.
(1986)

HORSESHOE QUARRY GRADED LIST

E4
Demolition Man (6b)
Physical Fizz (6b)
Southern Man (6b)
Private Prosecution (6b)
An Ancient Rhythm (6a)
Rain Dance (6a)
Legal Action (6a)
Megalithic Man (6a)
Dinky Toy (6a)
The French Connection (6a)
Say It With Flowers (6a)
Mr Blue Sky (6b)

E3
Lost Monolith (6a)
Nice Face, Shame about The Ledge (6a)
Cafe Bleu (6a)
Litany Against Fear (5c)

Shot Yer Bolt (5c)
Smoke Gets in your Eyes (5c)
Do Androids Dream of Electric Sheep (5c)
School's Out (5c)

E2
Conformist (6a)
The Party Animal (6a)
Rotund Rooley (5c)
Nijinsky (5b)

E1
Like Ice, Like Fire (5b)
Galening Crack (5b)
Spectrophotometry (5b)

HVS
Pot-washer's Wall (5b)
Spring Awakening (5a)

HORSESHOE QUARRY LIST OF FIRST ASCENTS

1982 Nov. 11   **Chocolate Blancmange Gully**   C Jackson, R Conway, R Small
A slither into the unknown slipping boldly where no man, or even woman, had gone before. The first ascensionists wore wellingtons and used sharpened limestone mud tools. This is now considered 'de rigeur'.

1984 Sept.   **Knight Rider**   S Hennassy, P Faulkner

1984 Dec. 10   **Legal Action**   C Jackson, R Conway

1985 March 25   **Litany Against Fear**   M Pretty, I Jones, Q Fisher

1985 March 26   **The Entropy Effect**   M Pretty, S Lewis
Superseded by Private Prosecution in 1986.

1985 March 27   **Hot Zipperty**   M Pretty (solo)

1985 June   **Do Androids Dream of Electric Sheep**   M Pretty, I Jones

1985 July   **School's Out**   I Riddington, G Radcliffe

1985 Nov. 31   **Cafe Bleu**   M Taylor, D Hawkins

1985 Dec   **An Ancient Rhythm**   I French, C Wright, S France

1985   **Nice Face, Shame About the Ledge**   S France, I French, C Wright

1985   **Rain Dance**   I French, C Wright

1985   **Megalithic Man**   I French, C Wright, S France
The original route up the fluting was harder.

1985 Dec. 12   **Nijinski**   D Hawkins, M Taylor

1985 Dec. 29   **Smoke Gets in Your Eyes**   S France, C Wright

1986 Jan. 7   **Shot Yer Bolt**   S France, I French, C Wright, M Pretty

1986 Jan. 15   **Lost Monolith**   I French, S France, M Pretty, J Godding

1986 Jan. 16   **The Party Animal**   M Pretty, S Coffey, J Godding

1986   **Esso Blue**   S France, I French

1986 Jan. 17	**Conformist** J Godding, R Brooks
1986	**Esso Extra** S France, I Barton
1986 Jan. 22	**White Dove** C Wright, I French, J Godding, R Brooks
1986	**Private Prosecution** I French, S France
1986 Jan. 25	**P.M.'s Question Time** M Taylor, D Hawkins, T Goodwin
1986 Jan. 25	**Southern Man** J Godding, M Pretty
1986 Jan. 26	**Into the Labyrinth** C Wright, M Pretty, A Goring
1986 Jan. 26	**Demolition Man** I French, M Pretty
1986 Feb. 13	**Say it with Flowers** M Pretty, I French, J Godding
1986 Feb. 16	**Blue Sunday** S France, M Pretty, C Wright, I French
1986 Feb. 19	**The French Connection** I French, C Wright (AL) M Pretty
1986 Feb.	**Pointless Plod** I Barton
1986 Feb. 21	**Rotund Rooley** M Pretty, D Whaley, J Dawes
1986 Feb. 23	**Mr Blue Sky** C Wright, S France
1986 Feb. 24	**Physical Fizz** M Pretty (unseconded)
1986 March 2	**Wall of Jericho** S France, C Wright, I French, A Goring
1986 March 2	**Golden Tights** and **Gold Label** S Ralph A Dight
1986 March 11	**While the Cat's Away** S France, B Hine
1986 March 22	**Liquid Engineering** T Kartawick
1986 April	**The White's Height** 'Chipper'
1986 April 20	**Like Ice, Like Fire** C Jackson, R Conway
1986 April 22	**Dalkon Shield** R Conway, C Jackson
1986 April 26	**Order Number 59** C Jackson, A Churcher
1986 April 26	**Galening Crack** W Wintrip, R Small
1986 April 30	**Spectrophotometry** S Hennassy, I Smith
1986 May 1	**Riser** S Hennassy (unseconded)

1986 May 2	**Spring Awakening** S Hennassy, I Smith
1986 May 3	**Pot Washer's Wall** W D Gregory, D Gregory
1984 May 24	**Gritstone Transplant** D Gregory, W D Gregory
1986 June 6	**Slabbering Slab** S Ralph
1986 June	**Shetland Chimney** S Ralph
1986 June	**Chicken** S Ralph
1986 June	**Little Damocles** S Ralph
1986 June	**Cob** S Ralph
1986 June	**Footprint** S Ralph
1986 June	**Pot-washer's Wall** S Ralph
1986 June	**Grockle's Gully** S Ralph
1986 June	**Golden Label** S Ralph
1986 June	**Bimbo on the Loose** S Ralph
1986 June	**Bimbo Drops his Codpiece** S Ralph
1986 June	**Bimbo's Off-day Route** S Ralph
1986 June	**Bimbo's Arête** S Ralph
1986 June	**Bimbo Has His Head Examined** S Ralph, A Dight
1986 June 26	**Dinky Toy** N Slater, P Grant
1986 Aug. 4	**First Day of Winter** W D Gregory, E Taylor
1986 Aug. 4	**Blade Runner** W D Gregory, D Gregory
1986 Oct. 1	**Heart to Heart** M Pretty, I French, C Wright, R Brooks
1987 Jan. 3	**Run For Your Wife** M Pretty, C Plant
1987 Jan. 6	**Screwy Driver** M Pretty, I French
1987 Jan. 25	**Sunday Sport** M Pretty

RAVENSDALE AREA

CRESSBROOK DALE
O.S. ref SK 172 733
by Andy Barker and Keith Sharples

SITUATION and CHARACTER
The crags are situated in a gorge downstream from Ravensdale.
Being below the level of the road the rocks are hidden from view
by foliage in the summer and the limited sunlight makes spring
the best time to visit. Once soaked by autumn rainfall the dale can
be virtually 'written off' until the following spring.
Notwithstanding this however, the solitude in the dale is a
pleasure to experience particularly when compared to its busy
neighbour, Water-cum-Jolly.

APPROACHES and ACCESS
APPROACHING FROM RAVENSDALE COTTAGES ONE HAS TO
WALK DOWNSTREAM ON THE LEFT BANK AND INTO THE DALE.
IN PARTICULAR DO NOT APPROACH DIRECT FROM THE ROAD.
THE CRAGS ARE WITHIN A NATURE CONSERVATION AREA AND
ACCESS IS A DELICATE ISSUE. THE NATURE CONSERVANCY
DOES NOT WISH CLIMBERS TO USE THESE CRAGS WHICH ARE
SITUATED IN A BOTANICALLY IMPORTANT SITE AND GREAT
CARE IS NEEDED TO AVOID DISTURBING THE ENVIRONMENT.
THE CLIMBS SHOULD NOT BE DONE AND IN PARTICULAR NO
NEW ROUTES SHOULD BE ADDED. THE DESCRIPTIONS ARE
ONLY INCLUDED FOR COMPLETENESS.

HISTORY
The 1980 Northern Limestone guidebook simply tacked
Cressbrook Dale onto the end of Ravensdale and only recorded
two aid routes.
Ed Wood, Chris Craggs and Mark Stokes were probably the first to
realize the dale's potential and in 1980 they added *Billy Two Hats*
and *Ed's Wall*. It wasn't until 1982 that further routes were added
when Keith Sharples and Ian Riddington climbed *Sloane Ranger*
and re-cleaned and climbed Billy Two Hats in mistake for a first
ascent. Sharples then cleaned but failed on 'the line', now *Hot
Rock*, but collected *The Plough* as a consolation prize. Andy
Barker and Paul Mitchell visited the dale and over the summer
added some shorter routes to the right bank. They culminated
their activities with *Belling the Cat* (Mitchell), *Doing the Business*
and *Square Hole, Round Peg* (Barker).

New route activity started early in 1984 when Martin 'Basher' Atkinson climbed *Hot Rock* up the wall left of The Plough. Misguidedly he used a blow torch to dry crucial holds before his ascent. Mitchell then added several hard routes including *Billy Bull Terrier* and *The Smoke and Noise Filled Room* to the left bank and then *Tax Dodge* to Speckled Egg Buttress. Barker produced another hard route when he succeeded in *Burying the Red Man* up the wall left of Mitchell's *Not a Patch on the Apaches*. During the summer months Quentin Fisher and Jerry Moffatt climbed regularly on the bouldering wall of Speckled Egg Buttress and between them produced some desperate, though thankfully short, routes. Fisher added *Cherokee Lane* and Moffatt obligingly gave it a direct start which he called *Jericho Road*. Fisher then climbed a dynamic problem, *Lift Off*, only to see Andy Barker repeat it statically. Moffatt added *Pink Indians* before he extended himself across the low level traverse, left to right, finishing up Jericho Road! *Moffattrocity* was the last addition in 1984.

THE CLIMBS: From Ravensdale cottages approach by following the stream. Skirt left around the waterfall, and pass a large fallen tree until, 7m over the crumbling dry-stone wall is:

HAS-IT-BUTTRESS.

1   Billy Bull Terrier   7m   E5   6b
A boulder problem start leads to a bulge at 2m. Laybacks and lunges around this lead to a peg. Climb blindly up the wall above then move right to a sapling to finish.   (1984)

14m to the right is a very overhanging groove leading to further overhangs. This is **Has It?**, *A3.*   (1966)

2   Billy Two Hats   15m   E3   6a   ★
Climb the fine steep crack 5m right of Has It?. A right-hand finish is also possible from half-height.   (1980)

28m farther on past dirty rock is a wide steep V-groove.

3   Disturbing the Daylight Owl   16m   E3   6c   ★
After a ridiculously fingery overhanging start, bumble up the groove above. If soloing beware the pigeon with a sense of humour at the top as it may fly out without warning!   (1984)

The Smoke and Noise Filled Room   13m   E5   6b   ★★
Start 5m right of the groove. Undercut flakes lead to a thread at
5m. Move slightly up, before going right to a peg. Layback the
thin flake above to a leaning groove which proves hard to enter.
(1984)

5m right is:

Square Hole, Round Peg   13m   E5   6b   ★ †
Climb around the bulge on very hidden holds to clip the peg.
Make a hard move up past this to the overhang. A long reach
rightwards round this brings a welcome jug and easier ground.
Move up the wall to a traverse leftwards into the finishing groove.
(1983)

Was Harpo a Trappist Monk?   12m   E1   5b
Climb the centre of the wall on good holds to a resting ledge
below a steep cracked wall. Climb this trending leftwards to the
top. (1984)

*The path continues rightwards downstream to **NOGBAD**
BUTTRESS which is just visible through the trees. The first route
starts at the very left-hand end of the buttress, near a tree with a
rather peculiar double trunk.*

Sloane Ranger   19m   E3   5c   ★
Climb the wall for 3.5m. Traverse 3m right and move over the
small overhang to a second traverse rightwards into a corner.
Follow this to the top. Easy for the grade. (1982)

*The buttress now overhangs dramatically and provides food for
thought. It also contains the aid route, **Nogbad**, A2. Where the
buttress returns to the vertical a flake splits the wall.*

Hot Rock   20m   E5   6b   ★★★
The classic of the dale without a doubt. Climb the flake for 4m and
place some gear. Traverse leftwards onto the wall and climb the
delicate groove to a thread above. Move left to another thread
then make hard moves to finish up the flaky wall above in a
magnificent position. (1984)

The Plough   20m   E3   6a   ★
As for Hot Rock until the first thread, then step right and climb the
flake above. (1983)

10   Ed's Wall   14m   E3   6b
Start 4m right at a red-stained wall/groove. Climb the boulder
problem wall to a frightening finish up a wobbly flake. A long
reach is an advantage.   (1980)

11   Eat the Rich   14m   E5   6b   †
The wall right of Ed's Wall with a loose jug and an appalling
finish.   (1985)

*The buttress peters out but by following the path rightwards
downstream an isolated overhanging buttress will be found.*

12   Mother's Milk   7m   E3   5c   †
Climb the obvious break in the overhang, half-way along the
buttress.   (1984)

*To gain the routes on the opposite side of the dale return to Hot
Rock and follow the path down the hill past some futuristic
walls.Cross the stream and ascend the slope to:*

SPECKLED EGG BUTTRESS

*The routes are described from LEFT to RIGHT. Since they are
mostly extended boulder problems, with the crux relatively low
down, they have not been given E grades. However many are
quite serious and would certainly rate as E5 in any other setting.*

The chossy corner bounding the wall is **Local Youth Dies – 24
Pints** as may anyone attempting a repeat.

13   Speckled Egg Indirect   10m   6c
Start just right of a grotty corner at the left-hand end of the
buttress. From a good hold a swing to the lip brings a poor hold to
hand. Somehow do something with this to reach a huge hold just
above. Finish 'eggsactly'as for the next route.   (1985)

14   Speckled Egg   9m   6a
From small holds by the initials 'S.E.' reach out behind or jump for
a good jug. Ape leftwards for 1.5m then make a hard pull to an
obvious traverse right. Follow this and finish straight up.   (1984)

15 Lift Off   8m   6c
Start to the right at a wire-brushed patch. Make a hard move up to good jugs(the small will have to use a rock or rocks to reach the first holds). From the jugs a monstrous leap to a very distant hold brings easy ground.   (1984)

16 Brain Pollution   9m   6c
Start at a steep brushed arête between Lift Off and Pink Indians. Either reach the first holds or use cheating blocks. A few moves lead up to a small bulge. Cross this rightwards to a hand traverse into Pink Indians.   (1985)

17 Pink Indians   8m   6c
3m right a ridiculous rock-over brings a small fingerhold to hand. A short pull brings the finish of the next route to foot.   (1984)

18 Tit for Tat   9m   6c
Start just right of Pink Indians. Make a long reach for a one finger hole (complete with blow torch scorch marks!) and lunge out backwards over the bulge. (Eyes in the back of your head seem to help.)   (1985)

19 Jericho Road   9m   6c
1m right, climb sloping holds above the initials 'C.L.L.H.'. These lead to small fingerholds below the overhang. Move slightly right to a flake. Strenuous moves above lead to a ledge and finish with the next route.   (1984)

20 Cherokee Lane   9m   6c
Start just right at a shallow brushed depression. A small flake at about 3m is reached after a rather perplexing start. Swing left from this for another small flake where long reaches and sharp pulls lead to the ledge of Jericho Road. Move up and left to the top.   (1984)

21 Doing the Business   9m   6b
Start 2m right. A series of hard full-stretch pulls brings a small flake halfway up the wall within reach. Better holds lead to a ledge where one can hopefully depump before the top.   (1983)

22 Tax Dodge   9m   6a
One metre right a long reach up the first wall brings dramatically steeper ground and speedy progress is needed up small flakes

past a hidden hold to the top. A left-hand start is called **Dodge City**, 6b.   (1984)

Just to the right is a short corner.

23   Avoiding the Issue   9m   E1   5b
Climb the corner for 3.5m until a move out rightwards brings a small ledge to hand. Finish straight up the wall above.   (1983)

Many other problems exist, and there are others to be discovered. The best existing problem is **Moffattrocity**, 6c — a traverse. This starts just left of Pink Indians at head-height. Traverse right and finish all the way up Jericho Road. Pumpy!

Someway upstream lies the next buttress. Just right of a steep muddy path is a very clean steep wall, with a tree at the top. This is:

24   Belling the Cat   13m   E5   6a   ★★
Very fine climbing up the centre of the wall. Start just left of a blocky corner and climb up to an undercut at just over half-height. Place some gear and get up and go.   (1983)

The next route stands some 3m right at the 'arête' of the buttress.

25   Opportunity Mocks   12m   E1   5b   ★
Climb the arête for 3m until it is possible to traverse right into a scoop. Climb this to a bulging crack which is followed to the top. A direct start, **Bleeding Scalp**, 6b, starts at the foot of the next route and goes up and left.   (1983)

26   Burying the Red Man   13m   E4   6b
Start at a flake just to the right. Attaining a position standing in the scoop proves to be quite problematical. The wall above leads into the final chimney/groove, 2 threads, and can be troublesome for the short.   (1984)

The following route starts at a thin flake 2m right.

27   Not a Patch on the Apaches   12m   E2   5c
Climb the small flake to its end, then move slightly leftwards to below an overhanging groove. Finish up the groove.   (1984)

m farther on is a small problem.

Hip Hop, Hip Hop, Hip Hop 7m HVS 6b
kip the pocketed bulging crack, to a grassy, disgustingly
egetated and tricky finish (marked by a blue arrow). (1983)

ome of the overhung small cracks to the right provide some
ouldering.

Flick of the Wrist 12m E2 6b
ontinuing rightwards the first obvious large corner to be
ncountered on the right is climbed by moving in low down from
e left arête. It can also be done direct. Finish leftwards from the
p of the corner. (1983)

More Me than Me 13m E1 5c
imb into the scooped groove just to the right of the previous
ute, and move onto the arête to the left. Ascend to the overhang
ast a thread, where a short traverse left leads to the finish of Flick
the Wrist. (1983)

RESSBROOK DALE LIST OF FIRST ASCENTS

66 June | **Has It** (A3) B Moore, J Ballard

e-1980 | **Nogbad** (A2)

80 Summer | **Billy Two Hats** E Wood, C Craggs, M Stokes, M Veale
Ed Wood starts the development of the dale with an overhanging crack.

80 Summer | **Ed's Wall** E Wood et al
Ed's final addition before leaving the dale.

82 April 16 | **Sloane Ranger** K Sharples, I Riddington (both led)
Sharples signals the start of the next phase of development. Billy Two Hats was recleaned and climbed by I Riddington in mistake for a first ascent.

82 Aug. | **The Plough** K Sharples
A consolation prize having failed on 'the Line'.

83 July 31 | **Flick of the Wrist** A Barker

1983 Aug. 13   **Square Hole, Round Peg**   A Barker

1983 Aug. 13   **Belling the Cat**   P Mitchell
Barker and Mitchell take up the mantle of the dale's main suitors, the development of routes continues and the 'bouldering wall' is opened up with Doing the Business, although an attacking wasp nearly spelt disaster as Barker was forced to jump off the final moves.

1983 Aug. 21   **More Me Than Me**   P Mitchell

1983 Aug. 27   **Speckled Egg**   P Mitchell

1983 Aug. 28   **Avoiding the Issue**   P Mitchell

1983 Aug. 28   **Doing the Business**   A Barker

1983 Aug. 30   **Opportunity Mocks**   P Mitchell

1983 Aug.   **Hip Hop, Hip Hop, Hip Hop**   P Mitchell

1984 Spring   **Hot Rock**   M Atkinson
So called because of the blow torch that was used t dry the rock prior to the first ascent.

1984 April 21   **Was Harpo a Trappist Monk?**   P Mitchell
Nearly the scene of a big fall as Mitchell, under a vo of silence for the day, couldn't warn Barker as he almost fell from the final moves.

1984 April 29   **Burying the Red Man**   A Barker

1984 April 29   **Not a Patch on the Apaches** and **Bleeding Scalp**
   P Mitchell

1984 May   **Lift Off**   Q Fisher
Quentin's first appearance on the scene.

1984 May 1   **Disturbing the Daylight Owl**   P Mitchell
A solo second ascent almost saw disaster as a pigeon nearly off-balanced Barker.

1984 May 5   **Mother's Milk**   P Mitchell

1984 May 16   **The Smoke and Noise Filled Room**   P Mitchell
Probably Mitchell's best effort to date.

1984 May 19   **Tax Dodge**   P Mitchell

1984 June 2   **Billy Bull Terrier**   P Mitchell

1984   **Cherokee Lane**   Q Fisher

1984	**Jericho Road** J Moffatt
1984	**Pink Indians** J Moffatt
1984	**Moffattrocity** J Moffatt

Jerry adds his weight to the effort before leaving for the States on his mega trip.

| 1985 | **Eat the Rich**   Q Fisher |

Fisher continues his 'socialist' routes.

1985	**Brain Pollution** Q Fisher
1985	**Speckled Egg Indirect** P Mitchell
1985	**Tit for Tat** A Ryan
1985	**Dodge City** G Griffiths

CRESSBROOK DALE GRADED LIST

E5
Billy Bull Terrier (6b)
Hot Rock (6b)
Square Hole, Round Peg (6b)
The Smoke and Noise Filled
    Room (6b)
Belling the Cat (6a)

E4
Burying the Red Man (6b)

E3
Disturbing the Daylight Owl
    (6c)
Ed's Wall (6b)
Billy Two Hats (6a)
The Plough (6a)
Sloane Ranger (5c)
Mother's Milk (5c)

E2
Flick of the Wrist (6b)

Not a Patch on the Apaches
    (5c)

E1
More Me Than Me (5c)
Was Harpo a Trappist Monk?
    (5b)
Opportunity Mocks (5b)
Avoiding the Issue (5b)
Bouldering Wall
Pink Indians (6c)
Tit for Tat (6c)
Moffattrocity (6c)
Brain Pollution (6c)
Jericho Road (6c)
Cherokee Lane (6c)
Lift Off (6c)
Doing the Business (6b)
Speckled Egg Indirect (6c)
Tax Dodge (6a)
Speckled Egg (6a)

RAVENSDALE
O.S. ref. SK 173 7?

by Mark Kemball and Trevor Langhorne

---

*'It was the groove on the left edge of Raven's Buttress
which stirred up renewed onslaughts. It was not easily
subjugated. Clive Rowland and his elder cousin Ted
barely avoided disaster in an attempt in June 1960. A
'good block runner' collapsed under Ted while he was
trying the second pitch, and he and the block hurtled
down. Clive, weighing scarcely half as much as the
leader, was swept from his stance and his low-level
belay was severed on two strands. Meanwhile the
boulder cut a swathe through the trees, brought out the
cottagers and made the Derbyshire Times the following
week.' An attempt on what became Conclusor.*

Paul Nunn, Northern Limestone 1969

SITUATION and CHARACTER

The crag stands in an impressive position high above Ravensdale
cottages on the eastern side of Ravensdale (Cressbrook Dale).
Several fine buttresses lie high above a wooded hillside, with
heights ranging from 23m to 43m on the large Raven's Buttress.
In general the rock is sound, but care must be taken on some of
the less popular routes as some loose rock still exists in places,
especially on the finishes. Above Raven's Buttress there are
sledge iron belays.

APPROACHES and ACCESS

By car, drive to Ravensdale cottages where there is limited
parking in a small car park. From Sheffield the T208 Trent bus
goes to Tideswell. It is then a walk to Litton where a footpath
leads down to Ravensdale Cottages (30 to 40 minutes). From
Manchester the X67 bus goes to Tideswell where the approach is
as above. From Bakewell a bus goes to Monsal Head. A pleasant
walk then leads down the dale to Cressbrook Mill and then to
Ravensdale Cottages. The most enjoyable approach is from
Wardlow (SK 182 745) along a signposted green track to the dale
rim and then south (left) along to the crag.

The crag itself is approached by a well-kept path starting at the
right-hand side of the Ravensdale Cottages car-park and
**CLIMBERS ARE REQUESTED TO USE ONLY THIS APPROACH
FROM THE VALLEY FLOOR**.

The main buttress, Raven's Buttress and the rocks between the two ways down on each side of it are the property of the Nature Conservancy. Although the presence of climbers conflicts with its aims, the Conservancy is willing to allow climbers to use these rocks provided that they only approach them along the clearly designated paths. On no account should climbers take independent lines up or down the slope below the crag. NO NEW ROUTES SHOULD BE UNDERTAKEN ON THE ROCKS OUTSIDE THESE LIMITS. Cave Buttress and any other rocks near it should not be used. As this situation is very delicate, care should be taken not to jeopardize the free access to this highly popular crag.

HISTORY

The recorded exploration of these fine cliffs began in November 1958 with the ascent of *Frore* by John Loy and Bill Woodward although some easy lines may already have been climbed. There were no more major additions until 1960. Then the obvious challenge of Raven's Buttress proved too much for Dave Johnson and Dave Mellor. Their efforts were well rewarded, with *Medusa* and *Delusor* as well as *Tria*. About the same time John Loy continued exploring and produced a number of shorter routes including *Amain* and *The Gymnic*. In September 1960 Loy and Mellor joined forces to produce the classic *Via Vita*, the hardest and most impressive route added at the time. The line of grooves destined to become *Conclusor* also received attention at this time, with nearly disastrous results for Clive and Ted Rowland. The following year saw a number of short routes added including *Y Chimney* by A. Wright, *Yew Cap* by J. Loy and *Bifurous Corner* by D. Morrison.

There was still a lot of steep virgin rock on Raven's Buttress; the period 1964-65 proved to be Ravensdale's 'golden age'. The grooves of *Conclusor* were finally climbed. A number of leaders had made attempts including Alan Clarke and R.D. Brown and they may have completed the pitch but Clive Rowland and Paul Nunn made the first recorded ascent. Also in 1964 Nunn joined forces with Oliver Woolcock to climb *Mephistopheles*. Obviously Woolcock liked the place as he returned to add *Ploy* and *The Girdle* (with R.D. Brown) and *Via Vita Direct* with J. Soper. The pace of exploration did not slacken as, in 1965, Bob Dearman added *Mealystopheles* (with R.D. Brown) and *Enigma* (with N Crowther). The shorter cliffs continued to attract John Loy who added a number of routes including *Thyrsus* and *Metronome*. The eliminate line of *Hades* was added by Wilf White and Ernie Marshall.

The chronology of events from 1965 to 1976 is uncertain but the birth of 'free climbing' led to the elimination of the aid points on routes such as Via Vita, Hades and Mephistopheles. Bob Dearman continued his association with the cliff by adding *Myopia* and *Purple Haze*. In 1976 J. Yates and C. Foord found the *Edge of Insanity* and D. Mithin and A. Crawley added *Critical Town*. There have never been many full aid routes in Ravensdale and they are all free climbs now. In 1977 Mike Browell and Giles Barker cleaned *Round the Bend* and Phil Burke with Keith Myhill had to *Cut Loose or Fly* on Twenty Minute Crack. In preparation for the previous guide Chris Jackson, Bob Dearman, Rod Haslam and Dave Sant added a variety of short routes including *Rockbiter* and *Beachcomber*.

As expected Gary Gibson has added some routes here, the best being *Tank, Vintage Two* and *Bullets* in 1980. The gaps between the lines are getting smaller. Mark Kemball added *Cold Shoulder* in 1981 but Ron Fawcett plugged a large gap with *Wilt* in 1982. The Wilt Wall has continued to attract attention and the scoop above the ledge on Wilt provided Johnny Dawes with *Pagan Man* in 1984. The line of Wilt has an obvious desperate direct start which was forced by Quentin Fisher in late 1985 to provide the *Wilt Alternative* which is probably the hardest series of moves on the crag.

There is still some unclimbed rock but the real attraction of Ravensdale is to the VS/HVS climber. There are days of fun at this level on steep, well-protected and exposed routes although many holds are becoming 'mirrors in the cliffs'.

THE CLIMBS are described from LEFT to RIGHT. At the left-hand end of the crag, left of the easy way down is a small scrappy buttress.

1   Raven Crack   10m   VD
Climb the crack up the left edge of the buttress from the lowest point.   (1970s)

2   Canopy Crack   10m   D
Scramble up the trees and chimney in the centre.   (1960s)

3   Unpleasant   10m   S   4a
The well-named crack 2m right.   (1960s)

The next route is just right of the easy way down.

4 True Lime 14m S 4b
Follow the corner to the overhang, traverse right below it to the
pedestal then go back left to finish up the arête. (1970s)

5 Bifurous Chimney 12m VD
The deep chimney in the corner needs a polished style. (1960)

6 Pedestal Branch 14m VD
Traverse left from 4m up the chimney to the pedestal. Finish up
the crack above. (1960)

7 Bifurous Corner 14m VS 4c
2m right of the chimney climb the corner direct, and finish up the
chimney. (1961)

8 The Bigot Direct 14m E3 6a ★
Climb the strenuous crack-line just left of the arête to the right of
Bifurous Corner. (1979)

9 The Original Start 15m HVS 5b
Traverse right into The Bigot from 5m up Bifurous Corner, just
above the overlap. (1976)

10 Forgotten Groove 20m VS 4c
The pleasant corner-crack right of the arête unfortunately ends in
dense jungle. (1964)

11 So-So 15m S ★
To the right, a crack behind the hawthorn leads to a flake behind
the yew. Suprisingly good. (1960s)

12 Ivy Corner 15m S 4a
6m right is a polished corner surrounded by encroaching ivy.
(1961)

To the right again is a prominent tower.

13 Tower Climb 14m VD
The corner on the left of the tower. (1961)

14 Beachcomber 21m VS 5a ★
Start at the lowest point of the face and climb it to the overhang
which is avoided on the left. Move back right to finish pleasantly
up the face. (1978)

Geraldine Taylor on Carl's Wark Crack, Stoney Middleton.
Photo: Ian Smith.

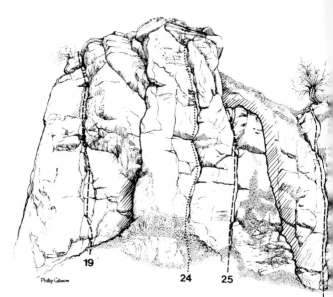

19

Philip Gibson

24   25

29

Flying Buttress

15 Tower Crack 15m VS 4b
Dirty loose cracks 2m right lead through vegetation to finish up a
steep flake crack. The start is best avoided as the finish (HS) can
be reached from the grass slope on the right.   (1960s)

16 Bosky 20m S 4b
10m left of the through arch is a V-groove. Follow the crack in its
left wall.   (1978)

17 Gruesome Groove 12m S 4a
Climb the V-groove, either moving left at the hanging flake or
continuing directly up the crack, moving left at the top.   (1965)

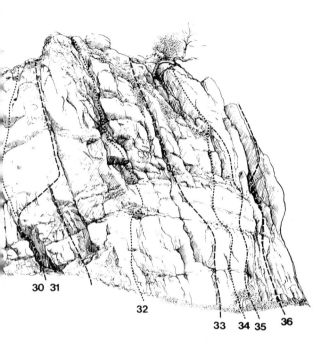

30 31

32

33 34 35 36

8 Scorpion 21m E2 5c ★
A very technical start leads to an excitingly loose finish. Start 2m
ight of the groove. Climb into a niche, move right with difficulty
to a flake crack, climb this then the arête above. (1966)

9 Gymnic 21m VS 4c ★★
A polished classic for gymnasts. Cracks just left of the cave lead to
an overhang. Continue up the corner above finishing either side
of the top overhang. (1960)

20   Amain   21m   VS   4c   *
Struggle up the hanging crack just right of the cave opening and
continue up the corner-crack more easily. The hanging flake on
the left provides a worthwhile alternative finish.   (1960)

21   Cold Shoulder   22m   E1   5b
Start up Amain, traverse left above the main overhang and round
the arête to a scoop. Climb the left arête overlooking Gymnic.
                                                                (1981)

22   Russian Roulette   21m   HVS   5b
Climb the crack between Amain and the arête moving onto the
arête at about half-height. Continue up this wearing blinkers.
                                                                (1978)

23   Looking at the Blue   20m   HVS   5b
The thin crack left of Impendent, finishing up Russian Roulette.
Contrived but technically interesting.   (1979)

24   Impendent   18m   VS   4c   **
The fine jamming crack in the outside face of the flying buttress
gives good value. A 'gritstone' classic.   (1960)

25   Shattered Crack   12m   VD
The wide crack right of Impendent is more solid than either its
name or appearance would suggest.   (1959)

26   Cave Corner   14m   S
The left corner of the square face to the right of the through arch.
                                                                (1959)

27   Ash Crack   15m   HS   4a   *
The central crack of the back wall of the alcove.   (1960)

28   Hydrolysis   18m   HVS   5b
A technically interesting eliminate up the thin crack and wall
between Ash Crack and Tria.   (1979)

29   Tria   18m   HS   4b   *
Ascend the right corner of the alcove.   (1960)

30   Cut Loose or Fly   18m   E3   5c   *
The crack 2m right is followed until it is possible to move right to
good holds. Continue directly up the wall.   (1978)

31 Wilt 20m E5 6b   **★★**
Move right from the initial crack of Cut Loose or Fly to good holds.
Traverse right to the improbable-looking faint crack-line. Climb
this or wilt! Very technical and strenuous, but well-protected if
you can stop to place the gear!   (1982)
The Direct Start, **The Wilt Alternative**, E5 6c, goes past a peg and a
thread.   (1985)
Pagan Man, E4, 6b, takes the scoop above the traverse.   (1984)

32 Malpossessed 21m HVS 5b   **★**
Start up the arête right of the alcove. Move right to below a block
overhang, cross this and move left into a groove. Finish straight
up. Rather tiring.   (1966)

33 Sneck 21m HVS 5b
Climb the wall 5m right of Malpossessed. Traverse left to below a
sharp groove in the overhang. Climb this, peg, and continue over
vegetation to finish over a small roof split by a crack.   (1970s)

To the right is an obvious V-groove, **The Wick**. *10m left of this is:*

34 The Watcher 20m E2 6a   **†**
Climb the wall to a groove in the overhang past two pegs. Climb
to a large tree then abseil off.   (1980s)

35 Tank 20m E1 5b
Climb the wall 5m left of The Wick to a bulge. Pass this on the
right by a short V-groove, then go diagonally leftwards across the
upper face to the arête of The Watcher.   (1980)

36 The Wick 20m MVS 4b   **★**
The obvious V-groove leads past a tree to finish over steep
pasture.   (1966)

37 Ice Cream Phoenix 20m HVS 4c
Start just right of The Wick. Climb up right through a rose bush to
a narrow ledge. (The loose block has joined its friends in the
woods below the crag!) From above this climb leftwards up a slab
to the pasture.   (1970)

38 Exfoliation 21m VS 4c
A flake system splits the upper wall about 8m right of The Wick.
Climb directly to this and follow it to the top.   (1970s)

About 30m right is an obvious descent gully. The steep wall 10m to the left of this has the following routes.

39 Troops of Tomorrow 20m E1 5c
Climb the wall left of the obvious cracks of Rockbiter which are joined near the top.   (1980)

40 Rockbiter 20m HVS 5a   ★★
Go directly up the steep thin cracks splitting the wall; well-protected.   (1978)

41 Plaque Crack 14m VS 4a
Start just left of the gully. Move to and round the right side of the plaque to a suspect finish.   (1960s)

42 Gorrah 14m HVS 5a
The clean-cut groove just right of the gully is followed direct.
                                                                       (1960s)

43 Begorrah 16m VS 4c
Mount the block a couple of metres to the right and climb cracks above. Near the top move left to finish at Gorrah.   (1960s)

Beyond vegetation is a slab bounded on its right by a curving crack.

44 Sagittarius 15m VS 4c
Follow the steepening crack and groove past an obvious block overhang. Strenuous. Finish slightly left.   (1960s)

The next climb is situated at the right edge of the bay and starts at a lower level.

45 Cracked Edge 18m HS 4b
Cracks 1m right of the arête lead to a ledge. The arête above is gained from cracks on its left.   (1960)

46 Round the Bend 20m E2 5c   ★
Start 2m right of Cracked Edge. After a short corner traverse right to a hanging corner move up and traverse back left to a thin crack. Climb this past a mantelshelf, finishing near the arête.   (1977)

Farther right a large tree grows at the base of the crag.

47 Hi-Fi   21m   VS   4c, 4c
1. 12m. Start up shallow grooves just left of the tree then traverse right to a flake stance.
2. 9m. Climb the slanting corner above.   (1966)

48 Boulder Problem   21m   VS   4c, 4c
Start in the corner 8m right of the tree.
1. 12m. Climb the corner, move left, loose, to a second corner which is followed to the Hi-Fi stance.
2. 9m. Pitch 2 of Hi-Fi or if 'bolder' the loose continuation of the second corner, which may give problems.   (1965)

49 Metronome   21m   VS   4c   *
Follow the first corner of Boulder Problem then step right and attack the wide impending crack above.   (1965)

50 Postern Crack   20m   VS   4c
Start on a higher ledge about 3m right of Metronome. Move directly up the wall to a crack which leads to a ledge. Finish by the yew tree.   (1960s)

51 Yew Cap   18m   VS   4c
The crack-line leading to the yew tree using the right-hand corner in the middle section.   (1961)

52 Y Chimney   15m   VS   4c
The chimney bounding the bay leads to a finish up the right-hand crack.   (1961)

The next climbs start directly below Y Chimney on the left side of an imposing crag which is **RAVEN BUTTRESS**.

53 Myopia   35m   HVS   4c, 5b
1. 14m. Climb the buttress by a line of grooves and belay right of Y Chimney.
2. 21m. The pillar above leads past 2 pegs to finishing cracks.
                                                              (1970)

54 Solitaire   12m   HS   4b
The crack splitting the wall right of Myopia. Walk off or climb Y Chimney.   (1960)

55 57

Raven Buttress

58 59

61

62 63 64 65 66 67

55 Conclusor 46m HVS 4c, 5a ★★
An excellent groove climb starting in a corner just right of Solitaire.
1. 14m. The steep corner leads to a cramped stance.
2. 32m. A slim groove line above gives enjoyable climbing to an exit right finishing up a wide crack. (1964)

56 Hades 46m E2 4c,5b
A hell of a climb with awful pegs. Start 4m right of Conclusor.
1. 14m. Climb the wall and two shallow grooves, peg, to belay on the left.
2. 32m. The flake crack is climbed to a pillar. Tackle the bulge above on the left past pegs to a steep groove which leads to a tree. The left-hand groove above is followed to the top. (1965)

57 Delusor 44m VS 4c,4c ★
Much better than it looks! The second pitch follows the steep groove right of Hades. Start as for Hades.
1. 12m. An ascending rightward traverse leads to a belay below a groove.
2. 32m. The groove is ascended passing a bulge to further grooves leading pleasantly to the top, reaching it at the same place as Medusa. (1960)

Variation Pitch 1(i) 12m 5b. The steep crack directly below the stance has a hard start. A good start to Via Vita.

To the right is a large tree. Starting 6m left of this is one of the Peak's classic VS routes, suitably polished of course!

58 Medusa 46m VS 4b,4b ★★★
1. 18m. A flake crack is followed to ledges. Move right and climb a suspect wall. Huge pinnacle belay on the right.
2. 28m. Attack the crack behind the pinnacle. The slabby gangway above is followed pleasantly. Step left into the final groove of Delusor to finish. (1960)

59 Via Vita 49m HVS 4b,4c,5b ★★★
Another classic with a short and safe crux. Start as for Medusa.
1. 15m. Follow Medusa to belay above the doubtful wall.
2. 11m. The steep groove above leads interestingly to Medusa's thread belay.

3. 23m. Climb the gangway of Medusa until a sensational swing right gains a ledge. Effecting a lodgement in the right-hand crack above the ledge gives a highly exposed crux. Finish more easily.

(1960)

Variations
3(i) **The Direct Pitch**   21m   E2   6a   *
The impressive overhanging groove above and right of the stance leads straight to the ledge and crux of the normal route.

(1964/1976)

3(ii) **The Sinister Finish**   23m   HVS   5a
From the ledge before the crux traverse left and climb a square corner to the top.

60   The Edge of Insanity   43m   HVS   †
A loose and potentially dangerous route which is perhaps best forgotten. Start at a shallow groove right of Medusa.
1. 17m. The groove and vegetation lead to the Medusa pinnacle stance.
2. 17m. Swing up onto the arête on the right and ascend past a shallow V-groove (peg). Keep close to the overhanging edge to a small ledge and peg belay.
3. 11m. Continue up just right of the arête until forced right to the foot of an obvious crack. Swing left and pull over the overhang to finish up a thin rib.

(1970s)

61   Mealy Bugs   46m   VS   4c,4c   *
The first pitch follows the prominent chimney crack-line just right of the tree.
1. 21m. The steep and pleasant chimney/crack-line leads to a belay on a little terrace on the right.
2. 25m. The groove above the belay leads into a large open scoop. Cross the scoop to finish up the superbly-positioned twisting crack on the left.

(1960)

62   Mealystopheles   46m   VS   5a,4c   *
Start below a shallow chimney left of the toe of Raven Buttress.
1. 22m. Shallow grooves give delicate climbing to the chimney which has a difficult move. Above the bulge, grooves are followed to the Mealy Bugs stance.
2. 24m. Follow the second pitch of Mealy Bugs into the scoop then traverse right around the rib, peg, to the obvious wide crack of Mephistopheles to finish.

(1965)

63 Bullets 45m HVS 5a,5b   *
Start at the toe of Raven's Buttress.
1. 22m. Climb the wall and very shallow groove to the break. Step
up and left onto a thin flake which leads left onto the arête. Go
delicately up this and over a bulge to belay as for Mealy Bugs.
2. 23m. Continue up the arête left of Mephistopheles to a peg. Pull
over the bulge to the finishing fist crack.   (1980)

64 Mephistopheles 45m HVS 5a,5b   **
This fine climb starts below a wedged block just right of Bullets.
1. 22m. Small holds lead past the block to a break. The thin crack
above is followed past a peg. Either continue direct or move right
and go up to a terrace. Belay on the left as for Mealy Bugs.
2. 23m. A few easy moves lead to an obvious thin crack. From its
top move right to some exciting moves past a bulge. Finish up a
wide crack (of Mealystopheles).   (1964)

65 Purple Haze 45m HVS 5b,5a   *
Another good route taking the groove line right of
Mephistopheles. Start behind a thorn bush.
1. 22m. A thin flake crack behind the bush leads to the
overhanging groove and then easier grooves above. Belay on the
terrace.
2. 23m. The wide crack goes to a yew tree (possible belay). The
steep wall above the tree is followed, crossing a bulge, to finish
up a steep corner.   (1970)

66 Ploy 50m VS 4c,4b,4c   *
Start in an overhung corner right of a thorn bush. Steep climbing.
1. 23m. The corner is climbed to an exit right into a niche. Follow
the crack springing from the niche to the terrace. Belay beside a
wide flake crack.
2. 14m. The crack leads to a yew tree. Easy rocks right and above
follow to belay below a groove.
3. 13m. Climb the groove, step left to a peg then move over a
slight bulge and finish direct in an exposed position.   (1964)

*The little terrace which has provided the first stance for the last
few routes now widens into a large grassy one splitting the
remaining climbs.*

67 Frore 43m VS 5a,4c   *
Start at a shallow groove 2m right of Ploy.
1. 21m. Gain a ledge below the scoop, bridge the scoop delicately

until a rising traverse to a tree on the terrace. Belay up and left to protect the second.
2. 22m. Easy rocks left of ivy lead to a junction with Ploy (possible second belay). From a few metres up the groove of Ploy a rising rightwards traverse goes enjoyably to the top.   (1958)

68 Thyrsus 41m HVS 5b,4c
Start from elder bushes right of Frore.
1. 21m. Climb ledges and a smooth wall to join Frore. Belay to trees up and left.
2. 20m. Climb the tree, ivy and eventually rock via a groove moving left to join the top pitch of Frore.   (1965)

69 Venous Return 20m HVS 4c
Start behind the tree left of Vintage Two and climb the groove to its top. Pull over the bulge above and follow the rightwards ramp to finish.   (1970s)

70 Vintage Two 20m E2 5b   *
An excellent pitch above the terrace. Start 7m left of a rib (pitch 2 Enigma). Gain a tree and climb a crack to the break. Move diagonally up and left to a flake below a thin crack and follow this to the top (2 pegs).   (1980)
The direct start is E3, 6a, **(For the Love of Ivy).**   (1986)

71 Enigma 37m HVS -,5a
Start in the ivy right of Thyrsus.
1. 14m. An easy chimney leading to the terrace. A better alternative is pitch 1 of Thyrsus or a walk in from the right.
2. 13m. Climb a rib to a fragile flake, move left and ascend the steep and strenuous wall (2 rusty pegs).   (1965)

72 Paupericles 17m HS 4b, 4b
Start at a crack on the edge of the buttress above the terrace.
1 8m. The crack then traverse right to a tree belay.
2. 9m. Move left past a flake to finish up a groove.   (1960)

73 Girdle Traverse 79m VS 4c,4c,4c,4b,4c   *
A left to right traverse offering good climbing. Best avoided on a busy day. Start as for Delusor.
1. 12m. 4c. Pitch 1 of Delusor.
2. 25m. 4c. Follow the second pitch of Delusor until Medusa is joined. Step right and make an intimidating swing (on Via Vita) onto an exposed ledge. Belay!

3. 15m. 4c. Traverse right around the rib to join Mealy Bugs below the final crack. Cross the scoop and descend the slab/groove of Mealy Bugs to belay on the terrace. A steady second is required as this is most of Mealy Bugs pitch 2 in reverse.
4. 13m. 4b. Pitch 2 of Ploy.
5. 14m. 4c. From the groove of Ploy the rising traverse of Frore is followed to finish. (1964)

74 Critical Town 55m HVS 5a,4c,5a
A high level girdle from right to left. Start from a thorn tree on the right of the terrace.
1. 21m. 5a. Traverse left below the overhang past the flake on Enigma. Follow the break then drop down to belay below pitch 2 of Frore.
2. 18m. 4c. Traverse around the arête to the scoop of Mealy Bugs, continue traversing to belay as for the girdle traverse on the exposed ledge.
3. 16m. 5a. Reverse the Via Vita swing and traverse left to finish up the final crack of Conclusor. (1970s)

*The wide gully right of Raven's Buttress contains a well-maintained descent route. No climbing should take place on the buttresses to the right of this gully. One of them, Cave Buttress has yielded three routes, **Waggs Groove** (HVD), on the left, **Choss** (VS, 4c) on the front and **Cave Crack** (VS, 4c) just left of the cave. THESE SHOULD NOT BE VISITED.*

RAVENSDALE LIST OF FIRST ASCENTS

1958 Nov.	**Frore**	J A Loy, W Woodward
		Recorded as 'Flypaper', climbed with some aid on a frosty day. Development begins.
1959	**Shattered Crack**	J A Loy, R Precious
1959	**Cave Corner**	J A Loy (solo)
1960 May 22	**Medusa**	D Johnson, D Mellor
		'The fierce looking jamming crack mentioned in the text was not led until 1963 by L Millsom.'
		Paul Nunn soloed the route on 9 June 1964.

1960 May 22	**Mealy Bugs** D Johnson, D Mellor

1960 June 5 **Delusor** D Johnson, D Mellor
The better first pitch was done by P Crew, B Ingle on 30 September 1962.

1960 June **Amain** J A Loy, D Johnson, D Mellor

1960 June **Gymnic** J A Loy, H Gillot, B Stokes, E Howard

1960 June **Tria** D Johnson, D Mellor

1960 June **South Crack** A Howard

Choss

1960 Summer **Pedestal Branch** J A loy (solo)

1960 Sept. 4 **Solitaire** J A Loy (solo)

Cracked Edge J A Loy, D Mellor

1960 Sept. 4 **Via Vita** (1 pt.) J Loy, D Mellor
The top pitch was climbed in boots with a peg, three falls and half a packet of fags for aid! This was undoubtedly one of the hardest limestone routes of its day and its ascent brought to a close developments for 1960.

The following routes were climbed before 1961 but with no available dates.

Bifurous Chimney (unrecorded)

Impendent J A Loy, D Mellor

Ash Crack (unrecorded)

20 Minute Crack (A2) J A Loy, R Precious
Free-climbed in 1978 by P Burke as Cut Loose or Fly.

Round the Bend (A1) G West, B Roberts

1961 **Bifurous Corner** D Morrison

1961 Autumn **Ivy Corner** J A Loy (solo)

Alcove Wall (A1)
An artificial route between Cave Corner and Ash Crack.

1961 Autumn **Tower Climb** J A Loy (solo)

1961 Sept.	**Yew Cap** J A Loy, D Mellor
1962 Sept. 30	**Y Chimney** A Wright, D Gregory
1964 May 14	**Mephistopheles** (1 pt.) P Nunn, O Woolcock *A peg was used on the second pitch. Nunn had a day off from revision for University finals.*
1964 June	**Ploy** O Woolcock, R D Brown
1964 Aug.	**Conclusor** C Rowland, P Nunn *This fine line had attracted considerable attention since the exciting times of the Rowland brothers in 1960. It was first attempted in 1959. Others who climbed all or part of the route prior to this ascent included R D Brown, C Curtis and A Clarke.*
1964	**Girdle Traverse** O Woolcock, R D Brown
1964	**Via Vita Direct** (aid) O Woolcock, N J Soper *Possible first free ascent by C Jackson in 1976.*
1964	**Forgotten Groove** P Newman, D Whittaker *A fine series of routes to rival those of 1960.*
1965 April	**Mealystopheles** R Dearman, R D Brown *Only the first pitch was new, the top pitch was climbed in 1960 by D Johnson and D Mellor (Adeste Fideles) as a variation finish to Mealy Bugs.*
1965	**Enigma** (2 pts.) R Dearman, N Crowther
1965	**Boulder Problem** J A Loy, G Armstrong
1965	**Gruesome Groove** J A Loy, G Armstrong
1965	**Thyrsus** (A1) J A Loy, G Armstrong
1965	**Metronome** J A Loy, B Moore
1965	**Hades** (1 pt.) W White, E A Marshall *Led with 1 peg for aid after gardening, considered to 'vie with Conclusor for the position of hardest route on the crag'. How things change!*
1966 May	**Hi-Fi** M Richardson, P Mason
1966 May	**Boulder Problem Direct** M Richardson, P Mason
1966 Aug.	**Scorpion** (2 pts.) M Quinn, J Dutton, B Samuels

The following routes were climbed between 1966 and 1976.

Critical Town   D Mithin, A Crawley

Edge of Insanity   J Yates, C Foord

The following routes first appeared in Northern Limestone (1969) therefore must have been climbed pre-1968.

Canopy Crack

Unpleasant

So So

Tower Crack

Plaque Crack

Gorrah

Begorrah

Sagittarius

Paupericles

968 July   **Malpossessed** (2 pts.)   E A Marshall, J A Loy
First free ascent by K Myhill, T King in 1970.

969 March 23   **Postern Crack** (1 pt.)   J A Loy, M Walsh, A Maskery

969 April 13   **The Wick**   J A Loy, M Walsh, G Armstrong

970 May 30   **Ice Cream Phoenix**   R Wallace, R Sedgwick

970 May 30   **Myopia** (1 pt.)   D Riley, R S Dearman

970 June 6   **Purple Haze** (2 pts.)   R S Dearman, D Riley
First free ascent by K Myhill, T Proctor on the second ascent.

976   **The Bigot**   J Fleming
Direct start added in 1979 by G Gibson.

977 May   **Round the Bend**   M F Browell, G Barker
The first of Ravensdale's few aid routes to go free. Also claimed by P Clarke on 29 May 1977.

| 1978 June | **Cut Loose or Fly**   P Burke, K Myhill |

This aptly named route free-climbs the aid route 20 Minute Crack.

| 1978 | **Beachcomber**   C Jackson, R Haslam |

| 1978 | **Rockbiter**   C Jackson, D Sant |

| 1978 | **Russian Roulette**   M Horlov, R S Dearman |

| 1978 | **Exfoliation**   C Jackson, D Sant |

| 1978 June 6 | **Bosky**   D A Whittingham, P H Hopkins |

The following routes appear in the previous edition of Northern Limestone for the first time and so are labelled 1970s.

Raven Crack

True Lime

Sneck

| 1979 April | **Hydrolysis**   G Gibson, J Norris |

| 1979 | **Looking at the Blue**   G Gibson |

| 1980 Jan. 4 | **Vintage Two**   G Gibson, D Williams |

| 1980 April 1 | **Venous Return**   G Gibson (solo) |

| 1980 May 15 | **Troops of Tomorrow**   G Gibson (solo) |

| 1980 May 15 | **Tank**   G Gibson (solo) |

| 1980 May 24 | **Bullets**   G Gibson, M Walton |

| 1981 Jan. 11 | **Cold Shoulder**   M Kemball, B McKee |

| 1982 | **Wilt**   R Fawcett |

Originally described as 'devastating' a fine contribution and combined with the direct start is by far the hardest route on the crag.

| 1984 | **Pagan Man**   J Dawes, T Kartawick |

| 1985 | **The Wilt Alternative**   Q Fisher |

| 1986 | **For the Love of Ivy**   N Dixon, S Lowe, S Hardy |

A direct start to Vintage Two.

RAVENSDALE GRADED LIST

5
Vilt Alternative (6c)
Vilt (6b)

4
Pagan Man (6b)

3
Cut Loose or Fly (5c)
The Bigot Direct (6a)

2
Scorpion (5c)
Round the Bend (5c)
Vintage Two (5b)
Hades (5c, 5b)
Via Vita Direct (5c)

1
Troops of Tomorrow (5c)
Cold Shoulder (5b)
Tank (5b)

HVS
Mephistopheles (5a,5b)
Bullets (5a,5b)
Malpossessed (5b)
Via Vita (4b,4c,5b)
Purple Haze (5b,5a)
Conclusor (4c,5a)
Rockbiter (5a)

VS
Beachcomber (5a)
Mealystopheles (5a,4c)
Frore (5a,4c)
Amain (4c)
Ploy (4c,4b,4c)
Gymnic (4c)
Metronome (4c)
Impendent (4c)
Delusor (4c,4c)
Mealy Bugs (4c,4c)
Medusa (4b,4b,4b)
The Wick (4b)

HAY TOP

O.S. ref. SK 176 726

This crag is below Cressbrook, at the bottom of Water-cum-Jolly, situated at the top of the tree line on the south side of Hay Top, and is the middle line of three buttresses. From right to left:-

Smokestack 10m HS
Climb the left-hand corner crack using the bottomless chimney which starts half way up the left-hand side.

Haystack 12m S
The overhanging crack to the right of Smokestack, finishing up a short wall.

3   Hay Wain   12m   VS
The overhanging flake crack 10m right of Haystack.

4   Arcadian   13m   VS
Start as for Hay Wain to the recess, traverse left for 3m to a
shallow corner and climb this to the top.

FIN COP   O.S. ref. SK 176 712

Situated at the Bakewell end of Monsal Dale and mainly hidden
from the tourist path, is a series of interesting blocks and
pinnacles formed by a landslip. Four routes are recorded, many
more are possible but on the whole the place is not much cop.

1   Overhanging Face   17m   HS
Start at the centre of the left-hand part of the main face. Climb 3m
to a narrow footledge; traverse right along this to an overhanging
crack leading to the top. A direct start is a touch harder.

2   Corner Crack   17m   D
The obvious corner right. Traverse left to an ivy corner to finish.

3   Right-Hand Face   13m   S
Climb the centre of the face right of Corner Crack.

THE CASTLETON AREA

O.S. ref. SK 138 827

'In the districts partly covered by this book there are a number of climbs on mountain limestone, some being very well known. The writer is satisfied that mountain limestone is beyond the border line of safety as that is understood by all the best and most experienced climbers; therefore mention of these climbs is omitted. The Dargai Crack for instance, is appreciably more dangerous than the Devil's Kitchen. Most climbers prefer difficulty without danger (by which one does not mean difficulty without exposure), but the limestone climbs are in large measure dangerous without being difficult, and frequently the only opportunity for the exercise of skill is afforded by the necessity of using loose holds safely, a proceeding rather edifying than pleasurable. It is safe to assume that all holds on mountain limestone are loose. There are nevertheless a few limestone climbs reasonably safe to the ordinary person; it is not proposed to specify'.

John Laycock in 'Some Gritstone Climbs'.

WINNATS PASS

SITUATION and CHARACTER

The 'windgates' is a narrow limestone gorge approximately 1km west of Castleton, running east-west. The main crags are high on the south side, while the popular ridges run from nearly road level on the north side.

The deeply cut gorge is the result of a collapsed cavern system, and this considerably increases the exposure on the steep faces. The routes are mostly loose and serious, being seldom frequented. No doubt they would improve with more traffic. They are in a fine position, and ideal for a hot summer's day, when shade is welcome. Elbow Ridge (3) and Matterhorn Ridge (5) give good sport in a hard winter.

APPROACHES and ACCESS

At the time of writing the Winnats is open to vehicles. When financial restrictions allow, a new road superseding the unstable Mam Tor road is to be built down Pin Dale. This may affect the status of, and approaches to, the Winnats.

The A265 leads to Castleton from Sheffield or Whaley Bridge. The A6 from Buxton or Stockport joins the A625. The Winnats Pass is reached from the old Mam Tor road, the A625. Castleton is served at present by the South Yorkshire Transport route 272 from Sheffield. Nearby Bamford is still served by trains from Manchester and Sheffield.

The land is the property of the National Trust which does not wish the Pass to be used for climbing because of the possible hazard of falling rock to cars and pedestrians. The route descriptions are included for completeness.

HISTORY

The 1910 Climbers' Club Journal records the ascent of *Elbow Ridge* and *Matterhorn Ridge*, probably by C.D. Yeomans, F. Winder and Douglass. Sometime early in the 1930s saw ascents of The Tourist Buttress routes and then for some time little is recorded. The next ascents were in 1969 when Keith Myhill climbed *Ginger Man* and with Tom Proctor did *Kaiser Bill*. *Pint of Blood* was free-climbed by Dave Mithen and Andy Crawley in the early 1970s. Inevitably hard modern routes were to appear on the steep walls of this neglected crag. In 1985 after five days of attempts Al Rouse, backed by T. Richardson, led *Rite of Way* and in the same year Craig Smith freed Bolt Route to give *Do Up Your Flies*.

THE CLIMBS are described from the easterly, Castleton approach. The pass begins at a cattle-grid just beyond the Speedwell Caverns. *Approximately 50m farther on the right is*:

TOURIST BUTTRESS

1   Tourist Crack   12m   VD
Climb the left-hand side of the buttress trending right.

(pre-1930)

2   Tourist Wall   13m   S
Climb the right-hand side of the front face, direct.   (pre-1930)

200m farther, at a bend in the road is:

3   Elbow Ridge   67m   D   *
Climb the pleasant ridge direct.   (pre-1910)

MATTERHORN RIDGE

This is 75m farther up the Pass. Its first tower is:

4   Cave Wall   20m   HS   4b
Start 2m right of the cave in the front of the buttress and ascend
direct.

5   Matterhorn Ridge   67m   VD   **
Climb the ridge, starting 17m above the road and taking the line of
least resistance.   (pre-1910)

6   Matterhorn Face   27m   HS   4b
Climb the ridge to a ledge at 7m, traverse left onto the face and
climb this trending left.

SHINING TOR

*The left-hand of the two large buttresses on the south side of the
Pass.*

7   Rite of Way   25m   E5   6b   ***
At the left-hand side of Shining Tor is a relatively new bolt ladder,
left of a line of old bolts. Start at a tiny vertical crack 2m left of the
bolts. Move right at 4m and follow the bolt ladder. Very sustained
and fingery on excellent rock. It is best to lower off from the top
bolts as the top is loose and dirty and belays are hard to find.
                                                    (1985)

8   Do Up Your Flies   30m   E5   6b
This strenuous route follows the line of rust 3m right of the cave.
                                                    (1985)

9   Aphrodisiac Jacket   30m   A2
Start at a shallow groove 10m right of the cave. Climb the corner
to the overlap and take this direct.   (1969)

Taking the impressive corner with caves at the foot and half-
height is:

10   Kaiser Bill   27m   HVS   5a
Start left of the cave and climb up 8m then traverse right to gain the crack. Ascend this, passing the cave, and exit right at the top.
(1969)

THE SHIELD
300m farther up the Pass is the characteristically shield-shaped buttress which has the following routes:

11   Ginger Man   25m   HVS   5a
Start on the left of the front face and climb to the groove. Go up this, moving right round the overhang to a small ledge. Go up to a pothole, peg, and with difficulty stand on the lip, and climb the shallow groove to a loose finish.
(1969)

12   Pint of Blood   23m   E1   5b   *
Start on the right and gain the ledge at 5m. Continue up the shallow groove, step right to the crack, and follow this to the top. Steep and loose.
(1969/1974)

13   Burning Giraffe   23m   A1   5b
Start right of the black circle on the right wall, and follow the horizontal weakness round the arête into Pint of Blood, using 4 pegs for aid. Finish up this.
(1970s)

WINNATS PASS LIST OF FIRST ASCENTS

pre-1910	**Elbow Ridge** J W Puttrell, H Bishop	
pre-1910	**Matterhorn Ridge** J W Puttrell, H Bishop	
1930	Routes done by C D Yeomans, Douglass, L Travis	
1969 Jan.	**Ginger Man** K Myhill, D Kichen	
1969	**Kaiser Bill** T Proctor, K Myhill	
1969 Feb.	**Pint of Blood** (6 pts.) Rev R Brownridge, T Mercer	
	First free ascent by D P Mithen, A Crawley in 1974.	
1969 July 13	**Aphrodisiac Jacket** (A2) R Buckley, P Abbot, L Bonnington	
1985	**Rite of Way** A Rouse, T Richardson	
1985	**Do up your Flies** C Smith	

Jason Myres reaching for the Black Kabul, Stoney Middleton.
Photo: Riche Brooks.

CAVE DALE

O.S. ref. SK 150 827

by Andy Barker

> 'So we went to the Peak Hotel and ate a sumptuous
> lunch, after which our inexorable leader drove us out,
> full of meat and sloth, back to the "Dargai". It is a climb
> that few men would try unroped. My acquaintance with
> its rickety joints and deceptive holds was made in a
> shower of fine rain that rendered it more slippery than
> ever; wet limestone is abominable stuff . . .
> . . . Midway in the final pitch a sapling sprouts from the
> cliff. Now according to the laws, written and unwritten,
> of the climber's art, this harmless vegetable must on no
> account be touched. But it is right in the way, and to
> make the difficulty of avoiding it greater its lithe trunk
> offers the only accessible hold for several feet. It would
> be "a touch beyond the reach of art" to leave it alone, so
> we fling scruples to the winds and push our way
> through the foliage up to the cliff's brow, where the
> gratified proprietor of the "Dargai" shakes each arrival
> by the hand.
> I know only one finer climb on mountain limestone, and
> that is far away in Somerset . . . '

> E.A. Baker. Moors, Crags and Caves of the High Peak.
> 1903

SITUATION and APPROACH

The Dale lies immediately south of Castleton village with Peveril
Castle's crumbling remains high on its right flank.
Approach the dale from the rear of the village square where a
signpost points up the steep narrow ravine at the start of the dale.

CHARACTER

Climbing here is very quiet and you certainly won't have to queue
for routes, although walkers and the dreaded day-trippers
constantly file up and down the dale. One consequence of the
unpopularity is loose rock which is quite bountiful. I can vouch for
that! Nature also seems to have quite a strangle-hold on most of
the easier routes. In winter the dale is very cold as it is a natural
wind funnel, but it can be quite pleasant on warm sunny days.

'The Famous Ed Wood' on Bubbles, Stoney Middleton.
Photo: Chris Craggs.

Belays are not to be found on a couple of routes but these are best avoided anyway due to the above-mentioned reasons.

HISTORY
As every budding climbing historian should know, Puttrell climbed his famous *Dargai Crack* at Christmas 1898 and it was so-named to commemorate the charge of the Cameron Highlanders at Dargai the previous year.

The rest of the dale's history is quite vague; some routes were mentioned in the 1910 Climbers' Club Journal, and West seemed to think that disillusioned pot-holers may have accounted for some routes and the occasional rusted piece of metal in the strangest of places. West and the Manchester Gritstone Club accounted for a few routes the best being *The Watchtower*, originally done with 5 pitons. Piton Route was eventually climbed free in 1979 by Roger Payne.

Nothing of note was claimed until the 80's when a direct route up the Watchtower was done, along with a couple of minor additions.

Paul Mitchell and Andy Barker discovered a handful of routes while Barker was working on the guide. The best of these, *A Friendly Chat with a Hungry Ghost*, which is the line of unclimbed pockets mentioned in previous guide, was climbed by Mitchell, chipping icicles off as he progressed!

THE CLIMBS are described from the narrow defile up the left-hand side (true right) of the dale and then back down the other side of the defile again. The first route is to be found on the left-hand side of a steep quarried wall on the left of the dale, 25m after the stile.

1   Dancing the Hard Bargain   9m   E1   5c
Follow the short leftward leaning groove to a finish up the wall.

(1984)

2   Alpha   10m   VS   4b
Just to the right ascend the twisting crack.

3   Dobbin   10m   HVS   5a
Climb the easier-than-it-looks wall from left to right.   (1984)

4   Beta   10m   VS   4c
Follow the fingery right-hand crack.

5   Scabby Buttress   33m   VD
100m past the second narrow defile, halfway up the steep slope,
is a large broken buttress. Follow the easiest line up this.   (1961)

Just down and right of Scabby Buttress is **RING BOLT BUTTRESS**.

6   Mr Jagger's Warning   10m   E3   6a   †
Climb the obvious central scoop on small pockets to a ledge. The
steep wall above is taken on large holds past a peg. Stake belay
well back.

7   Ring Bolt Buttress   17m   HVS   5a
Just right of the scoop is an old large ring-bolt. Climb the
awkward crack 2.5m right of this to the overhang. A quasimodo-
like traverse rightwards leads to a break in the overhang where
the top can be gained.

8   Barfleur   13m   VD
Follow the scrappy crack on the right of the buttress.

*Farther right a chain of small buttresses rises up the hill. These
buttresses provide about 20m of Diff climbing when linked
together. 250m farther on the dale closes with steep walls on both
sides.*

9   Moaning Groove   15m   S
Start from the small cave and follow the left-hand side of the deep
cleft. A finish can be made up White Ridge Crawl (18) V.Diff.
                                                                    (1961)

10   The Artery   13m   VS   4c
Start from the same cave and take a line up the left-hand side of
the fault. Hardest at the start.

11   Friction Wall   13m   HS   4b
The right-hand side of the cleft is taken via the wall and ledges.

12   Curving Crack   13m   S
The crack on the right. The White Mane (19) can be used as an
extension.

13   Green Groove   13m   S
Avoid this at all costs.

14   Scoop and Corner   15m   VS   4c
The deep corner to the right is climbed finishing up the scoop above.

15   Scoop Wall   15m   HS   4b
Climb the centre of the wall to the right directly up the centre.

16   Sycamore Groove   13m   HS   4b
A red paint spillage marks the start of this route. Move right beneath the overhang and ascend into the groove above to finish.
(1961)

17   V Groove   10m   D   .
15m right is an obvious groove which gives the route.

18   White Ridge Crawl   27m   VD
Take the most obvious line up the left-hand side of the ridge which is halfway up the hillside.
(1961)

19   The White Mane   35m   VD
The shallow groove on the front of the White Ridge is ascended to a small overhang. Turn this on the left and finish up the nose above.
(1961)

This area provides some spectacular winter 'poly-bagging', though at rather high speeds.

The next climbs are on the opposite side (true left). 12m down from V Groove (17) is:

20   Slab and Cleft   12m   HS   4b
Start from the right edge of the slab and climb up to a V-groove. Bridging up its outer edge brings the top.

21   Jaggered Crack   13m   HS   4b
The crack in the wall 3m right, with, surprise, surprise, a 'jaggered' rock on top.

22   Exide   13m   VS   4c
Start 2m right and climb direct to a small recess. Finish straight above.

The next route follows the obvious scooped, pocketed wall to the right.

23   A Friendly Chat with a Hungry Ghost   15m   E3   5c   ★★
An unusual-looking route, mentioned as unclimbed in the
previous guide. A mixture of undercuts, laybacking and bridging
lead past a tree and a peg to the finish.   (1986)

24   Goldfinger   17m   HVS   5b
Start right of the lower overhang at the foot of Dargai Crack and
climb diagonally up and left. The upper overhang is taken by a
good crack.

25   Dargai Crack   15m   VS   4b
'As a lead this is for none but the adept limestoner.' Charge up the
crack directly, passing a tree.   (1898)

26   Dargai Variant   17m   VS   4c
Climb the crack to the tree, then traverse leftwards to the finish of
Goldfinger.

27   Ivy Groove   15m   VS   4c
Pull over the overhang just right of the foot of Dargai Crack onto
the wall above. Climb the wall direct to finish up the overgrown
groove above.

3m right is:

28   Film   17m   VS   4c
Climb diagonally leftwards up the smooth slab on the right end of
the overhang to a weakness just left of the upper overhang.

29   Flam   17m   VS   4c
Take the right-hand edge of the slab to a slight groove in the arête
between the twin caves above.

30   Peak Climb   13m   VD
Climb the vegetated weakness leftwards above a concreted-up
cave, hidden up and round to the right.

10m down the dale is a smooth grey slab.

31   Belvedere   17m   E3   5c
The slab and wall left of Phone Home.   (1984)

32   Phone Home   17m   E3   5b
Follow the obvious line up the poorly-protected smooth slab.

33 Zorbit   17m   HS   4b
Start at the right-hand end of the smooth slab just left of the path
leading to the castle. Follow the uninteresting groove and crack.

The Keep and Keep Cleft have both been obliterated by a rock-fall
leaving quite an unstable mass for the moment. It is best avoided.

34 Keep Arête   18m   VD
The rounded easy-angled rib to the right of the rock-fall is taken past
much grass. Abseil off.

35 Jailer's Groove   18m   S
The groove right of the arête leads to horrendously steep grass.
(1961)

Round to the right is a bottomless groove; this is:

36 Jailer's Crack   20m   HVS   5a
Follow the corner/groove by quite pleasant climbing until vertical
grass is met. This section is possibly harder than the route!
(1961)

37 Jailer's Wall   20m   HVS   5a
The wall 4m right is taken direct on sharp pockets. Move leftwards on
obvious flakes to finish up Jailer's Crack.

38 Terrace Wall   20m   VD
The wall 10m right is taken direct.

39 Castle Groove   20m   HS
The wall just to the right is climbed, left of a small tree, finishing up a
groove.

40 The Watchtower   22m   VS   5a
This is the large buttress down and to the right (also the subject of
many Castleton post-cards). From its lowest point climb directly over
a small overhang to a stance and belay. Follow the flake crack round
to the left, to a recess around the arête. Move left for 2m and climb
direct to finish (the crux).
(1961)

41 All Along the Watchtower 22m   E2   5c
From the belay on the previous route, climb the hard looking wall
above past a bolt and a peg.
(1984)

42 Banana   17m   HS
From the same start again go direct to a short ramp. Follow this to finish up the right-hand side of the tower.

43 Pock Wall   12m   HVS   5a
Round the corner to the right by a recess is an obvious large thread. Follow the line of pockets leading left from this and finish through the ivy at its thinnest point. Poor.

44 The Letter Box   12m   E1   5c
Climb the overhang direct to finish up the groove on the right. Originally graded 4c!

45 Runts Grunt Stunt   12m   E4   6b
Start slightly to the right of the previous route below a peg. Climb the overhang past the peg trending slightly leftwards past another peg. Pumpy.

46 Belial   15   A2
The large overhang and overhanging wall is taken by a line of rusty bolts. Dubious marginal placements exist on the upper wall.

47 Piton Route   13m   HVS   5a
Ascend the wall just left of Puttrell's Crack.

48 Puttrell's Crack   12m   VD
Follow the obvious crack 7m right of Belial.

49 Puttrell's Arête   12m   VD
The arête right of the crack. Probably too loose to climb at present.

50 Banker's Climb   15m   VD
Farther down is an amphitheatre containing a cave. Moves lead from the cave onto a short wall. Climb this to a terrace and go up a short wall on the left to finish.

51 Borrower's Climb   10m   HS
Climb from the right of the cave to a small bush and up to a tree.

52 Crack and Nose   12m   VS   4c
At a lower level and to the right is a deeply undercut nose. From the recess take a crack to the nose and go direct up the wall above.

53   The Gangway   12m   M
The crack which runs diagonally leftwards to finish above the overhang. Garden rake may be useful.

The next two routes are completely overgrown and are merely described for completeness.

54   Thin Crack   12m   HS
The left-hand of two cracks is followed over a slight bulge.

55   Chastity   12m   VS   4c
The other crack is followed over some small roofs.

CAVE DALE LIST OF FIRST ASCENTS

1898 Christmas   **Dargai Crack**   J W Puttrell (solo)
Second ascent after gardening by H Bishop, C D Yeomans c1909.

pre-1910   **Cave Crack**   J W Puttrell

pre-1934   **Moaning Groove** (pegs used)   E Byne, C Moyer
First free ascent M Baxter, J Hayes in 1961.

1961   **Scabby Buttress**   M Baxter, J Hayes

1961   **Moaning Groove**   M Baxter, J Hayes
First free ascent. Two rusty pitons were found in the upper section.

1961   **Sycamore Crack**   M Baxter, J Hayes

1961   **White Ridge Crawl**   M Baxter, J Hayes

1961   **The White Mane**   M Baxter, J Hayes

1961   **Jailer's Groove**   M Baxter (unseconded)

1961   **Jailer's Crack**   G West (unseconded)

1961   **The Watchtower** (5 pts.)   G West, M Baxter

1961   **Spinal Finalé**   M Baxter, J Hayes

1979   **Piton Route**   R Payne (unseconded)
First free ascent.

1984	**All Along the Watchtower** D Kerr
1984	**Dancing the Hard Bargain** D Kerr. S Adderley, S Humphrey, P Mailor
1984	**Belvedere** D Kerr, S Humphrey, S Adderley, P Mailor
1984	**Dobbin** D Kerr (solo)
1984	**A Friendly Chat with a Hungry Ghost** P Mitchell

A small wall a couple of metres down provides a boulder problem.

PEAK CAVERN CLIFF

pre-1961   **Peak Cavern Cliff**   G West, J Taylor
An unsuccessful attempt on the superb weakness just left of the cavern entrance.
'We drilled our way up the overhanging side wall of the cave to the roof proper, then followed this round until the crack line was reached. At this point we abandoned the route for the following reasons: First was that up to the farthest point we had reached we had been able to use only three pitons, and as there was a hundred feet or so to go and not a chance of more than one or two pegs being used, we rejected the idea of spending days drilling up the wall. Originally of course we had though that it could be done with pitons, but our hopes never materialized. The second reason was that when the crack line was reached, the condition of the rock deteriorated a great deal, being in the form of a thick broken skin of loose rock over the solid underbelly. It was too expensive to knock away, and we considered it too dangerous to climb over. If a piece had broken off it would have swept us off the wall with the action of a gigantic guillotine. The last reason was the impending threat of prosecution by the owners of the cave'.

There was a second attempt in 1961 by G West, M Baxter and C Weston.

1961   **Peak Cavern Cliff**   G West, J Taylor, M Baxter, C Weston
On the second attempt the latter two climbers got halfway up the left wall while West was attempting the roof.

1981   *'Ian Buster Wright and Rob Harrison took five months to bolt the first ascent of Peak Cavern's 350-foot entrance, using some 250 bolts at a cost subsidized by Troll in excess of £100 . . . The pair finally made a complete ascent witnessed by a B.B.C. television crew. However, part of the agreement is that they must remove all the hangers to prevent any further ascents.*
Apart from being the longest roof climb ever it is also the longest line of continuous bolts placed'.

High no. 2

PINDALE QUARRY

O.S. ref. SK 160 823

The quarry is one of the least attractive climbing locations in the Peak. It is halfway between Castleton and Bradwell but is reached by the road from Hope. Park where a rough track (marked as Pindale Road on the 1:25,000 map) leaves the road at a sharp right-hand bend just past Pindale Cottage. Go up the Pindale road and the quarry is on the left. It is owned by the Earle's Cement complex.
On the far right of the quarry is a dark slab at the foot of the face. Routes at Very Difficult and Very Severe go up the right-hand corner and centre of this slab.
Towards the left of the quarry is a rusty projecting buttress. **Balbus**, Hard Very Severe, 5b, goes up the right wall of this. On the big wall containing a danger sign is **Fear and Loathing (In Las Vegas)** HVS, 4c. This climbs the wall slightly to the left of a thin quartz crack (peg) to a small niche followed by a steep crack to finish, (1986). The rest of the quarry is not worth consideration and there is little worthwhile rock on the other side of the dale on the small natural buttresses.

BRADWELL DALE

The rocks lie on both sides of the B6049 just south of Bradwell village. This road leaves the A625 along the Hope Valley at the Travellers' Rest. The rocks on the east side of the road are owned by the farmer at Hazlebadge Hall who does not want them to be used for climbing. In addition they contain much loose rock and are very near the road. They are now very overgrown. Those on the west side are cleaner, farther from the road and less open to view, but still of little interest.

EAST SIDE

1 Balcony Climb 30m HS
Climb over small grassy terraces to a good ledge at 20m on the first big buttress near the village, with a deep groove on its upper frontal face. Climb over the three balconies above to finish.

(1960s)

2 Hanging Garden 30m VS 4c
Climb to a platform at the foot of a short wall beneath the groove. Go up the wall to the groove and finish up this.   (1960s)

80m up the dale on the east side is a small parking space with a long overhanging wall hidden by trees behind it.

3 Rattan 30m HVS 5a
Climb to a break in the centre of the overhang and go direct over this to the terrace. Go up the bulging central wall to a tree on a ledge. Take the cleft on the left to a flake and vegetation to finish.

(1960s)

4 Mignon 33m HVS 5b
Climb the overhang 5m right and follow a line of calcite to a terrace. Climb a thin steep crack to a tree and ledge. Finish up the rib above diagonally right.   (1960s)

5 Cake Walk 33m HS
Climb the right-hand end of the overhangs to the terrace and go diagonally right over grassy ledges to a valley and exit left up a lead vein.   (1960s)

10m right is **Cave Crack**, an old aid route which is now free. 30m farther is **Angled Buttress**, 30m,S. Farther up the dale, behind another small parking place is:

6   Stack Wall   23m   HS
The small overhang and crack lead to a big ledge. Finish up the right-hand side of a second overhang.   (1960s)

7   Dysoning   17m   D
The wall to the right to a big ledge. Finish up the wall on the left, using lumps of spar.   (1960s)

8   Roof Route   23m   HS
Climb a crack to the right to the roof. Finish up the small overhang above.   (1960s)

9   Scoop Route   23m   VD
The scoop is followed to the top.   (1960s)

10   Bulging Wall   23m   S
Climb straight up the centre of the wall.   (1960s)

11   Flip Side   13m   S
The crack left of a tree. Finish direct up the wall.   (1960s)

12   Pinnacle Route   23m   HS
Climb the wall direct to the pinnacle on the upper tier. Finish up the cracks on the left of the pinnacle.   (1960s)

13   The Nose   13m   S
Climb the wall with a roof above it direct to a nose which is taken on its left.   (1960s)

14   The Platband   13m   HS
Climb up the right of the nose and take the roof at a weakness on the right-hand end.   (1960s)

15   Two Tier Climb   20m   HS
Climb the large buttress farther right on its right to a good ledge. Finish up the arête of the upper buttress.   (1960s)

Farther right is another but cleaner two-tiered wall giving the last and only clean climbs on this side of the road.

16 Direct Route 20m VS 4c
Climb the lower wall in line with the thin crack in the upper wall
and finish up that crack.   (1960s)

17 Indirect Route 20m VS 4c
Start just right and finish up the right-hand crack in the upper
wall.   (1960s)

WEST SIDE

*The rocks are best reached up a sloping track, closed by an iron
gate with a 'private' notice close to it, at their right-hand end. They
are, however, described from left to right. There is a jumble of
large blocks at the left above which is the deep overhanging
Chockstone Crack, 10m S.*

1 Elderberry Crack 10m S
Climb the crack on the left. Move left and finish up the centre.
                                                                (1960s)

2 Funf 20m VS 4c
The crack on the right to its top. Move left to a ledge and go
diagonally right to another ledge and up a weakness above.
                                                                (1960s)

3 Flake Crack 13m VS 4c
The crack just right to its top. Move left up the wall to an
overhanging flake and a big ledge.   (1960s)

4 Recessed Corner 20m VS 4c
The corner to the overhang and big ledge above. Finish up a thin
crack.   (1960s)

5 The Steps 10m VD
Follow the line of steps around the arête to the right to the top.
                                                                (1960s)

6 Two-Step 13m HS
From the second step go up the broken crack in the left wall.
                                                                (1960s)

7 Broken Crack 10m HS
The crack low down on the right. A hard mantelshelf right to
finish.   (1960s)

*Some distance right is a large grassy space where the 'private'
track finishes. At the left of the space is:*

8 Dragon's Back 33m VS 4c
Follow the saw-edged ridge.

(1960s)

9 Dragon's Side 33m VD
Take the easiest line up the wall on its right to finish up the ridge.

(1960s)

10 Amphitheatre Wall 33m VS 4c
Go up the centre of the wall opposite Dragon's Side to a ledge.
Mantelshelf onto the gangway. Go 15m left to a pock-marked
wall. Climb this to a ledge at the foot of a grooved corner. Finish
up this.

(1960s)

11 Amphitheatre Crack 33m VS 4c
Start just right and climb to a ledge below the crack. Follow the
crack to the gangway. Move 10m left and finish up the deep
overhanging crack.

(1960s)

12 Lefty 30m HS
Go up the wall to a ledge and take the left-hand groove to another
ledge. Finish up the left-hand crack.

(1960s)

13 Righty 30m VS 4c
Take the right-hand groove and finish up the right-hand crack.

(1960s)

BRADWELL DALE LIST OF FIRST ASCENTS

1930	Some early routes by Monty Granger.
1959/1961	Several routes done by M Baxter and the Manchester Gritstone climbers.
1965	Many of the easier routes by L Millsom, B Shirley.
1963/1969	**Hanging Gardens** M Baxter, E Jones
	Rattan M Baxter, B Duckworth

Mignon   M Baxter, E Jones

Cake Walk   M Baxter, B Duckworth

Cave Crack   M Baxter, E Jones
First free ascent.

Angled Buttress   M Baxter, E Jones

THE BUXTON AREA

PETER DALE

by Chris Craggs

SITUATION, APPROACHES and CHARACTER
This small cliff is about 2km west of Tideswell. Although the routes are short the setting is very pleasant and the crag gets all the sun that is going.
The nearest parking is on the minor road from Wheston to Smalldale where the road crosses Peter Dale. The cliff lies about 1km to the south down the valley (just round a bend). The cliff can also be reached by a longer stroll from the south from the direction of Monk's Dale.

HISTORY
There are several small buttresses in this valley, the most prominent contains *Peter Dale Chimney* and *Peter Dale Staircase*, put up by Henry Bishop, in 1908. Another seven routes were done by Chris Craggs, Mark Stokes, Colin Binks and Dave Spencer in early 1984.

THE CLIMBS start where a dilapidated dry-stone wall meets the crag, left of centre. 15m left of this are twin chimneys.

1 Sooty 12m VS 4b
Climb the left-hand branch.   (1984)

2 Sweep 12m VS 4b
Ascend the right-hand branch.   (1984)

3 Beef on the Hoof 15m E3 5c   *
The wall right of the chimneys has a prominent flat spike at 8m. Gain this directly (hidden peg), then move up left to a direct finish.
                                                              (1984)

4 Side Step 12m HVS 5a
Just left of the wall is a groove which is climbed until it is possible to pull into the continuation on the left.   (1984)

5   Peter Dale Chimney   14m   VD   *
Ascend the narrow chimney where the wall meets the crag.
                                                          (1908)

6   Diminished Responsibility   14m   HVS   5b
The right wall of the chimney has a crackline in it with an obvious
block. Take the crack direct.   (1984)

7   Peter Dale Staircase   14m   D
The blocky ramp gives a way up or even a way down.   (1908)

8   Fade to Grey   14m   E1   6a
The wall right of the Staircase has a prominent groove starting
8m up. Reach the groove directly and follow it easily.   (1984)

9   Drunk and Disorderly   13m   E1   5c
At the right-hand end of the wall is another groove that fades out
towards the bottom. It is approached from the ramp on the right
via a conspicuous hole.   (1984)

SMALLDALE and PEAK DALE QUARRIES

O.S. ref.
SK 097 771

by Chris Jackson

> 'Having been tipped off by the jackdaws the quarry
> inspector stormed angrily up the hillside and joined me
> at the top of the crag. After a lengthy tirade he was only
> placated when I agreed with him that we must have
> been mad to embark on such a death trap. With great
> conviction I promised to depart for good just as soon as
> (or if) Dave got up alive . . . but all I could see was that
> big and mean-looking wall which called to me every
> time we drove past the crag. I never did go back . . .

Geoff Milburn 1973.

SITUATION and CHARACTER
Smalldale Quarry is situated just south of the village of Smalldale,
approximately half way between Peak Forest and Buxton. It forms
several steep buttresses, some containing areas of flowstone, and

attains a height of 30m in places. As with many limestone quarries, the rock is of mixed quality and generally very steep. The crag faces north-west catching available late afternoon sun in the summer months. Peak Dale Quarry is the westerly extension of Smalldale Quarry.

APPROACHES and ACCESS

From Sheffield, pass through Stoney Middleton on the A623 as far as Peak Forest, and turn left a little way past the church. Follow this road for about 1km to a right turn leading to the village of Smalldale. Pass through the village, the quarry is on the left. Continue towards Peak Dale village for a further 500m for Peak Dale Quarry, also on the left along a short track.

From Buxton, take the A6 for 2km towards Dove Holes, then branch off right towards the villages of Peak Dale and Smalldale. Over the railway line, and opposite the pub is Peak Dale Quarry; continue along the same road for 500m and Smalldale Quarry will be seen on the right, beyond a new plantation.

Neither of these approaches can be easily accomplished using public transport.

The quarries are almost certainly private, and it is unlikely that permission would be given to climb there. No problem has yet arisen in Smalldale Quarry however; shouts of despair and the crashing of falling blocks has so far only raised perplexed smiles on the faces of the locals. Access is best accomplished via a gate at the Smalldale end of the quarry. Climbing in Peak Dale Quarry has been actively discouraged and climbers should consider carefully whether it is worth the possible conflict with the quarry owners.

HISTORY

Smalldale Quarry has almost certainly been climbed on in the past although ascents seem to have gone unrecorded. *Play it Again, Sam* and *Eeonefivebee* both showed signs of previous attention. Most of the remaining routes were climbed in the period May to July 1985.

Senan Hennassy claimed *Scott's Wall, Play it Again, Sam, Shanacie* and *Shae*; Bill Wintrip climbed *Little Lady, Diddyogger* and *The Ubiquitous*; Bob Conway *First Offence, Crooked* and *Going Straight*; Roy Small screwed it up with *Socket Set*; Les Naylor put up *Last Exit Going South*, and Chris Jackson did *Stainsby Girls, Eeonefivebee* and *Friend 15*.

In late 1986 Wintrip returned with Neil Foster and climbed the fine *Lost Contact* on the big wall, while Foster's addition *Can Boys* up the clean white wall is probably the Quarry's finest route making it well-worth a visit. Dedicated gardeners will discover that fine lines still remain to be discovered.

History records only one route so far in Peak Dale Quarry, although there is scope for more. An undercover attack by Geoff Milburn and Dave Gregory in May 1973 resulted in *Whispering Crack*.

THE CLIMBS
In Smalldale Quarry there are two main buttresses. The left-hand one, Arch Buttress, features an arch-shaped overhang at mid-height; the other, Truck Gully Buttress is some 100m right and is characterized by a gully at its left end containing a precariously jammed railway truck.

About 50m left of **ARCH BUTTRESS** *and at a higher level is a small buttress with a central crack.*

1   Scott's Wall   12m   HVS   5a
Climb the crack to the top.   (1985)

On the left (east) face of Arch Buttress is a prominent square groove.

2   Play it again, Sam   18m   HVS   5a
Climb the groove by bridging and jamming.

To the right is a sharp arête.

3   First Offence   21m   E4   6a
Start left of the arête. Climb to a ledge at 5m and continue to a bolt on the right-hand side of the arête. Move round the arête and climb boldly to a bolt. Continue just left of the arête to a peg then move right to finish up a crack.   (1985)

4   Stainsby Girls   26m   E4   6b   *
Steep and exciting climbing up the left side of the arch. Start on the front face below a discontinuous crack. Climb the crack to its top, (thread) and make reachy moves left to gain a ledge. Climb the wall above to a downwards pointing block and follow the overhang until a desperate move can be made into the final groove, 3 bolts. Easier climbing leads to the top.   (1985)

5   Lost Contact   26m   E4   6a   ** †
Start just right of the prominent central groove. Climb up to and
up a shallow groove, bolt, to a roof. Pull past this, bolt, and power
up the overhanging finger-crack finishing just left of the
watchblock.

6   Can Boys   20m   E5   6b   ***
A superb route. A few metres right, a wide crack rises from a
grassy bank. Climb the crack then move left and go up to a bolt.
Pass a second bolt to a flying layback and good hold on the left;
bolt. A downward-pointing spike is the key to the finish. Pass it
rightwards to a ledge and the top.   (1986)

7   Little Lady   18m   E2   5c
Start at the right-hand side of the buttress, a little way up the
grassy bank. Follow an obvious thin crack which leads to a wider
crack to finish.   (1985)

The next routes are on **TRUCK GULLY BUTTRESS.**

8   Diddyogger   16m   HVS   5a
Climb the obvious line just right of the gully.   (1985)

9   Crooked   18m   E1   5b
Start some 12m right of Jammed Truck Gully. Climb the left edge
of the deep crack line of Last Exit Going South, then trend left
after 6m and follow the curving line to the top.   (1985)

10   Last Exit Going South   18m   HVS   5a
Climb the obvious deep crack line direct.   (1985)

11   Eeonefivebee   18m   HVS   5a
Start just right of the last route and climb past huge threads until
it is possible to traverse precariously right to finish up a shallow
groove.   (1985)

12   Socket Set   18m   VS   4c
Thread your way up the obvious crack to the right, and make a
bolt for the skyline notch.   (1985)

13   Shanacie   30m   E2   5b
Start just right of the shattered groove which delineates the left
edge of the main face. Climb thin cracks trending right to a ramp
(psychological thread runners in-situ), go up this, then back left to
finish up cracks.   (1985)

14 The Ubiquitous 30m E1 5b
Start just left of a small cave at the foot of the buttress. Climb the
wall left of the crack/groove, thread at 5m, finishing up cracks just
left of the arête. (1985)

15 Going Straight 30m E3 6a ★★
Excellent climbing on essentially good rock, much better than it
appears. Start at an area of grey rock directly below the final
tower. Climb direct towards this, passing a peg at 15m. Move
slightly left just below the tower and finish up the front face. (1985)

16 Friend 15 30m E2 5b
Start some 6m right of the small cave and climb past a projecting
rusty peg to the left end of a wide dog-leg crack. Follow this to
finish up the waterwashed runnels to the right of the tower. (1985)

17 Shae 30m E1 5b
Start just right of Friend 15 and climb to a ledge at 6m. Move right
and head for the top. (1985)

PEAK DALE QUARRY   O.S. Ref. SK 095 770

*'I visited Peak Dale Quarry in 1962 but couldn't get
anyone to climb with me!'*

M Baxter.

Peak Dale Quarry is roughly formed by two walls at right angles,
and sports a pond in wet weather. The route is three-quarters of
the way along the right-hand wall.

1 Whispering Crack 24m VS 4c
The wide crack, is nothing to shout about. (1973)

SMALLDALE QUARRY LIST OF FIRST ASCENTS

1970s/1985 **Play it Again Sam** S Hennassy
Evidence of an earlier ascent.

1970s/1985	**Eeonefivebee** C Jackson
	Also probably done much earlier
1985	**Scott's Wall** S Hennassy
1985	**Shanacie** S Hennassy
1985	**Shae** S Hennassy
1985	**Little Lady** W Wintrip
1985	**Diddyogger** W Wintrip
1985	**The Ubiquitous** W Wintrip
1985	**First Offence** R Conway
1985	**Crooked** R Conway
1985	**Going Straight** R Conway
1985	**Socket Set** R Small
1985	**Last Exit Going South** L Naylor
1985	**Stainsby Girls** C Jackson
1985	**Friend 15** C Jackson
1985	**Lost Contact** W Wintrip, N Foster
1986	**Can Boys** N Foster

BIBBINGTON QUARRY   O.S. ref. SK 076 769

*"Bibbington? Bibbington! Where the hell's
Bibbington?" "You know . . . It's that horrible hole that
Al Evans discovered near Dove Holes – the one near that
big limestone slag-heap and the blue lagoon." "Oh . . .
THAT hole! I'm not going there." "It can't be that bad,
can it?" "Yes!" End of conversation.*

Anon.

SITUATION and CHARACTER
The quarry lies east of the A6 between Dove Holes and Buxton,
about 1km from the railway station.

Much of the rock is of reasonable quality, however the top of most of the routes is loose. There is a dry stone wall at the top of the main wall which has to be climbed after each route. Care should be taken that the rope running over it does not dislodge rocks onto the second. There are no belays at the top but a very solid fencepost at the right-hand end and in situ pegs in a boulder well back left of the main wall can be joined with a spare rope to form a continuous belay along the whole extent of the main wall.

APPROACHES and ACCESS

Trains run from Manchester and Buxton to Dove Holes every hour. From Dove Holes follow the A6 to Buxton. On the right is a large layby and about 400m past this the smaller faces of the quarry can be seen on the left. A rusty iron gate allows access to a track which leads through grassy hummocks to the top of the crag of which the main wall faces away from the A6. Walk back left (towards Dove Holes) along its top until one can see the huge blue/green pond and go rightwards over the angle of a fence and wall and down a grassy bank to the foot of the main wall.

HISTORY

The first probings here were by Tony Howard and friends but little was done and the details have been lost. The first recorded contributions were made by Ben Campbell-Kelly and 'Trig' Treglown. Their *Princess Anne's Crack* is perhaps the best line in the quarry and the amusing trio of routes on the left of the main wall is pleasant. Trig revealed the details of the quarry to Al Evans who enlisted a team and paid a visit one snowy day in January 1979. Alan Pierce and Paul Cropper did *Absolute Zero*, and Evans and Brian Cropper soloed *Winter's Tale*, an epic as it was choked with snow. Evans returned later with Martin Andrew and Nick Colton. Evans led *Black Holes, Werewolf Crack* and *The Skull* and Colton added *Alpinist's Dream* (named after its bivouac ledge). On another visit Evans and George Hardhill did *The Magnificent Concept* and some minor lines. Later Paul Cropper added *Mong Attack Crack* and *Psychodimbo*; Lim Burton added *Asylum* and *The Warder* while Al Evans and Nadim Siddiqui complicated matters with *Zen* etc.

THE CLIMBS are described from RIGHT to LEFT.

MAIN WALL

This is the 20m high wall just left of the grassy bank descent route. Facing it one has the huge blue/green pond on one's right. A fence runs up to the foot of Absolute Zero.

1 Psychodimbo 20m   HVS   5b
At the right-hand end of the main wall is a shallow green corner.
Follow this to the horizontal break and move out right to below
the obvious slim groove on the edge of the main wall. Gain this
and climb it to finish more easily over the wall.   (1979)

2 Alpinist's Dream 20m   VS   4c
As for Psychodimbo to the break. Move left to the good ledge and
climb the flake crack to a ledge. Follow the leaning crack to finish.
                                                                     (1978)

3 Princess Anne's Crack 20m   HVS   5a   *
The most obvious crack in the centre of the wall. Start up the
overhanging black corner. Move left into the upper crack and
follow this, taking care with the loose finish.   (1973)

4 The Asylum 20m   HVS   5b
Start 2m left at a shallow corner. Climb the corner to the break
then make difficult moves up the wall to the right-hand of two
hanging cracks. Climb this to an easier finish.   (1979)

5 Mong Attack Crack 20m   HVS   5b
Climb the wall 2m left again to the break and gain the left-hand of
two hanging cracks. Climb this to a difficult move onto a ledge.
Finish easily.   (1979)

6 Black Holes 20m   VS   4b   *
Start below obvious cleaned ledges and climb up left to a ledge at
7m. Climb up to the break, then up the scoop on good holds.
Move left at the top of the corner and climb ledges to finish.
                                                                     (1978)

7 Absolute Zero 20m   HS   4b
Start by the fence. Climb up the steep corner for 8m to a ledge on
the left. Climb the obvious stepped corner to the top, moving left
out of the final corner.   (1978)

8 Zen and The Art of Moving Horizontally 43m   VS   4b,4b
A girdle traverse of the crag. Start as for Absolute Zero.
1. 8m. Climb the corner and belay on the large ledge.
2. 35m. Step back down and traverse the obvious break
rightwards across the main wall.   (1979)

Emotional Rescue, Stoney Middleton.
Photo: Chris Jackson.

9   The Warder   20m   HVS   5a
Climb the corner as for Absolute Zero to the break. Move up and right to gain the hanging cracks on the arête. Follow these to the large ledge and an easier finish.   (1979)

10   Werewolf Crack   17m   VS   5a
On the wall right of the next corner is a hanging crack. Climb the lower wall awkwardly via discontinuous cracks to the break. Move up to the crack and follow it to the top.   (1978)

11   How Many people who have worked at Ellis Brigham's in Manchester have ever been out on a hill?   12m   VS   4b
Climb the corner with a deep crack. Starting direct or on the left.
                                                                      (1978)

12   One   10m   S
Follow the obvious flake crack on the left arête of the corner.
                                                                      (1974)

13   Or Perhaps None?   8m   VS   4b
The crack slanting slightly left in the wall at the top of the grass bank. Climb the crack and move left into a groove to finish.
                                                                      (1974)

14   Sad Crack   7m   VD
The bulging corner crack at the top of the grass bank.   (1974)

This ends the Main Wall and the ground now dips away and then rises again at a second grass bank, at the top of which is an obvious small corner, The Groove. The next climbs are described in relation to this from left to right.

15   The Skull   8m   VD
The obvious square-cut corner crack. 2m left of Subsidiary Groove.   (1978)

16   Subsidiary Groove   8m   VD
Climb the small corner immediately left of The Groove to a ledge (common with The Groove) and follow a crack in the left wall to finish.   (1978)

17   The Groove   8m   VD
The corner at the top of the grass bank is climbed direct.   (1978)

John Godding, Dreaming of Androids and Electric Sheep, Horseshoe Quarry.
Photo: Riche Brooks.

18   The Magnificent Concept   10m   VS   4b
5m right is an obvious crack with a bulge at 3m.   (1978

19   Titbit   8m   VD
The short flake crack 2m right starting from a ledge at 3m.

(1978

20   Niknak   8m   VD
The shallow gully 2m right.   (1978

*No more routes are described on this section of the crag. There
are two small routes on a small buttress 50m right of the Main
Wall above the blue/green pond.*

21   Springtime Fable   8m   VD
Ascend the pleasant crack just right of the arête.   (1978

22   Winter's Tale   8m   D
Follow the much wider crack 2m right.   (1978

BIBBINGTON QUARRY LIST OF FIRST ASCENTS

1973 Nov. 24	**Princess Anne's Crack** B Campbell-Kelly, R Treglown	
1974 Jan. 6	**Sad Crack** R Treglown, B Campbell-Kelly	
1974 Jan. 6	**One** B Campbell-Kelly	
1974 Jan. 27	**Or Perhaps None?** B Campbell-Kelly, Ida Niborg	
1978	**How Many People who have worked at Ellis Brigham's in Manchester have ever been out on a hill?** B Campbell-Kelly, R Treglown	
1978 Feb. 11	**Absolute Zero** A Pierce, P Cropper	
1978 Feb. 11	**A Winter's Tale** A Evans, B Cropper (both solo)	
1978 March	**The Groove** G Hardhill	
1978 March	**The Magnificent Concept** A Evans, G Hardhill	
1978 March	**Subsidiary Grooves** A Evans	
1978 March	**Springtime Fable** A Evans	

1978 April 5	**Black Holes** A Evans, M Andrew, N Colton
1978 April 5	**Alpinist's Dream** N Colton, A Evans, M Andrew
1978 April 5	**Werewolf Crack** A Evans, M Andrew, N Colton
1978 April 5	**Titbit** N Colton
1978 April 5	**Niknak** N Colton
1978 April 5	**The Skull** A Evans, N Colton
1979 June 20	**The Asylum** J Burton, R (Little Sid) Siddiqui
1979 June 20	**Mong Attack Crack** N Colton, P Cropper
1979 June 20	**The Warder** J Burton, R Siddiqui
1979 June 20	**Psycho Dimbo** P Cropper, N Colton
1979 June 20	**Madam Across the Water** A Evans, N (Big Sid) Siddiqui
1979	**Zen and the Art of Moving Horizontally** A Evans, N Siddiqui
1979 July 4	**Alpinist's Dream Direct Start** N Colton

HARPUR HILL QUARRY   O.S. ref. SK 062 704

*'On one occasion after completing several routes we
were relaxing on the hillside idly looking at a tunnel
opening below us. Suddenly without warning there was
a great roar and a huge horizontal flame (many yards
long) issued from the tunnel mouth. I was convinced
that we were looking at a secret underground rocket
launching site – which could be the only reason for
forcibly removing climbers from such a mediocre crag.'*

Geoff Milburn c.1970.

SITUATION and CHARACTER
The quarry lies 1.5 km due south of Buxton and is just over 1km
west of the A515 Buxton-Ashbourne road.
There are two tiers to the quarry and both are loose and require
care. The upper tier faces roughly north-west and is out of the sun
early on in the day. The climbs on Poised Block Buttress and the

Crazy Pinnacle should be treated with great caution – if the buttresses are still standing!

APPROACHES and ACCESS
A subsidiary road arcs off the A515 to the west at Brierlow Bar (SK 086 698) and rejoins it at SK 062 723. On the left of this road (travelling north) is a working men's club. One can usually park here. A path leads from the car-park over grassy spoil heaps to the quarry.
The quarry is owned by ICI and the company actively discourages climbing. The inclusion of these route descriptions is merely for completion and in no way implies that climbers have any right to climb in the quarry.

THE CLIMBS start at the left-hand end of the upper tier, to the right of a conspicuous cave, where a large buttress is split by a grassy ledge at two-thirds height.

POISED BLOCK BUTTRESS

At the centre of the face is a small shattered pinnacle.

1 Zebedee 33m   VS   4b
Step off the left side of the pinnacle and climb diagonally leftwards towards an overlap. Pass this on the right then go leftwards into a shallow groove which leads to the grassy ledge. Move right for 3m and climb a system of cracks trending left at the top.   (1960s)

2 Greensleeves 33m   VS   4b
Climb straight up from the pinnacle until it is possible to traverse right into an obvious crack which is climbed to a small overhang (thread). Move left and climb a thin crack to the grass ledge. Follow a wide crack containing several chockstones to the top.
                                                                           (1960s)

The next climbable rock to the right of Poised Block Buttress is a pinnacle behind which is a loose way down.

CRAZY PINNACLE

On the front of the pinnacle are two cracked grooves.

3   Slob Team Special   13m   HS
Climb the left-hand groove.   (1979)

4   Crazy Pinnacle Face   13m   HS
Ascend the right-hand groove to a compulsory perched block
then finish up an arête.   (1960s)

The next buttress on the right is the most obvious on the cliff.

PAPACY BUTTRESS

*On the left-hand side of the buttress, facing Crazy Pinnacle is a
water-worn crack splitting three bulges.*

5   Upthrutch   20m   VS   4c
Follow the crack to a fence-post belay.   (1960s)

6   The Seven Deadly Sins   33m   HVS   5a   **
Start in a small corner just left of an obvious wide crack in the
centre of the buttress. Climb the corner to a bulge, move left to a
small sloping ledge and climb a crack above to a slab. Move
diagonally left to another small ledge then climb the wall above,
peg, until a long traverse right can be made to finish up an
obvious groove.   (1966)

7   Lust   50m   VS   4b
Ascend the obvious wide crack.   (1966)

8   The Seven Deadly Virtues   33m   HVS   5b   *
Start as for Lust. Traverse right then climb up into a hanging
groove. Climb this to an overhang then move right to a small
ledge, peg. Climb diagonally right to a groove, peg, then go back
left over easier ground to the top.   (early 1960s/1967)

9   One Deadly Variant   33m   HVS   5b
Follow Seven Deadly Virtues to the overhang at the top of the
groove. Swing left and climb the wall above, peg, to finish.
                                                                        (1970s)

*To the right of Papacy Buttress is a zone of scree and rubbish. To
the right of and above is a steep buttress with a large shallow
corner.*

10   Lachesis   33m   E1   5a
Start by an elder bush. Climb the corner for 3m then traverse 5m left. Move up and rightwards towards a grassy ledge then climb a small overhang on the left. Move right into a crack which leads to the top. Loose.   (1970s)

17m right is a cave halfway up the face.

11   Z Victor 1   33m   HVS   4c
There are various ways into the cave. Move up the left wall of the cave until it is possible to stride back right into a groove to finish.   (1960s)

17m right is an obvious corner.

12   Inception   17m   S
Ascend the obvious corner.

The base of the crag drops steeply down to another area, and there is the hole of a miner's trial level which leads into the base of the crag for a few metres.

13   Two Cave Gully   27m   VS   4b
Start 2m right of the miner's hole. Traverse leftwards into the gully, above the overhang, and climb it if you must. Loose.   (1960s)

Several metres right is a small pocketed wall with problems for the connoisseur. 30m right of the miner's hole is a very clean slab of rock split by a thin diagonal crack.

14   Jam Butty Mines Crack   23m   VS   4c   *
Thin moves up the slab lead to a crack which is then climbed.   (1966)

15   Popeye   13m   VS   4b
Climb the obvious thin crack a few feet left of the previous route.   (1960s)

Just right of Jam Butty Mines Crack are two grooves.

16   Bluto   20m   HVS   4c
Climb the left-hand groove past loose blocks to a good ledge.   ·
Continue up steeply leftwards to another good ledge on the arête. Move right and finish up a short wall.   (1960s)

17 Avarice 20m VS 4b
Ascend the right-hand groove.   (1966)

Just to the right is another groove.

18 Gluttony 12m S
Climb the groove.   (1960s)

HARPUR HILL QUARRY — LOWER TIER   O.S. ref.
SK 064 707

by Malc Baxter

SITUATION and APPROACH
The left-hand part of this extensive quarry is split into two tiers.
These climbs lie on the right-hand side of the lower tier, near the
green pool and overlooking the college.
The usual approach is to drive up a track between the cottages,
opposite the garage, and park near the climbs. Gates are
sometimes locked however and a right of way is not presumed.
More general access is better by parking in the Harpur Hill Club
car park, for which permission has not been granted, but has not
been refused. A stile in a corner near the club, leads up two fields
to a quarry road. Follow the track left and into the quarry.

CHARACTER and ACCESS
The climbs are described from left to right facing the rocks, and
start from a pinnacle near the pool. There are ample belay stakes
for all the climbs which are low in the grass (This superb sentence
has been left unpunctuated for posterity and the edification of
future guide writers. Ed). All the climbs are on excellent steep and
often rough limestone, any loose rock having been cleaned.
After doing a couple of climbs without using bolts or pegs it
became a matter of pride to climb here with only natural
protection, so for the purists and upholders of tradition here is a
NO PEG and NO BOLT AREA which it is hoped will remain so.
Beware the lengths of the routes as the Glossop lads have not yet
been converted and can only climb in feet!
There is plenty of rock left for exploration.
CLIMBING IS NOT ALLOWED and the descriptions are merely for
completion.

HISTORY
by Mike F Browell

Harpur Hill Quarry is one of a number of recently abandoned workings which were barely clear of the quarrymen before climbers moved in. The quarry's reputation of being a perilously loose horror show has gone before it and each successive generation has been reluctant to pick up where the last one was scared off!

Initially the quarries were used for pegging practice and other than the rusting legacy of a few abandoned pitons no details of early routes were recorded. Joe Brown was however reputed to have climbed there. Even Graham West, who pioneered Derbyshire limestone climbing, neglected to record his aided ascent of *Seven Deadly Virtues*. Pegging activity commenced in the Fifties but the quarry was then left until 1966 before rediscovery.

Early in the Spring of 1966 Bob Dearman paid a visit to the quarry with three friends and climbed *Avarice*. He returned later, in August, with Bob Conway for the latter to lead the fine *Seven Deadly Sins*. Dearman even paid a third visit that year to record *Lust*. A glance at the Stoney First Ascent List shows that Dearman had completed his exploration there and had moved on to new pastures. These three routes were first recorded by Paul Nunn in New Climbs 1967.

Another climber who visited the crag was Chris Trotter of the Sheffield University Mountaineering Club who working at the nearby Safety in Mines Research Establishment (he should have known better!). He enlisted P Townroe of the S.U.M.C. to climb *Jam Butty Mines Crack*. This re-activated interest in the quarry and a short spate of activity produced the routes which appeared in the 1970 Southern Limestone guidebook. Shortly after Trevor Morris had freed Seven Deadly Virtues in 1967 access was clamped down and climbing became virtually impossible except for secret raids.

In 1979 Clive Jones was lumbered with the chore of checking the routes for the next guide and his enthusiasm for the task produced only one new route, *Slob Team Special*. So great was the response that no-one claimed any new routes until a marauding team visited from Glossop in 1985. Malc Baxter, Barry Duckworth, Ian Warhurst, Keith Ashton, Ado Garlick and Harry Venables re-discovered the Lower Tier and set to work to produce eighteen new routes within the space of three months. Despite tall stories in the Prince of Wales no other climbers were gulliblé enough to join the fray.

THE CLIMBS

1   Positive Discrimination   10m   VS   4c
Ascend the front face of the pinnacle from left to centre.   (1986)

To the right is a fine steep solid buttress called Pool Wall.

2   Cats 23   17m   HVS   5a
On the left end of the wall is an obvious crack. Start at a detached
block, moving left then right to follow the crack.   (1986)

3   Tricycle Man   18m   E2   5c
A few feet right of Cats 23. Climb the steep crack to the hole. Move
right and climb the headwall,   (1986)

4   Face Value   18m   E3   6a   *
Climb the sentry box and the thin crack to the centre of the wall.
Move right and climb the headwall right of Tricycle Man.   (1986)

5   College Crack   18m   E1   5b
Climb the obvious steep jamming crack.   (1986)

6   Permutation Wall   18m   HVS   5b
Climb the disjointed crack-line 2m right of College Crack to the
ramp at half-height, which is followed to the top.   (1986)

7   Upthrutch   17m   HVS   5b
The overhanging groove just right with an 'interesting' crack in
the back. Strenuous until a move left to the start of the ramp.
Move right and climb the worrying headwall.

8   Diamond Wall   17m   E1   5b
Start at an obvious hole about 8m right and just left of the right
end of Pool Wall. Climb up and right to reach a brushed diagonal
crack, then go left and up to the top.   (1986)

The next buttress right is called **RAILWAY BUTTRESS** *because of
the bits of railway line sticking out at the top right.*

9   Narrow Gauge   8m   S   4a
Ascend the pleasant flake crack, up left of the buttress.   (1986)

10   Wide Gauge   17m   VS   4c
Follow the wide crack on the left of the buttress.   (1986)

11   Railroaded   17m   HVS   5b
The central thin crack is followed over the overhang.   (1986)

12   Just The Ticket   12m   VS   4b
The wide crack on the right of the buttress with a short bit of
railway line to finish.   (1986)

The next climbing is on the walls to the right called the LONG
WALL AREA.

13   Malaido   17m   HVS   5a
Climb the gardened wall about 7m right of the left edge of the
buttress, and then the upper wall between the arête and the fine
upper crack of the next route.   (1986)

14   Malaise   17m   HVS   5a
Take the same gardened wall to start as far as the centre, then
move right and climb the fine finishing crack.   (1986)

*The next climbs are about 67m right on a buttress with an
overhang on the left front face, and a large flake balanced on top.
The overhang is split by two cracks. This is* **COLLEGE BUTTRESS.**
The right crack through the overhang is:

15   Merry Pheasant   22m   E1   5c
Technical wall climbing leads direct to the crack in the overhang,
then go direct up the strenuous crack.   (1986)

16   Frantic Manoeuvres   22m   E2   5c
Just right, climb the lower wall to a leftwards ramp which leads to
the central part of the wall. Climb up to an obvious thread and
continue to the top with interest.   (1986)

17   Bonedigger   22m   E1   5b
Ascend the finger-wide crack which splits the middle of the
buttress, moving slightly right at the top.   (1986)

18   Thirty Nine and a Half Steps   20m   E1   5b
About 10m right, climb the gardened lower wall to a narrow
rounded terrace and the upper wall to a tricky mantelshelf finish.
(1986)

HARPUR HILL LIST OF FIRST ASCENTS

1960s	**The Seven Deadly Virtues** (pegged) G West, B Roberts
1966 Spring	**Avarice** R Dearman, D Gill, D Goodwin, I Hartle
1966 Aug. 28	**Seven Deadly Sins** R Toogood, R Dearman
1966 Nov.	**Lust** R Dearman & party
1966	**Jam Butty Mines Crack** C Trotter, P Townroe
1967	**The Seven Deadly Virtues** T Morris *First free ascent.*

Other routes between 1966/1967; no first ascent details.

Zebedee

Greensleeves

Crazy Pinnacle Face

Upthrutch

One Deadly Variant

Z Victor 1

Inception

Pride

Two Cave Gully

Envy

Popeye

Bluto

Gluttony

1979	**Slob Team Special** C Jones
1986	**Positive Discrimination** I Warhurst, M Baxter, B Duckworth
1986 May	**Cats 23** M Baxter, K Ashton, B Duckworth

1986 May	**Tricycle Man**	B Duckworth, I Warhurst, M Baxter

1986 May   **Tricycle Man**   B Duckworth, I Warhurst, M Baxter

1986 June   **Face Value**   H Venables, M Baxter

1986 June   **Diamond Wall**   B Duckworth, I Warhurst, M Baxter

1986 June   **Narrow Gauge**   B Duckworth, I Warhurst

1986 June   **Wide Gauge**   B Duckworth, I Warhurst

1986 June   **Railroaded**   B Duckworth, I Warhurst

1986 June   **Just The Ticket**   M Baxter

1986 June   **Malaido**   M Baxter, A Garlick

1986 June   **Malaise**   M Baxter, K Ashton

1986 July   **College Crack**   H Venables, A Garlick, et al

1986 July   **Permutation Wall**   B Duckworth, M Baxter, et al

1986 July   **Upthrutch**   M Baxter, B Duckworth, et al

1986 July   **Merry Pheasant**   M Baxter, B Duckworth, I Warhurst

1986 July   **Frantic Manoeuvres**   B Duckworth, I Warhurst

1986 July   **Bonedigger**   B Duckworth, M Baxter

1986 July   **Thirty Nine and a Half Steps**   M Baxter

GRIN LOW

O.S. ref. SK 046 723

by Malc Baxter

ACCESS and SITUATION

Grin Low is a Country Park and caravan site off the A53 as it leaves Buxton. Follow the entrance road all the way to the car park at the bottom. From there walk back to the west end of the quarry.

At the far end is a large solid-looking tower. East of this is a green pool. Behind the pool is the obvious long narrow slab of The Grin Low Slide. Right of this are some large slabs on which are the following routes.

1 Cold Comfort 45m HVS 4c
Climb the centre of the wall by cracks and corner until a move
right is possible to the easy-angled slab which leads to the
terrace. Continue up a steep wide crack right of an impressive
arête.

2 The Grin Low Slide 25m HVD
Take a wandering line up the obvious narrow slide on the left
behind the pool to the terrace and stake belay.

3 Grin Low Crack 12m VS 4c
From the terrace above The Grin Low Slide, climb the steep crack
directly behind the belay stake. Hard to start.

4 Grin Low Wall 10m VS 4b
Start at the lowest point of the wall left of Grin Low Crack to a
small ledge and continue up the wall on sharp holds.

GRIN LOW LIST OF FIRST ASCENTS

1986 Jan. 28 **Grin Low Crack**   M Baxter, K Ashton

1986 Jan. 28 **Grin Low Wall**   K Ashton, M Baxter

1986 Feb. 1 **Cold Comfort**   M Baxter, I Lonsdale, K Ashton

1986 Feb. 1 **The Grin Low Slide**   K Ashton

*It is likely that the routes will all have been done at an
earlier date.*

ALDERY CLIFF — EARL STERNDALE

O.S. ref. SK 097 663

by Jim Rubery

---

*'This is a good little cliff and well worth a visit . . . All the
routes described were climbed from the bottom
upwards . . . The standardization will be found to be
somewhat easier than gritstone, probably more akin to
the Tremadoc cliffs, to which the crag has some
resemblance . . . Devotees of Tremadoc will like this
place'.*

Rock Climbs on the Mountain Limestone of
Derbyshire, 1961.

SITUATION and CHARACTER

The crag is on the right-hand side of the road, one and a half
kilometres south-east of Earl Sterndale, on the road to
Crowdicote.

The cliff is quite small, reaching about 35m at its highest point
and being about 80m long. It is an old quarry and this has given
rise to slabs at an angle of about 75°, rather unusual in a
limestone cliff. Its popularity has led to many of the holds
becoming very polished, but it has also resulted in the removal of
most of the loose material from the cliff.

The less frequented lines tend to become floral during the
summer and the nettle growth around the crag can be annoying,
however a rather palatable wine can be brewed from these weeds
if one is so inclined. It is hoped that future management policies
of the cliff will result in careful gardening and the felling of certain
trees and bushes which tend to shade the cliff and create mossy,
lichenous conditions. The cliff is fairly sheltered despite its
easterly aspect and catches the sun until mid-afternoon. Spring
and Autumn visits can be most pleasant.

APPROACHES and ACCESS

The crag is only 10m from the road with an area for parking
immediately below it. It has recently been acquired by the B.M.C.
and will remain in its care for the present at least. The land
surrounding the crag is owned by the farmer of Abbott's Grove,
Earl Sterndale, and care must be taken not to damage boundary
walls and fences, especially the wall above the crag.

Please keep the entrance gate to the crag closed during and after your visit as this helps to discourage tipping.
Camping is NOT allowed.

HISTORY

The dates of quarrying here are not known and neither is the onset of climbing, but *Clothesline* had been recorded prior to 1959.

May of that year saw members of the North Staffs M.C. at the cliff. They added a few routes and passed their information onto the Stockport Potholers and Climbing Club, who attacked the cliff in earnest and by July of 1959 over twenty routes had been done.

G.R. Fildes and A.T. Braddock's Aldery Cliff section of the 1961 Rock Climbs on the Mountain Limestone of Derbyshire guide included such routes as Clothesline, *Mitre Crack, The Cardinal, Nettlerash* and *The Spider*. Some of the routes needed aid, such as *Carmen, Surface Plate* and *The Arête*, but the cliff remained relatively unscarred from pegging. *A Girdle Traverse* was also recorded at this time but this has little to recommend it and does not appear in the route list.

The Southern Limestone guide of 1970 saw several obvious additions – *Broken Toe, Bishop* and *Sans Nom*. Surface Plate had its aid points eliminated whilst the only complete aid route, *Cooper's Peg Route*, was bashed into submission.

The ten years between the publication of the Southern Limestone Guide and the 1980 Northern Limestone Guide saw little real development, mainly due to the cliff being small and at slab angle, therefore not affording the modern, hard, uncompromising lines of many of Derbyshire's limestone cliffs. However, in 1977, Al Evans freed Cooper's Peg Route and added *November Wall* to give the cliff an 'Extreme' air. Gary Gibson visited the cliff in 1980 and amongst others, claimed *Yukio* and *Anti-Digestant*.

Very recent additions to the climbs are *Sword and Stone, The High Crusade* and *The Actress* by Richard Davies and *Chance in a Marillion* by Duncan Lee and Gary Thornhill.

THE CLIMBS are described from left to right. The descent is at the left-hand side of the crag, facing the rock, down a potentially dangerous path, especially when wet (crampons useful). Please take care not to damage the fence. It is probably best to abseil off just below the top for most of the climbs, as many of the finishes are poor and vegetated.

At the left-hand end of the crag is a dismal bay with a small cave in its bottom right-hand corner. The first climb starts just left of this corner.

1   Sword and Stone   8m   E2   5b   †
The thin crack in the wall left of the corner.   (1985)

2   The High Crusade   15m   E2   5c   †
Break rightwards from the last route to join Hidden Corner.
                                                                    (1985)

3   Hidden Corner   15m   HS   4a
From the cave climb the scrappy corner past large blocks and
often feathered species to a ledge and cave. Move left and up the
wall to finish.   (1960s)

Around the arête to the right is another wall.

4   Therianthropic   15m   HVS   5a
7m right of the arête is an obvious crack. Climb this with a hard
move at 5m and a jungle bash to finish.   (1974)

5   Jackorner   17m   VS   4c
Climb the obvious corner with a move right onto the arête at the
top. Finish up vegetated rocks.   (1974)

*Just right again is another wall and the crackline right of the arête
is:*

6   Cooper's Route   17m   E2   5c   *
Make very hard moves to start the crack and follow this past a
peg. Strenuous moves lead to a tree. Finish up the wall or abseil
off the tree.   (1960s/1977)

7   November Wall   17m   E2   5b   *
Start 2m right at a crack. Climb this and go directly up the wall on
good holds but with poor protection to a ledge. Trend leftwards to
finish.   (1977)

The leftward slanting groove just right of the last climb is taken by
Lethanol *HVS 5a. 8m right up the mud slope is a series of cracks.
The first is taken by*:

8   Timber   15m   HS   4a
The thin crack running up the slab to a tree with a wider
continuation crack.   (1974)

9   Rent a Ghost   15m   S
One metre right is a wider crack finishing at the same tree. Finish
as for Timber.   (1974)

10   The Clone of Jeremiah   14m   VS   4c
Immediately right is a very thin crack. Follow this to a ledge.
Continue up the wall and enter a loose groove to finish.   (1979)

11   Nazi Baby   14m   S
The tip of a gully to the right. Recommended for those conversant
in jungle warfare. May improve with napalm.   (1979)

At a lower level is a smart arête and clean face.

12   The Arête   20m   HVS   5a   ★★
Follow the arête first on its right then its left to a large ledge and
trees. Easy rock to finish.   (1959)

A sloping crack joins The Arête from the left at 7m. This is **Lost
Thread** *5b. A poor alternative.*

13   Mitre Crack   20m   VS   4c   ★
A good climb following the zigzag cracks just right of The Arête.
                                                             (1959)

14   Chance in a Marillion   20m   E3   6a
A direct line between Mitre Cracks and The Cardinal. Deviations
onto either of these routes reduces the grade.   (1986)

15   The Cardinal   20m   VS   4c
Start as for Mitre Cracks but follow the rightwards slanting crack
into the corner and onto a ledge. Climb the corner to finish with
the crux near the top. (1959) **The Actress** 5c † is a direct start.
                                                             (1985)

16   The Bishop   23m   HVS   5b
Start in the corner below the block overhang and move up to it on
very polished holds. Step right onto the arête and continue up the
wide crack onto the ledge of The Cardinal. Finish with awkward
moves up the arête and cracks.   (1960s)

17   Sycamore Crack   23m   HS   4c
2m right of Bishop is a crack splitting the overhang. Muscle up
this (crux) to the tree. The easy slab above the tree is used to

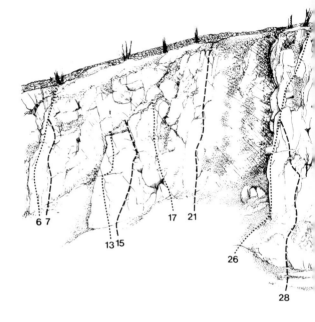

6 7   13 15   17 21   26   28

Aldery Cliff

finish. The crux can be avoided by stepping in from the next
route, VD.   (1959)

18 Jeremy's Jungular Jaunt   22m   S
Start at the foot of Jackdaw's Gully and move left to a crack. Climb
this to the top.   (1979)

19 Jackdaw's Gully   22m   HD
The obvious vegetated gully. Beware of tarantulas.   (1959)

The crag steps forward here to give a longer slab.

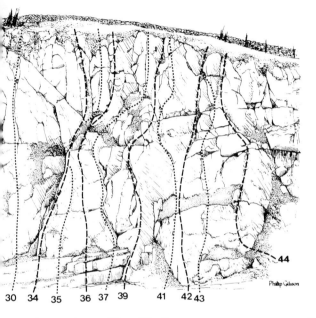

30 34   35   36 37 39   41   42 43

Philip Gibson

20 Carmen Jones 25m VS 4b ★
A very pleasant affair taking the left arête of the slab to the right,
direct.   (1978)

21 Carmen 25m VS 4c ★
Start 5m right of the arête. Climb the left of two cracks to a
polished rightward slanting crack (crux) and go up to the tree.
Easy rocks to finish. The arête can be climbed direct at 4b.
                                                                     (1959)

22 Deceptor 23m VS 4c
Start 4m right at a thin crack and move up to an undercut flake 8m
up the wall. Pass this on its left and continue up the wall trending
right to finish – dubious rock.   (1973)

23 Sans Nom 20m VS 4b
Slightly higher up the dirt slope is a vegetated crack leading to a tree. Climb this and a shallow flake-filled groove until forced right almost into Central Gully.   (1960s)

24 Central Gully 20m VD
Another tip of a gully, giving more arboreal meanderings.

25 Black Country Rock 15m HVS 5a
Start in the centre of the side wall to the right and up a thin leftward sloping crack via a very creaky flake to a cave. Step out right and finish up cracks.   (1979)

To the right is a large slab.

26 Ash Tree Arête 25m HVD
Follow the grassy left-hand arête of the slab into a bay. A groove leads to the top.   (1959)

27 Anti-Digestant 25m HVS 5a
A few metres right of the arête is a bald slab. Climb this to an awkward move at 3m and then go slightly right to a thin crack leading to a ledge. Continue up the slab above via the thin crack.   (1979)

28 Ash Tree Slab 25m HS 4a
7m from the arête is a small polished leftward facing corner. Ascend this to its top and follow the crack above moving left of the trees to finish up the arête.   (1959)

29 Nettlerash 30m VS 4c
The crack 3m right has a polished move at 4m. From the trees several finishes are available.   (1959)

The wall between Ash Tree Slab and Nettlerash can be taken at 5a
— **The Nonsense Man Start**.

30 Broken Toe 35m VS 4c   *
A good climb starting at a hairline crack immediately right. Climb the bald slab to a wider crack passing right of the trees and through a small overhang.   (1960s)

31 Formic 35m VS 4c
Take the first section of Broken Toe to finish up the slab and corner on the right.   (1981)

32 Venom 35m HVS 5b   (1981)
Ascend the slab just right of Broken Toe.

33 Yukio 35m VS 4c
Just right again is a small leftward facing groove starting 2m from
the ground. Go up to and past this to a long thin ledge with a thin
continuation crack and corner.   (1979)

*The corner gives another scrappy route. To the right is a slab
facing the car park.*

34 Central Arête 35m HVD
Climb the arête for 10m, step left and use the tree to reach the
ledge. (The arête direct is 4b). From the back of the ledge climb
the obvious pillar and flaky crack above.   (1959)

35 Janbaloo 35m HVS 5b
Climb the slab between Central Arête and Surface Plate starting at
a sawn-off tree stump, moving left onto the arête near the top.
Finish up the arête on the right-hand side of the large ledge.
                                                              (1978)

36 Surface Plate 35m HVS 5a   *
Ascend the polished scarred crack in the centre of the slab to the
large ledge. Climb the crack and corner 1m right of Janbaloo to
finish.   (1959/1960s)

37 Clothesline 35m S
The polished corner crack leads to the large ledge. Continue up
the brown flaky crack in the centre of the right-hand side back
wall.   (pre—1959)

38 The Fly 35m HVS 5a
Follow Clothesline for 3m and move right along the crack. Go
direct up the wall into a corner and then onto a large ledge. Finish
left of the right arête by a cracked groove.   (1977)

39 The Spider 35m VS 4c
Climb the broken groove just right or the arête to the top of the
groove. Make an awkward step left onto the nose and go up to the
tree. Finish as for The Fly.   (1959)

40 Burst 35m HVS 5a
Just right and at a lower level is a leftward facing corner. Climb
this to its top and follow the short leftward slanting crack to the
tree of The Spider.   (1978)

41 The Bender 33m HVS 5a
Just left of the arête of Terrace Wall is a shallow brown scoop.
Follow this, quite awkward, to the terrace. From the back left-hand
side of the terrace climb the groove of Terrace Wall for 4m then
break left up the shallow corner to a ledge. Move right round the
arête and climb cracks left of the tree.   (1978)

42 Terrace Wall 35m VS 4b
Follow the arête moving slightly left near the top. From the
terrace two finishes are available:
i. Climb the shallow groove in the back left-hand side of the
terrace moving rightwards into a corner. VD.
ii. Climb up to the square overhang 4m right and follow the flaky
crack emerging from its left-hand side to a ledge. Cross it at a tree
and move onto a thin ledge to finish up cracks right of The
Bender. Contrived at HS.   (1959)

43 A Question of Palance 30m VS 4b
The shallow groove just right to the terrace. Move up the
rightward facing corner (left of Terrace Wall pitch 2) to an
overhang. Step left onto the face and go to the top using the best
available rock.   (1979)

44 Right Arête 30m VS 4b
The blunt arête leading to the right-hand end of the terrace.
Continue in the same line with an awkward mantelshelf to finish
up a groove.

*The rocks further right are vegetated and loose and no routes
have been recorded here.*

ALDERY CLIFF LIST OF FIRST ASCENTS

1959 May	*Several routes by members of the North Staffordshire M.C.*
1959 May/June	**The Arête**
	Mitre Crack
	The Cardinal
	Sycamore Crack
	Jackdaws Gully
	Carmen
	Ash Tree Route
	Ash Tree Slab Climb
	Nettlerash
	Central Arête
	Surface Plate (HS & A1)
	Clothesline
	The Spider
	Terrace Wall
	Girdle Traverse

All the above routes by G R Fildes, A T Braddock and members of the Stockport Potholers and Climbing Club.

'By July the crag boasted over 20 routes' – but only 15 appeared in the guide!

1964	**Bouncing Crack** (A2) E Ward, J Loy, D Morrison
pre-1970	**Cooper's Peg Route** (A1) *First free ascent by A Evans in 1977.*
	The Bishop
	Sans Nom
	Central Gully

Broken Toe

Surface Plate free – many claims

Right Angle

1969 June 15	**Blind Faith**	R Treglown, G Holden (AL)
1973 Summer	**Deceptor**	P Ashton, B Duckworth
1974	**Jackorner**	J Woodhouse, A Sansom, G Hoey
	Theriantropic	J Woodhouse, A Sansom, G Hoey
	Timber	J Woodhouse, A Sansom, G Hoey
	Rent a Ghost	J Woodhouse, A Sansom, G Hoey

1977   **Cooper's Peg Route**   A Evans
First free ascent.

1977 Nov.   **November Wall**   J Holt, I Barber, K Yates

1977   **The Fly**   J Holt, I Barber, K Yates

1978   **Janbaloo**   P Barber, R Shaw

1979 March 14 **Burst**   G Gibson (solo)

1979 March 20 **Clone of Jeremiah**   G Gibson

1979 March 20 **Nazi Baby**   G Gibson

1979 March 30 **Anti-Digestant**   G Gibson, D Beetlestone

1979 March 30 **Lethanol**   G Gibson (solo)

1979 Dec. 13   **Yukio**   G Gibson (solo)

1979 Dec. 16   **A Question of Palance**   G Gibson (solo)

1981   **Formic**   R Shaw, A Jackson

1981   **Venom**   R Shaw, A Jackson

1985   **Sword and Stone**   R Davies (on-sight solo)

1985   **The High Crusade**   R Davies (on-sight solo)

1985 Aug. 1   **The Actress**   R Davies

1986   **Chance in a Marillion**   Duncan Lee, G Thornhill

Wall of Jericho, Horseshoe Quarry.
Photo: Riche Brooks.

ASHWOOD DALE

O.S. ref. SK 073 727 to 076 727

by Simon Nadin

'Unfortunately its close proximity to the A6 road and the fact that there is a sewage works close by deters climbers from spending more than a few hours at a time. Not that the sewage works smells to any degree, it is just the fact that it is there, and I have always believed that a crag's situation has a large influence on its popularity. Taking these things into account however, it is still an excellent place to while away a few hours on a leisurely afternoon, or when one is waiting for the night life to begin in Buxton!'

G. West, 1961 guide.

SITUATION and CHARACTER
The cliffs of Ashwood Dale are situated beside the A6 Buxton to Matlock road, 1km from Buxton. The cliffs are generally fairly sound though the vegetation becomes a little overpowering during the summer.

APPROACHES and ACCESS
The cliffs are easily gained via the A6 from Buxton or Matlock, being virtually on the roadside. For this reason care must be taken not to dislodge any rock onto passing traffic. Little is known of the ownership of these cliffs apart from the lineside faces which are owned by British Rail and these cannot be used unless British Rail workers are on strike! Parking for these cliffs is below Lovers' Leap, 1km out of Buxton on the A6.

HISTORY
Most of the routes in the dale were climbed by Gary Gibson though some of these may have been climbed before. On the Railway Buttress Steve Bancroft added *Ashwood Crack* in 1974. Later, in 1979 Gibson added *Z.C.T.* and *Down in the Sewer*.

THE CLIMBS
1km from Buxton on the right-hand side i.e. south side of the road, is a very deep cleft:

Chris Wright, Mr Blue Sky, Horseshoe Quarry.
Photo: Brooks/Wright Collection.

LOVERS' LEAP

> 'On the right of the cleft is the steep vegetated wall
> which starts immediately from the edge of the road . . .
> If one did climb here, fell, and escaped serious injury, no
> doubt a passing motorist would finish him off.'
>
> G. West, 1961 guide.

1   Down in the Sewer   18m   E1   5b   *
Climb the obvious flake on the left wall about 20m into the ravine
direct to a bulge. Finish up an obvious groove, 2 pegs. A good
route.   (1979)

2   Z.C.T.   15m   E1   5b
Climb the wall to the right of the last route. Finish direct over the
bulge to a small tree.   (1979)

*50m down the road towards Matlock and on the same side as
Lovers' Leap, but up the bank, is a buttress split by a gully.*

3   Full Frontal   10m   HVS   4c
Go direct up the centre of the buttress right of the gully.   (1978)

4   Activator   10m   VS   4c
Climb the crack to the left of the gully using a tree high up.
                                                               (1978)

5   Samson   12m   VD
To the left ascend a wide crack. Best avoided after a hair-cut.
                                                               (1950s)

6   The Urge   12m   VS   4c
Climb the shallow groove left of Samson.   (1978)

*100m left past numerous bays and pinnacles is a buttress with an
obvious layback flake on its left side.*

7   Free 'em   17m   VS   4c
Ascend the right-hand arête of the buttress moving slightly left
near the top.   (1978)

8   Feed 'em   15m   S   4b
To the left follow twin broken cracks.   (1978)

9   Boogie Flake   15m   E1   5b   ★
Climb the flake on the left, reaching a wide crack higher up.

10   Boggle Tower   12m   HVS   5a
20m left ascend the front face of the tower.   (1978)

11   The Growl   10m   VS   4c
7m left ascend the tower.   (1978)

15m left is a steep buttress near the road.

12   Right Groove   20m   S
Follow the steep wide groove at the right-hand side of the
buttress.   (1950s)

13   Central Crack   20m   VS   4c
Climb directly to a V-groove 7m left of Right Groove   (1950s)

14   Left Route   20m   HVS   5a
Start 2m left of Central Crack and climb direct to a crack system.
                                                                 (1950s)

*On the other side of the road, river and railway and slightly
downstream of Lovers' Leap is a large buttress. 7m to the right is:*

15   Sergeant Pepper   20m   VS   4c
Climb a wall into a groove, which is followed to the top.   (1967)

16   Ashwood Crack   20m   HVS   5b   ★
Climb the pleasant finger jamming crack right of Sergeant
Pepper.   (1974)

ASHWOOD DALE LIST OF FIRST ASCENTS

1950s   *'Michael Roberts, Tom and Graham West, B Ritson, F
               Walker and Roy Brown climbed in Ashwood Dale,
               reputedly attacking even the left-hand crags, a few
               feet from the railway line. Michael Roberts acquired
               both home-made pitons and a passion for loose
               rock. Here perhaps was one beginning of an impetus
               towards the later limestone invasion.'*

1950s	*Many routes were done on the cliffs of Ashwood Dale 'The Buxton Pinnacles', varying from Difficult to VS but only three routes were recorded in the 1961 guide.*
1950s	**Right Groove**
1950s	**Central Crack**
1950s	**Left Route**
1950s	**Samson**
1967 July 6	**Sergeant Pepper** J Morgan, R Mares
1974 May 18	**Ashwood Crack** S Bancroft, J Allen
1978	**Full Frontal**
1978	**Activator**
1978	**The Urge**
1978	**Free 'em**
1978	**Boggle Tower**
1978	**The Growl**
1979	**Down in the Sewer** G Gibson
1979	**Z.C.T.** G Gibson

COW DALE – CRAIG Y BICEPS   O.S. ref. SK 084 721

by Gary Gibson

'The autumn saw the closing of another prolific season of new climbs on limestone. Gary Gibson returned to the crag Chris Jackson drove past. Actually he drove past it twice: the second time was to check whether Gary had found the same crag!'

Climber and Rambler, May 1984.

SITUATION and CHARACTER
Whilst only being a small crag in comparison to most Derbyshire limestone crags, Craig Y Biceps offers two very good and relatively unusual routes which make it well worth one visit.

The small bulging cliff lies to the left of the road running up from the A6 (Buxton to Bakewell road) to Cow Dale cottages. This road leaves the A6 3km east of Buxton and cuts sharply up the hillside via two hairpin bends. The crag is clearly visible on the left just before the bends.

For the most part the crag overhangs somewhat alarmingly and offers very few lines for most of its length. The weaknesses that do exist offer only high standard challenges. The routes done so far have been thoroughly cleaned and have little loose rock or vegetation, but the rest of the crag is thickly cloaked in flora and fauna in summer, both underfoot and overhead.

APPROACHES and ACCESS
Once located it is best to park cars at the top of the hill in Cow Dale as for Staden Quarry and then to walk down. A path will have to be made through the heavy vegetation below the cliff to get to it.

HISTORY
The crag was undoubtedly the scene of numerous aided routes in the past, but who did what is unclear. Gary Gibson started a slow campaign of free-climbing in 1979 and added all of the routes so far.

THE CLIMBS
In the centre of the crag is a large roof with a block on the ground below it. Breaching the roofs at this point is a superb crack.

1   The Main Motor Mile   18m   E5   6a   ***
Exhilarating climbing up a stunning line. Follow the crack with difficulty to the roof and use huge jugs to cross it. Finish up a short wall. Two pegs and three threads are in place.   (1982)

2   Much Monkey Magic   20m   E4   6a   **
An exciting pitch. Start 18m left of The Main Motor Mile at a thin line of resistance through the largest part of the overhangs. An initial awkward wall leads to a break, threads. Continue up the steepening crack to the roof and pass this rightwards onto the lip. Continue direct to the top.   (1983)

3 Phaseout   15m   E1   5b
The hanging corner bounding the overhanging section to the left.
Gain it direct and finish on the right.   (197?

4 Burning Rubber . . .   12m   E3   5c
Start 4m left of Phaseout and climb direct into a vegetated sentry
box. Exit awkwardly to the top. Serious.   (197?

COW DALE LIST OF FIRST ASCENTS

1960s	*Early aid routes.*
1979 Oct. 6	**Burning Rubber** G Gibson (solo)
	Originally known as Burning Rubber, Blubber, Blackout!
1979 Oct. 6	**Phaseout** G Gibson (solo)
1982 July 12	**The Main Motor Mile** G Gibson (unseconded)
1983 Sept. 19	**Much Monkey Magic** G Gibson (unseconded)

STADEN QUARRIES

STADEN MAIN QUARRY   O.S. ref. SK 080 72?

by Adey Hubbard

SITUATION and CHARACTER
The two quarries are situated to the south of the A6 road from
Buxton to Bakewell, close to the hamlet of Cowdale. The rock is
similar in both quarries and, on first acquaintance, much of it
looks very loose. However, many of the faces consist of excellent
rock and a number of the routes have become classics of their
kind. The best climbs are on the north-facing sections of the upper
quarry, which in winter can become bitingly cold. In summer,
they provide high quality climbing often of a highly technical
nature and sometimes also quite strenuous. The farmer has made
an excellent job of levelling and grassing the floor of the upper
quarry and seconds frequently have to contend with a herd of
inquisitive Friesians.

APPROACHES and ACCESS
IT IS VITAL THAT THIS SECTION IS READ AND ADHERED TO IF ACCESS IS TO BE MAINTAINED.
Both quarries must be approached only from the hamlet of Cowdale, which is reached by a very narrow road leading off the A6, past Craig Y Biceps, at a big bend at O.S. ref. SK 087722. As the road widens between the houses an entrance on the right leads to Cowdale Hall. This is owned by Mr. Morton who tenant-farms the land in which the quarries lie. He may be willing to allow small groups of climbers into the quarries if permission is sought. PLEASE DO NOT ENTER THE QUARRIES WITHOUT THIS PERMISSION which is usually freely granted. The BMC, via its Peak Area Committee, put many hours of negotiation into achieving this access agreement with Mr. Morton, and with ICI Ltd., who own the quarries. **We hope that it will not be put in jeopardy by the thoughtless actions of a few**. Rock debris is gradually spreading into the field from the crag foot and the farmer would be grateful if it could be thrown back out of the way of his vehicles.

HISTORY
These quarries received no attention, perhaps because of their loose appearance from afar, until 1966 when Paul Nunn and John Smith climbed *Solo*. The true potential of the beautiful, solid walls on the south side of the upper quarry was not discovered until three years later, when Bob Dearman climbed the classic *Joint Effort*, using a point of aid low down. This was later removed by Tom Proctor. *Charas* required four aid nuts and *The Nails*, another Nunn contribution, also needed a nut.
The next few years saw little development until the mid-seventies when Jon and Andrew Woodward climbed *Bimbo* etc., *Rupert Bear, Hammer into Anvil* and the very difficult *A Game of Chess*, which was much undergraded in the previous guide. The main action began in 1977 with the removal of the aid on Charas by Steve and Jim Worthington with Giles Barker, after a busy gardening session. At this time also, spurred on by guidebook writing in the following year, Barker began to develop the Solo area with his ascents of *Solar Plexus, Solo Man's Ploy* and a free ascent of the previously aided *Fixation*. After a long afternoon putting the route together, Tony Freeman, Pete Brayshaw and Barker produced the magnificent *Welcome to Hard Times*. This was quickly followed by Phil Burkes's *Captain Reliable*, another fine route.

New routing continued apace as Gary Gibson began an association with the quarries by soloing *Xenophobia* and digging out *Titanic Reaction*. The Yellow Wall area gave several good routes to the team of Chris Jackson and Malc Battersby, including the fine *Ground Zero Man*. Gibson, with Derek Beetlestone, put up *Liquid Courage* in June 1979 and returned in August to solo *Waterloo Road* and *Great Expectations*. He also added three excellent routes on the Charas slab with Phil Wilson and Mark Walton. These were *Bicycle Repair Man*, named after the battered cycle which still resides at its foot, *Wipe Out* and the reachy *Telescopic Demand*. Determined to do the last routes before the guide went to print Gibson crept in with *Paraplege* and *Roman Numeral X*.

The appearance of the new guide in 1980 brought an unprecedented wave of climbers to sample the routes. It also brought an unprecedented furore in the shape of a total ban on climbing by ICI, the quarry owners, who were concerned about liability, trespass and a whole host of other things. The farmer, Mr. Morton, found himself in the unfortunate role of temporary unpaid ICI policeman and access was no more. This situation prevailed for almost two years, when patient negotiating by the BMC and especially by Lyn Noble, then chairman of the Guidebook Executive, finally bore fruit in the shape of an access agreement with ICI subject to the conditions stated in the approaches and access information. In addition, the BMC erected information notices at strategic entrances to the quarries.

Upon the reopening of access further development took place with Gary Gibson completing his almost systematic working out of the black walls. Phil Burke created the excellent *Cathy's Clown*, previously cleaned by Chris Jackson, before Gibson added a whole string of routes and eliminates. The exquisite though serious *Silent Manoeuvres*, *Cross Purposes*, *Telescopic Demand Direct* and *Mozaic Piece*, on which he utilized a bolt runner. The following day Gibson soloed the route rendering it obsolete but left it in place for a proposed girdle. Richard Davies and Simon Nadin won the race for this, and the bolt was used for protection. However it was later felt unjustified by one climber who promptly removed it in complicated circumstances. Richard Davies added the esoteric *Psychological Warfare* and finally in 1986 added the quarry's hardest route with *Private Gripped* a bold and uncompromising route on one of the quarry's smallest remaining gaps.

THE CLIMBS are sheltered and south-facing which is an advantage in winter and they lie below a public footpath marked by the old railway line fence posts. Descent into the quarry is easy to the right, and is down a steep earth bank. The routes described follow the most obvious features on the soundest rock, although lines have been recorded almost everywhere. The first route starts 12m to the left of a small cave at the foot of the right-hand end of the wall, where there is a steep, grey wall of clean rock above a clump of trees. The routes are described from RIGHT to LEFT.

THE SOLO AREA

1   Solar Wall   10m   HVS   5b
Climb a broken groove to a ledge at 5m and then the wall above finishing leftwards.   (1977)

45m farther left is a smooth grey wall, just to the right of a loose-looking groove capped by a square-cut overhang.

2   The Solo Man's Ploy   10m   VS   4c   *
Climb the short rib right of the groove to a small ledge and over the bulge to follow the sharp arête to the top.   (1978)

3   The Orange-Throated Gonk   10m   VS   4b
Climb the loose-looking groove to the overhang. Traverse left to finish up the corner and crack.

4   The Wry-Necked Gonk   10m   VS   5a
Go up the crack to the other Gonk and traverse right under the overhang to its right-hand crack.

5   Solo   10m   HS   4a
This is the next corner to the left, containing a sapling.

6   Fixation   10m   VS   5a
Follow Solo to the sapling then move right to finish up the arête.
                                                                         (1969)

7   Emergency   10m   E1   5a
The arête just right of Fixation. Do not fall off!   (1978)

8   Sun Crack   10m   HS   4a
The steep, clean crack 6m to the left.   (1977)

9   Generosity Exists   10m   HS   4a
The cracked groove in the arête just to the left.   (1979)

10   Friendly Local   10m   S
Climb the next right-angled corner via a ramp.   (1979)

11   Diaphragm   9m   VS   4b
Just left is a sapling in a blocky groove. Take a deep breath and
climb cracks in the wall to its right.   (1979)

12   Solar Plexus   10m   VD
Starting from a boulder below the blocky groove climb the arête.
(1978)

*To the left is an area of loose rock on which routes have not been
described.*

YELLOW WALL AREA

*At the far end of the quarry is an enormous, stepped flake above a
large block in the rubble slope.*

13   Giant Staircase   15m   HS   4a
Reach the pinnacle, atop the large flake, via the crack on its right
and finish up the right-hand crack in the wall above.   (1979)

14   Boomerang   15m   VS   4c
The wall and corner to the ash tree 4m left and then the left-hand
side of the pinnacle flake and the left-hand crack to finish.
(1979)

15   The Heron   12m   VS   4c
The dirty corner and flake 4m to the left.   (1979)

16   Kellogg's are on Strike   12m   VS   4c
Climb the steep wall to a thin, horizontal crack below the big flake
and finish up its left-hand side into the sunshine.   (1979)

*45m left is an obvious arête which is left of a big corner at the top
of a rubble slope.*

17   Roman Numeral X   18m   E3   5b
Gain the arête from the left and follow it to the top. Hard and
rather dangerous since a rockfall.   (1979)

18 Ground Zero Man   18m   VS   4c
Gain and follow the obvious, wide crack left of the arête.   (1978)

*The next four routes are best approached via a loose rising
traverse from below Roman Numeral X.*

19 Rising Potential   12m   VS   4b
The leftwards slanting crack from the foot of Ground Zero Man.
(1979)

20 Great Expectations   12m   HVS   5b
Climb the steep groove 5m left to the overhang and go over this
strenuously by a superb crack.   (1979)

21 Halcyon Drift   12m   HVS   5a
The twin cracks and short corner at the left-hand end of the
overhang.   (1978)

22 One Step from Earth   12m   VS   4c
Climb the crack to a sandy pod 3m to the left.   (1978)

23 Pig Sick   8m   VD
Trot groggily up the short blocky corner at the left end of the
rubble terrace.   (1979)

35m to the left, past vast piles of rubble, is a series of grooves.

24 Broken Hammer   18m   HS   4a
Scramble up grassy ledges to climb the right-hand groove past its
diamond-shaped hole.   (1979)

25 Throwback   18m   VS   4c
The obvious wide crack in the next groove but one.   (1979)

26 Psychological Warfare   12m   E4   5b
The obvious, isolated arête well to the left again. Reach it via a
crack in the left wall and traverse out to below a bulge. Pull round
this and continue direct.   (1983)

JOINT EFFORT WALL

*A long way to the left is an obvious grey slab, bounded on its right
by a large, white pillar and opposite the bottom entrance to the
quarry. This marks the beginning of the climbs of real quality.*

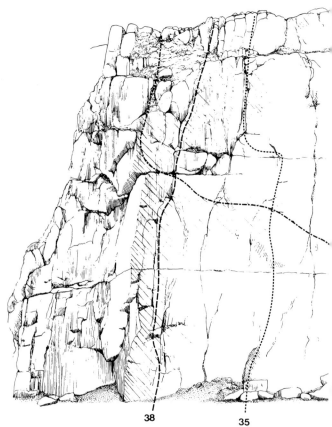

38   35

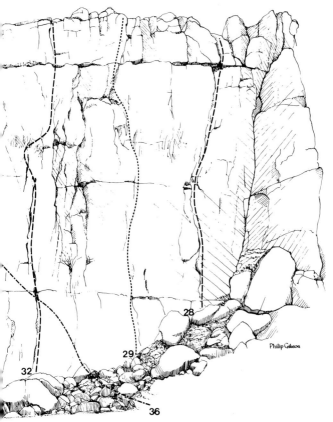

Philip Gibson

Joint Effort Wall

27 Waterloo Road 30m E1 5b
Follow the low level break crossing the face from right to left to
join and finish up Fiat. Alternatively, to reduce drag, at the
junction of Nails go up that route or diagonally left to finish up
Suscipiat. A poor route.   (1979)

28 Liquid Courage 24m E2 5c   ★★
5m left of the corner formed by the pillar and the main face is a
series of thin cracks up the yellow-streaked wall. Climb via a
shallow groove to a bulge. Hard moves right lead to a deep crack
which is followed strenuously to the break. Finish left of the gully.
                                                            (1979)

29 Cathy's Clown 25m E3 5c   ★★
Superb sustained wall work. Start 3m left of, and down from,
Liquid Courage. Follow a system of discontinuous cracks over a
bulge to a standing position in a horizontal break, below a second
bulge. Cross the bulge leftwards into a scoop which leads quickly
to easy ground and the top.   (1981)

30 X Certs 33m E1 5c
A diagonal eliminate starting from the foot of Liquid Courage and
following a vague line to the groove of The Nails. Finish maturely
across the slab on the left.   (1981)

31 Investal 24m HVS 5a
Follow the line of vegetation to an obvious niche and climb out of
it to a grassy ledge and finish up the capping wall. Better than it
looks.   (1969)

32 Captain Reliable 24m E2 5c   ★
Gain the wide crack, left again, and climb it easily to a bulge. Go
over this then up the wall on its right-hand edge to a grassy ledge.
Finish on trustworthy holds up the crack.   (1978)

33 Private Gripped 25m E6 6b   ★ †
Follow Captain Reliable to the top of the crack, below the bulge.
Move left and climb thinly up the smooth headwall via a faint line
of flakes and with a distinct lack of protection.

34 Joint Effort 27m HVS 5b   ★★
Climb the obvious crack 2½m left, difficult at first, to steady 4c
climbing past a horizontal break to the top.   (1969)

35   Welcome To Hard Times   25m   E2   5c   ★★★
Technically superb with cunning but good protection. Follow a
line more or less up the centre of the wall to the left to a thread at
the bulge. The difficulty soon eases and a move left leads to the
obvious final groove of The Nails. A direct finish from the bulge is
possible at a sustained E3, 5c.   (1978/1983)

36   Cross Purposes   35m   HVS   5b   ★
A parallel line to X Certs, starting 3m right of Captain Reliable and
finishing up the arête of Xenophobia.   (1980)

37   The Nails   25m   HVS   5b   ★
Climb the vague crack and follow it to the final white groove.
Finish up this in a fine position.   (1969)

38   Suscipiat   25m   VS   4c
Start 2m to the right of the main slab's left arête at some thin
cracks. Climb these and the crack above.   (1966)

39   Xenophobia   25m   E1   5a
Climb the flake crack in the arête of the slab for 6m then move
slightly left and continue up the arête, avoiding the little green
men, to finish at a sapling. Often done with protection in
Suscipiat.   (1978)

40   Fiat   26m   HVS   5a
Not surprisingly this pitch falls apart quite easily. Climb the
slabby corner 3m left to a bulge which is surmounted to find a peg
at the top of a slab. Gain a niche above, then traverse right to
finish up the previous route. Serious.   (1966/1973)

*Farther left, past horrible-looking walls is another grey slab with a
tree at its foot and a protruding buttress 15m to its right. This has
a crackline starting 6m up with a wider one to the right.*

41   Titanic Reaction   15m   HVS   5b
Gain the crackline in the protruding buttress after a few moves up
Insidious Iceberg and follow it to the top.   (1978)

42   Insidious Iceberg   15m   VS   4c
Gain and climb the widening crack to a muddy ledge. Finish up
the corner behind.

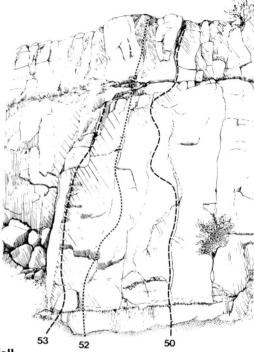

53   52   50

Charas Wall

43 My Tulpa   19m   E2   5c
From a muddy ledge, climb the obvious arête and thin crack to
gain an overhang and loose rock above.   (1981)

44 Amatarasu   19m   VS   4c   ★
At the right-hand side of the grey slab is a corner capped by an
overhang. Climb it, pull round the overhang and finish up the
groove.   (1969)

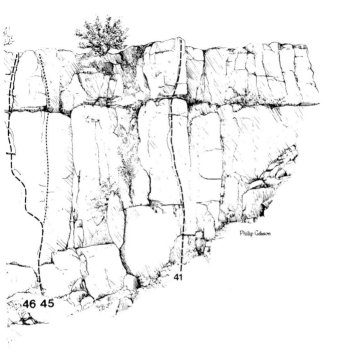

Philip Gibson

45 Wipe Out 21m E3 5b   ★
Ascend the very thin crack on the left to a ledge. Move diagonally
left to a shallow groove capped by an overhang. Go over this via
an obvious crack.   (1979)

46 Paraplege 19m E3 5c   ★
As for Wipe Out to where it goes left then go direct up the obvious
but painfully thin crack to a large flake crack finish. The upper
section of the flake is a Kellogg job — loose!   (1979)

47   Action Potential   25m   E4   5c
Follow Wipe Out to the shallow groove then go left, into Charas
and, similarly, into the 'Bicycle'. Pedal left to the arête to finish
then, having had a lot of fun, abseil off.   (1983)

48   Mozaic Piece   18m   E4   5c
A direct line left of Wipe Out leads to bolder moves up the faint
pillar above. Side runners reduce both the seriousness and the
grade.   (1981)

49   Charas   18m   HVS   5b   ⋆
A fine route offering a short, well protected section of finger-
jamming. From the tree follow the thin crackline and short corner
to the top.   (1969/1978)

50   Bicycle Repair Man   18m   E1   5b   ⋆⋆
Go direct up a thin crack just left of Charas to a ledge, then follow
the wall slightly leftwards to ledges and an overhang. Crank over
this on the right and free wheel up the wide crack.   (1979)

51   Swan Song   18m   E2   5b
Gain the obvious ramp left of Bicycle Repair Man and follow it
almost into that route. Step left then up the wall via a very thin
crack to easy ground and a junction with Bicycle Repair Man.
                                                             (1983)

52   Telescopic Demand   18m   E3   6a   ⋆⋆
Reach the left-hand of two very thin cracks direct and climb it with
extended arms to a finish on the left.   (1979/1981)

Variation. The original route started up Swan Song then moved
left into Telescopic Demand at E3, 5c.

53   Silent Manoeuvres   18m   E4   5c   ⋆⋆
Climb the right side of the arête to the left by some strange
layback moves to gain a large block. Continue, or abseil off.
                                                             (1980)

54   Somebody's Trademark   18m   HVS   5a
Climb a thin crack, just left of the arête to finish via the right arête.
                                                             (1979)

*Across a loose gully to the left is a smaller slab containing two
cracks.*

**55   Bimbo the Exploding Lorry Driver's Gulch
Eliminate**   12m   HS   4b
The right-hand crack is easy with the correct gear.   (1976)

56   Rupert Bear Goes Hiking   12m   VS   4c
The left-hand crack is finished by an amble up the middle of the
slab.   (1976)

*6m left is yet another smaller slab with a tiny overlap and sentry
box on its left, low down.*

57   Nice 'n' Sleazy   15m   E2   5b   *
Pull over the right end of the tiny overlap to climb the slab slightly
leftwards to a finishing flake. Pleasant.   (1979)

58   Hammer into Anvil   18m   E2   5c
From under the small overlap move awkwardly left to the sentry
box. Easy ground above leads to the top.   (1976)

59   A Game of Chess   18m   E5   6b   ★★
"It's all in the mind!" Climb the faint, almost non-existent, crack in
the holdless slab to the left, to a bulge; check. Pull round this and
carry on direct; check mate!   (1976)

60   Tout Comprendre   15m   HVS   4c
Climb the left arête of the slab starting off a boulder and finishing
first right, then up.   (1981)

STADEN LOWER QUARRY   O.S. ref. SK 083 723

by Richard Davies

SITUATION and CHARACTER
A track inclines down from the Upper Quarry to the A6. The
quarry is situated behind dense vegetation to the left of the track.
There are two steep walls separated by a series of corners and
grooves, which tend to be loose and vegetated. The steep walls
are of sound rock characterized by small finger holds. The finishes
of the easier routes demand care.

APPROACHES and ACCESS

The Lower Quarry must be reached via the Upper Quarry. The track is opposite the Joint Effort wall and to the right of the Solo area. IT MUST NOT BE APPROACHED FROM THE A6.

HISTORY

The first routes to be done were by Paul Nunn and John Smith in 1966 when all the easier routes were climbed. No further development occurred until, in 1978, Mike Horlov and Bob Dearman added *Route 1* and, with a point of aid, *Soft Mick*. After the guide was published nothing happened until late 1982 when Simon Nadin and Richard Davies freed Soft Mick and added *Restive Being*. Realizing the further potential they returned and added *Silent Fear*. Their hardest route, *Invisible Limits* was led by Nadin who also recorded *Bandobras Took*, whilst Davies led *Death's Retreat*. The development drew Gary Gibson to the quarry and he repeated most of the new additions and added *Leningrad*. The gap right of Ephemeral Groove was plugged by Nadin and *Levant*, the last obvious line, was soloed by Davies in July 1983.

THE CLIMBS are described from LEFT to RIGHT. The left-hand wall of the quarry is characterized by a terrace above and a muddy slope on its left. Towards its left-hand side is a steep calcite crack-line; the wall to its left gives:

1   Leningrad   21m   E1   5b,5b
1. 9m. Climb the calcite wall past a thread to the terrace.
2. 12m. Continue up the centre of the upper wall between obvious cracks.   (1983)

2   Route 1   24m   HVS   5b,4c
1. 12m. The calcite crack with an awkward start leads to the terrace.
2. 12m. Follow the obvious crack-line above.   (1978)

3   Death's Retreat   12m   E4   6a
Gain the thread just to the right and pass it to a small ledge. Reach an isolated hold on the arête to the right and semi- mantelshelf (crux). Easier climbing remains.   (1983)

4   Soft Mick   13m   E3   5c   ★
The best pitch in the lower quarry. Climb the shallow depression in the wall to the right passing a peg and thread runners and an array of interesting holds.   (1978/1983)

5 Bandobrass Took   13m   E3   5c
Gain a flake and thread in the wall 2m right, from below, and
move up into the small groove above. Steep climbing up this line
leads to the terrace.   (1983)

6 Taxing Times   12m   E3   5b
Gain the thread on the last route from the wall on the right then
step back right and finish up a short crisp wall.   (1983)

7 Indictment   30m   VS   4c
A poor route taking the first corner to the right of the left-hand
wall and the wide crack above.   (1966)

8 Leper's Groove   30m   VS   4c
As its name implies it is best avoided. Follow the leftwards-
trending groove right again with any crack finish above.   (1966)

9 Marmoliser   15m   HS
The appalling corner to the right leads to a vegetated struggle.
                                                            (1966)

*The wall to the right sports an old peg in the break at 4m. Both the
next two routes pass near here.*

10 Invisible Limits   12m   E5   6a   *
Gain a large jug just left of the peg via the wall below then launch
up the wall above.   (1983)

11 Silent Fear   13m   E3   6a
Finger holds allow access to the break right of the peg on Invisible
Limits. Stand in the break via a precarious manoeuvre, crux, and
tiptoe up the ramp above.   (1982)

12 Levant   13m   E2   5c
To the right is a small loose overhang. Climb a short wall to reach
holds in its left side and pull rightwards across it to finish back
left.   (1983)

13 Ephemeral Groove   14m   HVS   5a
Ascend the wall to reach the prominent groove.   (1966)

14 Before the Storm   15m   E3   6a
From a sapling just to the right, ascend the awkward wall to the
break. Breach the roof and finish up the cracks (crux).   (1983)

15   Restive Being   14m   E1   5b
Climb the groove and crack to finish up a short corner, 2 pegs.

(1982)

A traverse of the right-hand wall, **Progression**, HVS, 5a, leads
along the obvious break. The left wall awaits a lead to complete
the girdle.

(1983)

STADEN QUARRY LIST OF FIRST ASCENTS

1966 April	**Solo** J Smith	
1966 July	**Fiat** P Nunn, M Rowe	
1966 July	**Indictment** J Smith, P Nunn (AL)	
1966 July	**Leper's Groove** P Nunn, J Smith	
1966 Aug.	**The Marmolizer** J Smith, P Nunn	
1966 Aug.	**Ephemeral Groove** P Nunn J Smith	
1966 Aug.	**Suscipiat** P Nunn, W Ward, J Smith	
	Started direct at a later date.	
1969	**Baang**	
	A loose groove and arête 20 metres right of Solo.	
	Joint Effort (2 pts.) R Dearman	
	Fixation (1 pt.) R Dearman	
	Charas (4 pts.) R Dearman	
	Investal J Morgan	
1969 July	**The Nails** (1 pt.) P Nunn, R Olliphant	
	Amatarasu (1 pt.) K Bridges	
1970 Feb.	**Wooden Leg** T Proctor, K Myhill (AL) C Jackson	
1974	**Bimbo the Exploding Lorry Driver's Gulch Eliminate** J R Woodward, A Woodward	
1974	**Rupert Bear Goes Hiking** J R Woodward, A Woodward	

974 **Frozen Assets** J R Woodward, A Woodward
The HVS arête 7m right of Solo.

974 **The Orange Throated Gonk** J R Woodward, A
Woodward
The steep HS crack just right of Solo.

974 **Outer Plasmic Membrane** J R Woodward, A
Woodward
The fine HVD crack right of The Gonk.

976 **Hammer Into Anvil** J R Woodward, A Woodward

976 April **Captain Reliable** P Burke, G Cooper
Also recorded as Clank. Possibly done in June, 1977.

976 **A Game of Chess** J R Woodward, A Woodward

977 **Charas** S Worthington, J Worthington, G Barker
First Free Ascent.

977 **Solar Wall** G Barker, A Hildred

977 **Sun Crack** G Barker, A Hildred

978 May 24 **Xenophobia** G Gibson (solo)

978 Dec. 13 **Emergency** G Gibson (solo)

978 Dec. 13 **Titanic Reaction** G Gibson (solo)

Solar Plexus G Barker, A Hildred

The Solo Man's Ploy G Barker (solo)

Fixation G Barker, A Hildred
First Free Ascent.

Welcome to Hard Times A Freeman, P Bradshaw, G
Barker

Ground Zero Man C Jackson, M Battersby

One Step From Earth C Jackson, M Battersby

Halcyon Days C Jackson, M Battersby

Soft Mick (1 pt.) M Horlov, R Dearman

Route One M Horlov, R Dearman

1979 March 20 **Somebody's Trademark** G Gibson (solo)

1979 June 28	**Liquid Courage**	G Gibson, D Beetlestone

1979 June 28   **Liquid Courage**   G Gibson, D Beetlestone

1979 Aug. 12   **Bicycle Repair Man**   M Walton, G Gibson, P Wilson

1979 Aug. 12   **Telescopic Demand**   P Wilson, G Gibson, M Walton

1979 Aug. 12   **Wipe Out**   G Gibson, M Walton, P Wilson

1979 Aug. 16   **Waterloo Road**   G Gibson (solo)

1979 Aug. 16   **Great Expectations**   G Gibson (solo)

1979 Aug. 16   **Nice 'n Sleazy**   G Gibson (solo)

1979 Sept. 23   **Generosity Exists**   D Gregory, J Rubery

1979 Sept. 23   **Friendly Local**   J Rubery, D Gregory

1979 Sept. 23   **Giant Staircase**   D Gregory, J Rubery

1979 Sept. 23   **Boomerang**   D Gregory, J Rubery

1979 Sept. 23   **The Heron**   D Gregory, J Rubery

1979 Sept. 30   **Kelloggs Are On Strike**   D Gregory, J Rubery

1979 Sept. 30   **Rising Potential**   A Ward, C Darley

1979 Sept. 30   **Broken Hammer**   A Ward, C Darley

1979 Sept. 30   **Throwback**   A Ward, C Darley

1979 Sept. 30   **Pig Sick**   J Rubery, D Gregory, A Ward

1979 Oct. 6   **Paraplege**   G Gibson, D Williams

1979 Oct. 6   **Roman Numeral X**   G Gibson, D Williams

1980 March 30   **Silent Manoeuvres**   G Gibson, D Beetlestone
After top-rope practice.

1980 May 11   **Cross Purposes**   G Gibson, P Gibson

1981 March 25   **My Tulpa**   G Gibson, H Carnes

1981 March 25   **Mozaic Piece**   G Gibson, D Beetlestone, S Frazer
Soloed without the bolt by G Gibson on 26 March, 1981.

1981 March 25   **Telescopic Demand Direct**   G Gibson, D Beetlestone, S Frazer

1981 April 4   **X Certs**   G Gibson (unseconded)

1981 June   **Cathy's Clown**   P Burke, G Cooper

Bill Wintrip on the first ascent of Diddyogger, Small Dale Quarry.
Photo: Chris Jackson.

982 Aug. 18	**Soft Mick** free	S Nadin, R Davies
982 Aug. 18	**Restive Being**	R Davies, S Nadin
982 Aug. 30	**Silent Fear**	S Nadin, R Davies
983 April	**Welcome to Hard Times Direct**	P Stidever, R Beadle
983 April 3	**Invisible Limits**	S Nadin, R Davies
983 April 12	**Bandobras Took**	S Nadin, R Davies
983 April 12	**Death's Retreat**	R Davies, S Nadin
983 May 15	**Swan Song**	R Davies, S Nadin

Now incorporates Telescopic Demand's old start.

983 May 20	**Action Potential**	S Nadin, R Davies
983 June 8	**Leningrad**	G Gibson (solo)
983 July 17	**Before the Storm**	S Nadin, R Davies
983 July 27	**Levant**	R Davies (solo)
983 Aug. 1	**Taxing Times**	R Davies, S Nadin
983 Aug. 16	**Progression**	R Davies, S Nadin
986 Aug. 20	**Private Gripped**	R Davies (unseconded)
983 Sept. 12	**Psychological Warfare**	R Davies (solo)

TADEN QUARRIES AND COW DALE GRADED LIST

6
rivate Gripped (6b)

5
. Game of Chess (6b)
he Main Motor Mile (6a)
nvisible Limits (6a)

4
1uch Monkey Magic (6a)
ilent Manoeuvres (5c)
eath's Retreat (6a)
ction Potential (5c)

Psychological Warfare (5b)
Mozaic Piece (5c)

E3
Welcome to Hard Times
Direct (5c)
Before the Storm (6a)
Cathy's Clown (5c)
Soft Mick (5c)
Paraplege (5c)
Silent Fear (6a)
Bandobras Took (5c)
Wipe Out (5b)

artin Atkinson on an early ascent of Rite of Way, Winnats Pass.
1oto: Neil Foster.

E2
Captain Reliable (5c)
Liquid Courage (5c)
Levant (5c)
Hammer Into Anvil (5c)
Swan Song (5b)
Welcome to Hard Times (5c)
Nice 'n Sleazy (5b)

E1
Bicycle Repair Man (5b)
Restive Being (5b)
Waterloo Road (5b)
Leningrad (5b,5b)

HVS
Charas (5b)
The Nails (5b)
Joint Effort (5b)

DEEP DALE
O.S. ref. SK 086 698 to SK 103 724

by Alan Wright

---

*'Deep Dale, which had been neglected up to 1960 owing
to its relative shortness, came in for its share of visits.
Most of the routes here have been done by Jack
Arrundale, B Roberts, M Blackwell and G West. Jack
Arrundale came to like Deep Dale so much that the rest
of us very nearly had to ask permission to climb on
"his" crag.*

Graham West. 1961

SITUATION
Deep Dale is the valley which runs between Brierlow Bar (SK
086 698) on the A515 Buxton – Ashbourne road, and Topley Pike
Quarry (SK 103 724) on the A6, Buxton – Bakewell road. The
climbing is divided between the routes of the upper dale, on Two
Tier Buttress, Long Buttress, and Secret Garden Buttress, and the
lower dale routes overlooking Topley Pike Quarry, on Windy Slab,
The Rim and The Cove.

APPROACHES and ACCESS
All the areas can be reached from the Topley Pike Quarry
entrance. Windy Slab can be seen overlooking the entrance on
the left and The Rim contours the hillside behind. To reach The
Cove follow the path which starts to the left of the settling ponds
and continue straight ahead. To reach the upper dale from this
end, start as for The Cove and follow a path round to the right,

behind the Quarry, passing larger redundant settling ponds to reach the path up the dale. Alternatively the upper dale can be reached via a footpath from King Sterndale Church (SK 094716) to the edge of the dale, zig-zagging down to the stream near Thirst House Cave.

The lower part of the dale belongs to the quarry company, which seems to tolerate climbing. The ownership of the upper dale is not known.

HISTORY

The first recorded climbs in the dale were done by Jack Arrundale, Barry Roberts, Mike Blackwell and Graham West in 1960. They discovered such routes as *Egg an' Onion Crack*, *A Reet Treet* and *Blueberry Tower* on The Rim, and routes around Windy Slab. The area seems to have remained dormant until 1977, when a visit by Jon Woodward resulted in *Second Lesson* on The Rim. In the same year Phil Burke visited the dale and led the difficult *Half Way Crack*, *Stroll Way*, *Bill's Crack* and *Parrot Crack*, a route subsequently claimed by several parties. During the next two years periodic visits by Graham Warren uncovered *Robin Hood*, *Maid Marion* and *Lost Chimney* on Secret Garden Buttress. He also discovered *Nancy Boy* and *Town Hall Clerk* in The Cove. Preparation for the 1980 Northern Limestone guide gave Bob Conway and Chris Jackson the opportunity to develop the remaining stretches of rock, producing a string of routes. Tom Proctor helping out on a couple of evenings, to produce *Tom's Off Day Route* and *Midge Dance*, then the hardest route in the valley. Most of the post 1980 guide activity has been on the Long Buttress with ascents of *Antidote*, *Deep Throat*, *Deep Thought*, *Hazy Day* and *Scent of Spring*. In the same period The Secret Garden Buttress yielded *The Abbey Habit* to Mark Kemball and Dave Abbey. Another visitor was Dave Lee who took a break from his Chee Dale exploration to free the technical *Thunderball*. As a fitting climax to the current phase Phil Swainson and Mike Richardson snatched the plum from The Cove named *Polymath* while Paul Mitchell climbed *Too Mellow to Bellow* up the left side of the cave.

THE CLIMBS are described from RIGHT to LEFT.

WINDY SLAB

This is the prominent slabby buttress which lies about halfway up the narrow ridge of Topley Pike, above the quarry entrance.

1   Big Ears' Crack   7m   HVD
To the right of the slab the buttress is split by a crack from top to
bottom.   (1960)

2   Windy Slab   8m   HVD
Climb the right-hand end of the slab.   (1960)

3   Very Windy Slab   8m   VD
                                                               (1960)

4   Porthos   12m   HVD
The first leftwards slanting chimney round the corner from Windy
Slab.   (1960)

5   Aramis   12m   VD   *
One metre left of the chimney, a crack leads to a ledge at 5m.
Above the ledge, climb the corner crack between the wall and the
rib on the left.   (1960)

6   D'Artagnan   13m   D
3m left of the chimney, a groove with a large tree at the bottom.
Climb round the trunk and ascend the slab on the left.   (1960)

*Climbing farther left is not recommended because of the likely
hazard to users of the road below.*

THE RIM

*150m right and at a higher level is an obvious line of crags
extending along the rim of the dale beyond Windy Slab. The
climbs are described from left to right. The first climbable buttress
is 15m along the crag past some small outcrops. It has an
overhang at the top, and an overhanging rightward slanting crack
on the left-hand side of the front face.*

7   Brutal Brutus   8m   VS
Climb the steep crack to the overhang which is passed on the left.
                                                               (1960)

8   Gentleman Jim   8m   VD
Just right of the middle of the buttress ascend via a short groove
to the overhang which can be passed on the right or the left.
                                                               (1960)

3m right, past an easy groove is a V-arête.

9 Rambler's Arête 7m VD
This arête is climbed directly.   (1960)

A short way right, past a subsidiary corner is a bigger corner with a large tree. The slab behind the tree has an obvious crack.

10 By-Pass 8m D
Climb to the top of the crack, finishing rightwards. Alternatively, hand-traverse into the corner (harder).   (1960)

7m right of the corner there is a small cave below a crack.

11 Floating Rib 10m VD
Climb the rib to the left of the cave, just right of the tree.   (1960)

12 Ostrich's Throat 10m HVD   *
Climb out of the cave and follow the crack directly.   (1960)

The next buttress is the highest and most prominent on The Rim. On the front of the buttress there is a tree stump on a ledge at about 3m. On the left of the tree stump is a steep crack.

13 Egg an' Onion Crack 13m VS 4b
Climb the broken wall to the crack and continue up to a tree belay.
                                                                        (1960)

14 A Reet Treet 15m VS 4c   *
Right of the tree is a steep clean crack. Climb the lower wall to the ledge and swing right into the crack. Follow the crack, moving left at the overhang to easier ledges.   (1960)

15 Direct Start 5m HVS 5b
Climb the thin crack to gain the main crack.

16 Second Lesson 17m HVS 5b
Gain a groove on the nose of the buttress to the right of A Reet Treet, by a diagonal leftward line. Up the groove, finishing to the right of the overhang.   (1977)

17 Right Slab 7m D
The slab right of the corner.

A few metres right is a twin-towered buttress, divided by a square corner.

18   First Day Tower   10m   S
The front face of the left tower is climbed on small holds.   (1960)

19   Second Day Crack   10m   S
Climb the corner between the two towers.   (1960)

20   Lazy Day   10m   VS   5a
Just right of the corner is an indefinite crack which ends in a small overhang. Follow the crack with a hard layaway at the top.
(1960s)

21   Third Day Tower   10m   HVS   5b
An old peg route following the centre of the right-hand tower.
(1960s)

The next prominent buttress is 10m right, past bushes. On the left is a steep slab with a tree well up on the left.

22   Early Bird Wall   8m   VD
A thin crack up the slab leads to a shallow groove on the left. Go up the right-hand side of the groove and over steep blocks to finish.   (1960s)

Farther right is another large tower, the last of any size on The Rim.

23   Blueberry Tower   10m   S
Start at the lower part of the buttress and take a short steep section of rock to a narrow slanting groove. Continue up the slab above to a series of loose blocks.   (1960)

The Rim beyond here consists of many short walls, pinnacles and buttresses which offer a variety of boulder problems.

About 300m up the valley from the road, the main valley curves round to the right behind the quarry workings. A short valley continues to the left. The head of this is known as The Cove and it contains a cave, known as the Churn Hole.

THE COVE

On the east side of The Cove is **Thunder Buttress**. From left to right:-

24   Thunder Buttress Route   17m   VD
Go left up a steep groove, climb a steep rib to a rake, then traverse right to a block and crack. Pull round the block and climb to a tree belay.   (1960s)

25   The Primrose Path   17m   VS   4b
Climb the groove 13m left of Thunder Wall, follow the undercut flake rightwards and finish directly.   (1977)

26   Old Nick   20m   HVS   5b   *
3m left of Thunder Wall a crack splits the overhang. Climb this and follow it up the wall above, finishing up a steep slab.   (1979)

27   Thunder Wall   23m   E3   6a
At the highest part of the buttress. Climb the lower wall trending rightwards to a thin crack in the bulge. Climb the crack and wall above to a yew tree. A corner leads to the top.   (1979/1983)

28   Jack Frost   22m   VS   4c
Start at the lower wall of Thunder Wall and follow its right-hand edge to an overhang. Step right to a crack, and follow it to a good ledge. Continue to the top.   (1960s)

29   Thunder Chimney   15m   D
The easy chimney in the corner right of Jack Frost.   (1960s)

At the head of The Cove opposite the Churn Hole is a slabby buttress. Starting in the centre of the slab at a pointed boulder is:

30   Nancy Boy   20m   HVS   5b
Climb the wall directly from the pointed rock passing a sapling and move slightly left at a bulge. Traverse right across the slab and finish up a crack in the arête.   (1978)

31   The Fop   20m   HVS   5b   †
The wall and flake crack left of Nancy Boy.   (1985)

32   Polymath   20m   HVS   5a
Start about 3m left of the pointed boulder of Nancy Boy. The obvious groove is hard to start and leads to an overhang. Go over this to the wide finishing crack.   (1985)

33   Town Hall Clerk   20m   D
The deep crack 7m right of Nancy Boy.   (1978)

UPPER DEEP DALE

About 1km up the main dale from the quarry on the left there is an outcrop in two tiers. The upper tier contains various short problems.

34   Hangman   10m   VS   4c
Climb the undercut crack which splits the prominent centre of the tier.

35   Queer Tree Groove   8m   D
The groove 3m to the right with a tree at its base.

Farther right the tier forms a leaning wall with two grooves. The left-hand one is:

36   Ash Gash   17m   HD
Go up a steep corner, past a tree and onto the steep slab above.
                                                                      (1960s)

The lower tier consists of four isolated towers, each with Very Difficult routes up their fronts. A farther 150m upstream the dale takes a bend left, round which is Thirst House Cave. From here can be seen Long Buttress on the left and Secret Garden Buttress upstream on the right.

THIRST HOUSE CAVE *gives the following climbs:*

37   Too Mellow to Bellow   12m   E5   6a
On the left side of the Thirst House Cave; an obvious line of situ gear points the way of this route.   (1985)

38   Zany Pop   15m   E1   5a
The right wall of the Thirst House Cave.   (1985)

39 Gam 11m HVS 5a
Climb the right-hand corner of the cave.   (1985)

*The following five climbs described from right to left are to be
found on the rocks forming the entrance to the cave opposite the
Thirst House Cave.*

40 Doggy's Roof 12m E3 6a
Take the obvious line across the roof of the cave past three
threads.   (1985)

41 Figment of Imagination 12m E3 6a   †
Climbs the roof crack at the left side of the cave. Gain it from the
left and move leftwards at the lip of the roof. Up the easy corner,
then traverse left along a break to finish at a sapling.   (1985)

42 Forging the Chain 12m E4 6a   †
Climb the wall 4m left of the last route to a slanting break. Climb
the overhanging wall to an obvious groove and finish at the
second sapling. Abseil off or scramble to safety.   (1985)

43 Blue Adept 12m E3 6a   †
Climb the wall to a flake 3m left again and continue up the shallow
groove to a traverse right and junction with the previous route.
                                                                 (1985)

44 Rated X 12m E2 5c   †
The obvious groove 3m left of Blue Adept to finish at a tree.
                                                                 (1985)

LONG BUTTRESS

*The climbs are on the upper tier. The most prominent feature here
is a corner with a wide crack leading to a square-cut overhang,
Vulture's Crutch. This is about halfway along the tier, and the
climbs are described in relation to this feature. To the left of the
corner there are many short buttresses, cracks and chimneys. At
about 22m left there is a groove containing two trees, Megsy.*

45 One Night Stand 13m E1 5c
Climb the system of thin cracks and a bulge 3m left of Megsy.
Convenient tree for abseil.   (1985)

46   Megsy   13m   HS
Steeply enter the groove and follow it to the top.   (1979)

47   Vulture's Crutch   15m   VS   4c
Climb the crack to the roof then move left into a steep flake crack
to finish.   (1979)

48   Antidote   12m   E3   5c
The short sharp and technical groove left of Vulture's Crutch.
                                                                      (1980)

49   Deep Throat   11m   HVS   5a
The overhanging crack-cum-groove, left of Antidote.   (1982)

50   Deep Thought   11m   HVS   5a
The next groove left.   (1982)

51   Hazy Day   11m   VS   4c
A left to right line across the buttress to the left of the
chimney/gully left of Deep Thought.   (1982)

52   Scent of Spring   11m   HVS   5b
Climb the right arête of the buttress left of the chimney left again.
Right of Vulture's Crutch.   (1982)

53   Classical Gas   10m   VS   4b
Immediately right of the corner is a shallow groove. From the
bottom of the crack step right into the groove and follow it to the
top.   (1979)

*Right again the crag forms an undercut arête with a tree in a small
cave.*

54   Knee Trembler   17m   VS   4c
From the tree traverse right for 2m and climb the bulge. Move
back left into a groove on the arête and follow this to the top.
                                                                      (1979)

55   Alexander Beetle   20m   VS   5a   *
3m right of the arête, a shallow groove leads to a small roof at the
horizontal break. Climb the groove, moving right to take the crack
through the bulge.   (1979)

56 A Private Cosmos 20m HVS 5b
3m right again there is a small yellow hanging flake. Climb the
wall above the flake to the rake, and follow the crack directly
above.   (1979)

57 A Poke in the Eye with a Sharp Stick 23m HVS 5b
As for A Private Cosmos to the rake, then traverse right to the tree
to gain a crack above. Follow the crack to the top.   (1979)

58 Happy Humphrey 20m VS 4c
A further 15m right there is a tree at the foot of the crag. Climb the
wall behind the tree to the rake. Traverse 3m left to a tree and
climb the crack behind it.   (1979)

59 Emmaline 23m HVS 5b
As for Happy Humphrey to the tree on the rake. To the left again is
a bulge in the wall. Take this on the left and climb past a pocket to
the top.   (1979)

SECRET GARDEN BUTTRESS

*The buttress is on the west side of the valley opposite Long
Buttress. Walking up the dale, it is just before the power line
which crosses the dale at a leftward bend. It has two tiers, all the
climbs being on the clean upper tier. The right-hand patch of
jungle is the Secret Garden. The climbs are described from left to
right starting from where the main crag meets the steep rising
bank.*

60 Little Weed 12m HVS 5c
The front feature is a short bottomless groove which is entered
with difficulty. Move right above the groove into a short crack to
finish.   (1979)

61 Bill's Crack 13m HVS 5a
3m right, climb the wall, trending right until below a hanging
crack. Climb the crack to the top.   (1977)

62 Ben's Groove 13m VS 4b
3m right, climb the wall trending left to meet Bill's Crack then
trend rightwards into the groove and follow it to the top. (1979)

63   Stroll Wall   13m   S
Climb the obvious corner groove and crack to the right of Ben's
Groove.   (1977)

64   The Abbey Habit   12m   E1   5c
The line up the wall 3m left of Half Way Crack via a slight crack
and groove.   (1982)

65   Half Way Crack   13m   E1   5c
5m right of the corner is an obvious crack in the upper wall.
Ascend the steep lower wall to the horizontal break. Use a good
layaway hold to reach a hold on the bulge which is climbed with
difficulty to the crack.   (1977)

66   Tom's Off Day Route   17m   E2   5c   *
Start 2m right of Half Way Crack, just right of a shallow groove.
Climb to the right-hand crack. Traverse left and use hidden flake
holds to gain the groove on the left which relents only towards
the top.   (1979)

67   Tree and Leaf   17m   VD
Start below the tree left of the jungle. Climb the lower wall past a
rockfall scar and continue up a groove to the right of the tree.

68   Holiday Home for Pets Pie Company   17m   VS   4c
A shallow groove right of the jungle patch. Climb the scooped
wall to a bulge. Climb this on good holds, then to the top trending
left.   (1979)

69   Midge Dance   17m   E2   5c
Start 5m right, below the prominent hanging in the upper wall.
Climb straight up to the small overlap, peg, go over this to the
right, and then back left to the black undercling. A deep flake crack
gives the finish.   (1979)

70   Touch and Go   17m   E1   5b   *
The prominent groove left of the Secret Garden. Go up the pillar
and into the Secret Garden via two trees. Climb the obvious
chimney on the left.   (1979)

71   Congealed Chimney   20m   VD
Start at a shattered pillar below the left-hand end of the Secret
Garden. Go up the pillar and into the Secret Garden via two trees.
Follow the obvious chimney on the left.   (1979)

72 Summertime 23m VD
Start 3m right of Congealed Chimney. Climb diagonally
rightwards to a thin bedding plane. Swing right to a hawthorn
tree and into the Secret Garden, finishing up the V-groove behind
the trees.

73 Maid Marion 23m VD
Below the right-hand end of the Secret Garden is a large detached
flake. Climb the stepped flake to a large ledge and follow the V-
groove on the left to a grassy ledge, finishing up the wall behind.
(1978)

74 Parrot Crack 23m VS 4c
As for Maid Marion to below the ledge. Traverse right and move
up to the bottom of an obvious cleft. Follow this to the top.
(1977)

75 Cock or Two 23m VS 4c
As for Parrot Crack to the foot of the cleft. Traverse left round the
nose to a series of cracks which are followed, swinging right to
the top.

76 Robin Hood 23m HVS 5b
Start up the broken wall immediately below a short groove in the
wall to the right of Parrot Crack. Go up the wall and move left
towards the foot of Parrot Crack. Move right into a shallow groove
and climb this to reach a crack which leads to the top.   (1978)

77 Tourist Groove 20m HVS 5a
Right again is a fine shallow groove. Climb the wall below the
groove, trending right to the horizontal break. Traverse left into
the groove, and follow it to the top. Worth a passing visit.

DEEP DALE LIST OF FIRST ASCENTS

by Geoff Milburn

1960   The first development was very much the work of
             Jack Arrundale who was convinced of its worth for
             novices or a pleasant evening.

             Windy Slab

Big Ears' Crack

Porthos

Aramis

D'Artagnan

Brutal Brutus

Gentleman Jim

Ramblers' Arête

By-Pass

Floating Rib

Ostrich's Throat
All routes by a combination of J Arrundale, B Roberts, M Blackwell, G West.
'Jack Arrundale was called "Ostrich" because he was reputed to be able to hold a half-pint pot sideways in his mouth.'

Egg an' Onion Crack

A Reet Treat

Easy Chimney

First Day Tower

Second Day Crack

Third Day Tower (A1)
'This route is the only piton route on the Rim. It has also been free-climbed in 1969.

Early Bird Wall

Eaglet Corner

Apple Pie Buttress

Blueberry Tower

Thunder Buttress Route

Thunder Chimney

1967   **Thunder Wall** (S, A1)   R S Dearman
Reduced to 1 pt. by R Conway, C Jackson in 1979.

First free ascent by Dave Lee in April 1983.

pre- 1969	**Lazy Day**	
	Jack Frost	A Howard
	Queer Tree Groove	
	Ash Gash	
	Fox Hole Groove	
1967	**Second Lesson**	J Woodward
1977	**Half Way Crack**	P Burke
1977	**Stroll Way**	P Burke
1977	**Bill's Crack**	P Burke
1977	**Parrot Crack**	P Burke
1977	**The Primrose Path**	G Warren, M Kaye
1978	**Robin Hood**	G Warren
1978	**Maid Marion**	G Warren
1978	**Lost Chimney**	G Warren
1978	**Nancy Boy**	G Warren, Susan Russell
1978	**Town Hall Clerk**	G Warren
1979	**Old Nick**	R Conway, C Jackson
1979	**Megsy**	R Conway
1979	**Vulture's Crutch**	C Jackson, R Conway
1979	**Classical Gas**	C Jackson, R Conway
1979	**Knee Trembler**	C Jackson, R Conway
1979	**Alexander Beetle**	C Jackson, R Conway
1979	**A Private Cosmos**	C Jackson, R Conway
1979	**A Poke in the Eye with a Sharp Stick**	C Jackson, R Conway
1979	**Happy Humphrey**	R Conway, C Jackson
1979	**Emmaline**	R Conway, C Jackson
1979	**Little Weed**	R Conway, C Jackson

1979	**Ben's Groove** R Conway, C Jackson
1979	**Tom's Off Day Route** T Proctor, C Jackson
1979	**Holiday Home for Pet's Pie Company** C Jackson, R Conway
1979	**Midge Dance** T Proctor, C Jackson
1979	**Touch and Go** C Jackson, T Proctor
1979	**Congealed Chimney** C Jackson, R Conway
1980	**Antidote** J Woodward, I Maisey
1982	**Deep Throat** M Kemball (unseconded)
1982 March	**Deep Thought** D Abbey, S Hughes, M Kemball
1982 March	**Hazy Day** R Jarratt, J Marks, S Finch, M Kemball
1982 March	**Scent of Spring** S Finch, M Kemball, R Jarratt
1982 March	**The Abbey Habit** M Kemball, D Abbey
1983 April	**Thunder Wall** Dave Lee *First free ascent.*
1983 June 24	**Old Nick** S Nadin, R Davies *First free ascent.*
1985 June 28	**Figment of Imagination** D Kerr, I Wyatt
1985 June 28	**Doggy's Roof** D Kerr, I Wyatt
1985 June 28	**Forging the Chain** D Kerr, I Wyatt
1985 June 28	**Blue Adept** D Kerr, I Wyatt
1985 June 29	**Rated X** D Kerr, I Wyatt
1985	**One Night Stand** D Kerr, I Wyatt
1985	**Zany Pop** I Wyatt, D Kerr
1985 Sept. 10	**Too Mellow to Bellow** P Mitchell
1985 June 29	**The Fop** M Richardson, B Griffiths *'Veteran's team.'*
1985	**Gam** A Barker, C Ellis, I Taylor

UPPER WYE VALLEY CRAGS

GREAT ROCKS DALE

O.S. ref. SK 112 730

by Gary Gibson

'All the climbs were led on sight and few have been repeated . . . '

1980 Northern Limestone Guide.

SITUATION and CHARACTER
This is the very obvious and heavily quarried dale which runs south-east from Peak Dale to end above the railway cottages at Chee Dale. The climbing area is situated above the cottages and is very conspicuous from the layby at the top of Topley Pike. Part of the quarry is now being filled in by tipping.

The rock here is very blocky and for the most part very, very loose. However, some of the gardened routes, especially on the white wall, offer good climbing in hostile situations! Many of the more hazardous-looking routes are still unrepeated and are perhaps best left that way.

APPROACHES and ACCESS
These quarries are owned by I.C.I. THE MANAGERS DEMAND THAT NO CLIMBING IS TO BE UNDERTAKEN IN THE QUARRY. ON NO ACCOUNT SHOULD PEOPLE CLIMB HERE AND THE CLIMBS ARE ONLY INCLUDED FOR COMPLETENESS. For this reason some routes have not been given stars.
The normal approach is direct from Chee Dale cottages into the quarry base, which is increasing in height with the years! It is also possible to reach the top of the quarry from the bank opposite Plum Buttress in Chee Dale and to abseil into the routes.

HISTORY
Climbing in Great Rocks Dale was, up until 1980 dominated by employees of Troll Safety Climbing Equipment, especially Tony Howard. 1964 was the year in which interest first started with the aiding of *Double O* and *M*. 1965 also saw new routes with Bill Tweedale joining in and Tony Howard and Tony Nicholls accounting for three more routes. One of these, *Samedi*, was free-climbed to give *The Merger* in 1970, which proved to be a bumper

year; all the routes on the loose wall on the left side of the Main
Wall were done but the girdle which was tried, had to wait.
Nandin was also climbed. The girdle was completed by Tony
Howard and Mike Shaw in 1976 and the following year saw four
other routes as well as the free-climbing of M as *The Rubber Ogre*
by Howard and Tut Braithwaite.
1978 saw the remaining obvious gaps being filled in, notably
Sunshine Superman by Howard and Shaw. At this point a new
guide appeared and the gaps were duly noted by Gary Gibson. He
came up with the quarry's best route in *Nuclear Device* a classic of
its type. At the same time Howard and J Smith bagged *The
Gibbet*. 1981 saw more routes from Gibson with the unusually
named *No Cure for Gangrene, Slow Like Strychnine* and others.
Gibson's final offering came in 1983 in the form of a superb wall
climb, *A Recipe for Paralysis*. Also in 1983 Steve Lewis stepped in
to bag the first (and last?) free ascent of Double O.

THE CLIMBS are described from RIGHT to LEFT.
At the right-hand end of the crag is a boulder slope right of which
is an undercut buttress. A steep wall on the right offers two routes
with a common start.

1 Onga   19m   HS   4a
Climb the right-hand crack in the wall.   (1978)

2 Up and Coming   25m   VS   4b
From the horizontal break on Onga traverse left 2m and follow the
flaky crack to the top.   (1978)

3 Rhombus   19m   VS   4c
Just left are some zig-zag cracks. Follow these through a bulge to
the top.   (1966)

4 Rainy Day Ramble   25m   VS   4b
From a ledge at mid-height on Rhombus move left and climb to
the top via the arête.   (1978)

5 Sensayuma   22m   VS   4c
Left again. Climb the right-hand crack and knobbly wall to gain a
broken corner crack which leads to the top.   (1965)

6 Hot Legs Special   12m   VD
Climb the open corner-line starting up the right-hand crack.
                                                                 (1978)

7 Chikka 14m VS 4b
Climb a crack just left of Hot Legs Special and move left to gain its
thinner continuation. This leads to a finish on the right arête.
(1978)

8 The Marmaliser 12m VS 4c
3m left is a wide crack. Climb this to an overhang and move up
right to pass it. Move back left to finish on the arête.   (1978)

*Left of the boulder slope is an area of broken rock forming the
right-hand section of* **WHITE WALL.**

9 Green Onions 22m VD
The shattered cracks in the wall between the boulder slope and a
sandy chimney.   (1966)

10 October Crack 18m VD
Climb broken rock just left of the gully into the gully and continue
up a crack passing a small tree.   (1966)

11 Arch Wall 22m VS 4b
Climb the wall just left of the sandy cleft and move left after a few
metres to finish up its centre.   (1970s)

12 Solitaire 18m S
The wide corner crack up the left side of the wall.   (1965)

13 Neptune's Bellows 18m VS 4b
Just left again a groove leads to a roof. Climb the groove and
avoid the roof on the left.   (1970)

14 Skywalker 19m HVS 4c
3m left again. A thin finger-crack leads to the roof on the last
route. Finish up this. A good route.   (1978)

15 Griffon 22m VS 4b
Just left. An awkward jamming crack leads to a ledge on the left.
Move up right to a steep finishing crack.   (1966)

16 Pussy Galore 22m VS 4c
Climb the crack just left of the arête to a niche. Move left, go up via
a hanging corner and finish up the corner left of the roof.   (1965)

17   As Happy as a Pig in   30m   E2   5c   † † †
The roof crack left again provides this route; formerly Double O
but now free. The grade carries a government health warning and
soon the roof may not be around for you to try it!   (1964/1983)

*To the left is a prominent wall, which offers the best climbs on the
crag.*

18   Sunshine Superman   33m   E1   5b
Start below the very left end of the large roof and climb the wall to
a bulge. Traverse left along the horizontal break to a shallow
crack. Climb this passing some ledges onto hanging flakes to
finish. A fine route.   (1978)

19   The Merger   33m   E1   5b
From the bulge on Sunshine Superman continue up a thin crack
above to twin horizontal breaks. Traverse left passing Sunshine
Superman and finish up a slabby left-trending groove.   (1970)

*To the left a thin ledge runs across the wall low down and ends at
a tree.*

20   Let Me Introduce You To The Family   30m   E4   5c
Start 5m along the thin ledge on some perched flakes. Take a
belay! Step right off the flakes onto the wall and climb boldly to
the break. Step 2m left, then go up the wall, peg, to easy ground.
Move right to finish up the big flake-line.   (1981)

21   The Rubber Ogre   30m   E1   5c
Behind the tree a shallow groove and thin cracks split the wall.
Climb the groove and cracks passing the roof. Move right above
this to a steep finishing crack, just left of an easy groove.
                                                        (1964/1977)

22   Nuclear Device   30m   E2   5c
The centre of the white wall; superb. From just left of the tree
climb a thin crack and wall directly above to a bulge, peg. Climb
over this, crux, and finish directly to the top.   (1980)

23   Slow, Like Strychnine   35m   E3   6a
Excellent climbing. Start 5m left of Nuclear Device at a thread in
the wall on the thin ledge. Climb directly up the wall, bold, past a
break to a second break. Traverse 9m right past Nuclear Device to
a tiny groove. Go up this for 5m, step right to a peg then go direct
up the smooth wall above.   (1981)

24 Nandin 45m VS 4b
The left arête of the wall taking one section via the obvious jam crack to finish. The route is getting shorter!   (1964/1970)

The wall left of Nandin contains a number of groove-lines and is called the WALL OF GROOVES. *All the routes start about 12m left of the arête, part way up the scree slope.*

25 The Temple of Lara Jongrang 48m HVS 4b,5a
From 2m up the scree slope traverse right for 9m to a groove just left of the arête. Climb up this to a ledge at two-thirds height, on the arête, belay. Move left and go up the corner to the top.
(1970)

26 Visions of Vishnu 35m HVS (2 pts. aid) 4c,5a
Climb a left-slanting crack to belay below an overhanging groove. Cross the wall on the right with two aid pegs to a steep crack. Climb this.   (1970)

27 Kali 35m HVS 5a
As for Vishnu to the belay and continue up the overhanging groove above.   (1978)

28 Govinda 48m HVS 4c,5a
As for Vishnu to the belay. Move 2m left to a hanging groove. Up this to a roof and traverse left across a slab to an exit gully.
(1978)

29 The Sanctuary of Siva 46m HVS 4b,5a
Climb the big corner on the left behind the elders to a roof at 5m. Traverse up right to the belay of Vishnu. Continue up right below the roofs to a big corner (left of Lara Jongrang). Climb this.
(1970)

Left again is a wall at right angles to the Wall of Grooves.

30 Brahma 30m VS 4b
Climb the centre of the wall to a groove part way up it. Climb this to the top.   (1970)

31 Total Haemorrhage 33m E2 5b
From the foot of the corner on Brahma step right round the arête onto a pillar. Climb the centre of this to the top.   (1981)

Philip Gibson

White Wall

32 Dismembered 35m E1 5c
From the foot of the corner on Brahma climb the thin crack on the left to a break. Step up right and climb the huge flake to the top.
(1981)

33 A Recipe for Paralysis 35m E5 6a
An excellent route taking the centre of the very impressive wall. Climb Dismembered to the break and move left to a peg in its centre. Step up then climb direct, with a lunge or two, past a thread, to the top.
(1983)

34 No Cure for Gangrene 37m E2 5c
Dramatic and unusual. From the foot of the corner on Brahma step down left onto the wall and ascend leftwards onto the arête. Climb this past a wide crack and a wild move to easy ground.
(1981)

6m left of the elder trees is an open hanging groove.

35 Zyklon B 33m VS 4c,4c
Climb a crack in black rock then the left arête to ledges, belay. Finish up the right-hand of two cracks.
(1977)

36 Help the Poor Struggler 33m HVS 5a,4c
Start at the next obvious corner 8m left of Zyklon B. Step off a pedestal and climb a crack. Traverse right between overhangs to the groove left of Zyklon B. Go up this to a belay. Gain the rib on the right and climb the steep crack and chimney above.
(1978)

37 Sergeant Mold 30m HVS 4b,4c
Start as for Struggler. Step off the pedestal into the corner and climb this past two bulges to a ledge. The steep corner leads to a large roof. Traverse left and go up a groove.
(1977)

38 The Gibbet 35m E2 5c,5c
The large wide crack splitting the roofs of 'Struggler'. Climb the crack initially through two overhangs to a belay. The thin crack in the centre of the leaning wall above leads to a finish over a protruding block.
(1980)

39 Albert Pierrepoint 30m HVS 5a,4c
Start just left of Sergeant Mold. Climb the leftward leaning crack to a roof and move right to some ledges. Continue up a broken groove and its left arête above.
(1977)

40 Hsiao Mieh 30m HVS 5a
Climb the broken groove 2m right of Scaramanga to a roof and
by-pass this via the left arête and easy broken rock above.
(1977)

41 The Scavenger's Daughter 33m VS 4c
The broken wall right of the corner of Scaramanga starting up
Scaramanga for 5m.   (1978)

To the left is a long wall running up the dale; **THE MAIN WALL.**

42 Scaramanga 35m VS (1 pt. aid) 4c,4b
Climb the obvious corner bounding the wall on the right with an
aid peg at half-height. Belay below the obvious roof. Traverse
12m left below the roof and finish up a steep wall.   (1965)

43 Indirect Start 20 HS 4a
The pinnacle and groove left of the normal start to the belay.

44 Kundalini 30m VS 4c
Start 6m down and left. Climb a small pinnacle and step left and
go up a shallow groove. Move left again at its top to join the
traverse and finish of Scaramanga.   (1970s)

*45m farther left is a cone of broken rock at the base of the wall.
Above this are some loose hanging corners and a curving crack to
their right.*

45 Ourobouros 38m VS 4b,4b
Gain the curving crack from the left, follow it and go up a vertical
crack to a corner. Move right from the top of this to belay ledges.
Continue leftwards up grass and corners to a horizontal break.
Move right to finish.   (1960s)

*30m left again is a second mound of broken rock. There is a roof
above and a long crack in the buttress to the left.*

46 Will O' The Wisp 38m VS (2 pts. aid) 4c,4c
Gain the long crack with an aid peg and follow it to grass. Climb
the wall above, just left of its centre, with another aid peg to gain
the groove above.   (1970)

*Another 320m left above a sycamore and elder tree is a pedestal
on a smooth wall.*

Martin Atkinson on Wilt, Ravensdale.
Photo: Neil Foster.

47   Natty Dread   40m   VS   4b,4b
Climb the obvious wide corner on the left, gaining it from 6m up
the broken gully. Move right along the upper of two traverse lines
below the roofs, belay. Traverse right past the precarious
pedestal and descend to another pedestal. Move up and right to a
belay ledge. Finish by climbing diagonally left via a crack or, safer,
rightwards.   (1978)

48   Hot to Trot   50m   VS   4b,4b
Start just right of the lowest point of the buttress, just right of the
trees. Trend up left to twin horizontal cracks and then move up
right to a belay below a corner on the right wall of the pedestal.
Climb the corner to an overlap, traverse right and go up to finish.
                                                  (1970s)

49   Bon-Bon   35m   HS   4b
Start from the top of the brown scree fan on the right. Climb the
leftward leaning groove to a loose bulge. Move right and go up
cracks to the top.   (1970)

Some 25m farther left, on the left side of the buttress is:

50   Shaken Not Stirred   38m   S   4a
Climb slabby rock to a rake below a leaning wall. Follow the rake
rightwards past a tree to ledges and a slab leading up to a terrace.
Finish up the steep wall behind.   (1970)

There are two girdle traverses starting behind the trees, as for The
Sanctuary of Siva.

51   Forbidden Fruits   60m   HVS   4b,4c,4c
Now slightly shorter since the disappearance of the upper wall of
Double O. Pitch 1 of Siva. Move right to belay below the final
groove of Lara Jongrang and belay. Reverse Lara Jongrang and
go round the arête onto the white wall. Move up this to a traverse
line 3m from the top. Go right on this to a belay on a good ledge.
Continue traversing but just before a rock fall ascend direct to the
top.   (1976)

52   Death Row   110m   HVS   5a
Traverse left from behind the trees. From 6m up Siva traverse left
past Brahma to the left arête of the large wall. Move left and belay
in the recess of Zyklon B. Follow Zyklon B to a ledge then cross
the slab to the rib. Continue into the corner of Sergeant Mold to

belay. Climb the corner for 3m then reach the undercut on the left. Move up this and continue down to Scaramanga, belay. Follow Scaramanga but continue left to belay in the grassy gully. Step down past blocks to a foot traverse. Follow this past a red corner. Go up this to a higher traverse and finish up a short corner.

(1978)

53 Great Rocks Girdle 180m HVS
It is possible to combine both traverses starting from the top of Forbidden Fruits and joining up with Death Row at The Sanctuary of Siva: A veritable expedition.

(1978)

GREAT ROCKS DALE LIST OF FIRST ASCENTS

by Geoff Milburn and Chris Hardy

1964	**The White Edge** Unknown
	Eventually became Nandin.
1964	**The Rubber Ogre** Unknown
1964	**Double O** (S A3)
	'The roof on the verge of collapse . . . Eventually did so!'
	First free ascent by S Lewis in October 1983, named As Happy as a Pig in . . . .
1964	**M** (VS A1) A Howard, B Hodgkinson
1965 May	**Samedi** (HVS A1) A Howard, B Hodgkinson
	The aid was reduced by A Howard, P Seddon in 1970 and the route renamed The Merger.
	The early aid routes were mostly done by A Howard, J Amatt, A Waterhouse and A Nicholls of the Rimmon M.C.
1965 May	**Solitaire** W Tweedale, R Flemming
1965 May	**Sensayuma** W Tweedale, R Flemming
1965	**Pussy Galore** A Nicholls, A Howard
1965	**Scaramanga** (some aid) A Nicholls, A Waterhouse

1965	**Ourobouros** A Howard (solo with a peg runner)
1966 Oct.	**Rhombus** B Richardson, P Oldham
1966 Oct.	**Green Onions** P Oldham, B Richardson
1966 Oct.	**October Cracks** B Richardson, P Oldham
1966 Oct.	**Griffon** W Tweedale, J Finnigan
1970 March 22	**Neptune's Bellows** W Tweedale, P Hayward
1970 March 29	**Nandin** A Howard, W A Birch (AL) *A free ascent of The White Edge.*
1970 April 4	**The Temple of Lara Jongrang** (1 pt.) W A Birch, A Howard *Free the same year by K Myhill, B Crown.*
1970 April 5	**Will o' the Wisp** (2 pts.) A Howard, W A Birch (AL)
1970 May 2	**Visions of Vishnu** (3 pts.) A Howard, W A Birch (AL)
1970 May 4	**The Merger** (2 pts. + rest) P Seddon, A Howard (AL) *Originally climbed as Samedi. The route was re- named when the aid was reduced to a nut to place a peg for tension on pitch 1 and nuts were used for resting on pitch 2 – a curious reason for re-naming in 1970.* *The route was later freed by A Howard.*
1970	**The Sanctuary of Shiva** (some aid) A Howard, W A Birch (AL)
1970 June	**Bon Bon** P Hayward, R Treglown
1970	**Wall of Grooves** Unknown
1970	**Brahma** W A Birch, P Seddon *Peg marks indicated an earlier ascent.*
1970 Nov. 1	**Boo-Boo Pongo** J R Barker, W Phillips
1970	**Shaken Not Stirred** A Howard, R Treglown
1976 Aug. 7	**Forbidden Fruits** A Howard, M Shaw
1977 Sept.	**Albert Pierrepoint** A Howard, M Shaw
1977 Sept.	**The Rubber Ogre** P Braithwaite, A Howard *First free ascent of M.*

1977 Sept.	**Zyklon B** A Howard, P Braithwaite
1977 Oct.	**Hsiao Mieh** A Howard, M Shaw
1977	**Sergeant Mold** A Howard, P Braithwaite
1978	**Up and Coming** A Howard, Diana Taylor
1978	**Hot Legs Special** A Howard, Diana Taylor
1978	**Chikka** M Shaw, A Howard
1978	**Sunshine Superman** M Shaw, A Howard
1978	**Govinda** A Howard, M Shaw, Diana Taylor
1978	**Help the Poor Struggler** A Howard, M Shaw, Diana Taylor
1978	**The Scavenger's Daughter** A Howard, Diana Taylor
1978	**Kali** M Shaw, A Howard
1978	**Onga** M Shaw, A Howard
1978	**Rainy Day Ramble** A Howard, D Taylor
1978	**The Marmaliser** M Shaw, A Howard
1978	**Natty Dread** A Howard, D Taylor
1970s	**Hot to Trot** A Howard, M Shaw
1978	**Death Row** M Shaw, A Howard
1978	**Skywalker** A Howard, D Taylor
1978	**Great Rocks Girdle** A Howard, M Shaw
1970s	**Kundalini** A Howard, M Shaw
1970s	**Arch Wall**
1980	**The Gibbet** A Howard, J Smith (AL)
1980 Feb. 22	**Nuclear Device** G Gibson, A Hargreaves, D Williams
1981 Feb. 14	**Slow Like Strychnine** G Gibson, S Horridge
1981 April 11	**No Cure for Gangrene** G Gibson, D Beetlestone
1981 Sept. 5	**Total Haemorrhage** G Gibson (solo)
1981 Sept. 5	**Dismembered** G Gibson, G Jewson, C Parkin

1981 Oct. 18 **Let Me Introduce You to the Family**   G Gibson, H Carnes

1983 Oct.   **As Happy as a Pig in . . . .**   S Lewis, B Moon
A free ascent of Double O.

1983 Dec. 27 **A Recipe for Paralysis**   G Gibson (unseconded)
After top-rope inspection.

PREVIOUS EDITIONS

1913 Some Gritstone Climbs by John Laycock included climbing on the dolomitic limestone of Harborough and Brassington Rocks.

1950 A Climbing Guide to Brassington Rocks by Eric Byne, M.A.M.

1961 Rock Climbs on the Mountain Limestone of Derbyshire by G.T.West.

1965 Climbs on Derwent Valley Limestone by D.K. Scott. N.C.C.

1966 Stoney Middleton Dale by G.B. Birtles.

1969 The Northern Limestone Area (Rock Climbs in the Peak. Vol. 5) edited by Paul Nunn. Authors included: Len Millsom, A. Howard, G.T. West, R. Dearman, M. Baxter, C. Jackson, J. Loy, O. Woolcock, B. Moore, J. Street, and G. Birtles.

1970 The Southern Limestone Area (Rock Climbs in the Peak. Vol. 8) edited by Paul Nunn. Authors included: D.K. Scott, R. Leeming, D. Carnell, J.R. Allen, D. Burgess, R. Dearman, Jeff Morgan, Trevor Morris, David Thorpe and D. Gregory.

1971 The Chatsworth Gritstone Area (Rock Climbs in the Peak. Vol. 4) edited by Eric Byne included Harborough and Brassington Rocks.

1980 Northern Limestone by Chris Jackson (Rock Climbs in the Peak. Vol. 4) edited by D. Gregory. Authors included: Tom Proctor, Geoff Birtles, Al Evans, Clive Jones, Gary Gibson, Giles Barker, R. Conway Dave Gregory, Tony Howard, Gabriel Regan, Geoff Milburn, Jim Moran, Adey Hubbard, Dave Sant, Rod Haslam and Mike Browell.

1981 Derwent Valley by Jim Ballard and Ernie Marshall (Rock Climbs in the Peak. Vol. 5) edited by D. Gregory. Authors included: Alison Hargreaves, Paul Howarth, Len Pearson, Bob Conway and George Fowler.

1981 Staffordshire Area by Mike Browell, Steve and Brian Dale and Nick Longland (Rock Climbs in the Peak. Vol 6) edited by Geoff Milburn. Authors included: Chris Calow, Dave Gregory, Giles Barker and John Codling.

THE PEAK DISTRICT GUIDEBOOK PATTERN

First Series — 'Climbs on Gritstone'.
Volume 1 – Laddow Area (1948)
Volume 2 – The Sheffield Area (1951)
Volume 3 – Kinder, Roches and Northern Area (1951)
Volume 4 – Further Developments in the Peak District (1957)
Volume 5 – West Yorkshire Area (1957)

Second Series — 'Rock Climbs in the Peak'.
Volume 1 – The Sheffield – Stanage Area (1963)
Volume 2 – The Saddleworth – Chew Valley Area (1965)
Volume 3 – The Sheffield – Froggatt Area (1965)
Volume 4 – Chatsworth Gritstone (1970)
Volume 5 – The Northern Limestone Area (1969)
Volume 6 – The Bleaklow Area (1979)
Volume 7 – The Kinder Area (1974)
Volume 8 – The Southern Limestone Area (1970)
Volume 9 – The Staffordshire Gritstone Area (1973)

Third Series — 'Rock Climbs in the Peak'.
Volume 1 – Stanage Area (1976)
Volume 2 – Chew Valley (1976)
Volume 3 – Froggatt Area (1978)
Volume 4 – Northern Limestone (1980)
Volume 5 – Derwent Valley (1981)
Volume 6 – Staffordshire Area (1981)

Fourth Series — 'Peak District Climbs'.
Volume 1 – Stanage Millstone (1983)
Volume 2 – Derwent Gritstone (1985)
Volume 3 – Peak Limestone – Stoney (1987)
Volume 4 – Peak Limestone – Chee Dale (1987)
Volume 5 – Peak Limestone – South (1987)
Volume 6 – Moorland Gritstone
Volume 7 – Western Gritstone

INDEX

Climb	Page
A Friendly Chat with a Hungry Ghost	173
A Game of Chess	235
A Poke in the Eye with a Sharp Stick	251
A Private Cosmos	251
A Question of Palance	214
A Recipe for Paralysis	264
A Reet Treet	245
A.N. Other	52
Abbey Habit, The	252
Absolute Zero	192
Acrophobia	80
Action Potential	234
Activator	218
Aerospace	73
Aga	42
Albert Pierrepoint	264
Alcasan	43
Alexander Beetle	250
All Along the Watchtower	174
All Systems Go	72
Allergy	87
Alpha	170
Alpinist's Dream	192
Amain	148
Amatarasu	232
Amphitheatre Crack	182
Amphitheatre Wall	182
An Ancient Rhythm	121
Anti-Digestant	212
Antidote	250
Anything Corner	53
Aphrodisiac Jacket	167
Aquiline	32
Aramis	244
Arbeit Macht Frei	90

Climb	Page
Arcadian	164
Arch Wall	259
Arête, The	209
Armageddon	47
Artery, The	171
As Happy as a Pig in . . .	260
Ash Crack	148
Ash Gash	248
Ash Tree Arête	212
Ash Tree Slab	212
Ashwood Crack	219
Asparagus	70
Aspirant Desperado	80
Asylum, The	192
Atropos	33
Au Gratin	64
Au Revoir Monodoigt	73
Augean	53
Aurora Arête	42
Aurora	42
Aux Bicyclettes	67
Avarice	199
Avoiding the Issue	138
Babylon By-Pass	52
Balbus	178
Balcony Climb	179
Banana	175
Bandobrass Took	237
Banker's Climb	175
Barfleur	171
Bay of Pigs	59
Bay Rum	89
Bayliff	89
Beachcomber	145
Beanstalk	56
Beef on the Hoof	184
Before the Storm	237

Climb	Page	Climb	Page
Begorrah	150	Blue Sunday	127
Belial	175	Blueberry Tower	246
Belinda	57	Bluefinger	57
Belling the Cat	138	Bluto	198
Belvedere	173	Boat Pusher's Wall	62
Ben	66	Boggle Tower	219
Ben's Groove	251	Bon-Bon	266
Bender, The	214	Bonedigger	202
Benstirer	92	Boogie Flake	219
Beta	170	Boomerang	226
Bicycle Repair Man	234	Borrower's Climb	175
Bifurous Chimney	145	Bosky	146
Bifurous Corner	145	Boulder Problem	151
Big Chiv	92	Brahma	261
Big Ears' Crack	244	Brain Pollution	137
Big Nose	36	Brassiere Strap	71
Bigot Direct, The	145	Breathing Underwater	43
Bill's Crack	251	Broken Crack	181
Billy Bull Terrier	134	Broken Hammer	227
Billy Two Hats	134	Broken Toe	212
Bimbo drops his Codpiece	126	Brown Corner	83
		Brutal Brutus	244
Bimbo Has His Head		Bubbles Wall	73
Examined	126	Bulging Wall	180
Bimbo on the Loose	126	Bullets	156
Bimbo Strikes Again	127	Burning Giraffe	168
Bimbo the Exploding Lorry		Burning Rubber . . .	222
Driver's Gulch	235	Burst	214
Bimbo's Arête	126	Burying the Red Man	138
Bimbo's Off-day Route	126	By-Pass	245
Bingo Wall	58	Cabbage Crack	86
Bishop, The	209	Cafe Bleu	127
Bitter Fingers	56	Cake Walk	179
Black Bryony	92	Can Boys	188
Black Country Rock	212	Candy Store Rock	88
Black Holes	192	Canopy Crack	144
Black Kabul	73	Captain Reliable	230
Black Teddy	49	Cardiac Arrest	77
Blade-runner	124	Cardinal, The	209
Blisters	62	Carl's Wark Crack	72
Blue Adept	249	Carmen Jones	211
Blue Banana	40	Carmen	211

Climb	Page
Castle Groove	174
Cathy's Clown	230
Cats 23	201
Cave Corner	148
Cave Crack	89
Cave Wall	167
Centimetre Diédre	91
Central Arête	213
Central Crack	219
Central Gully	212
Chance in a Marillion	209
Chantrelle	49
Charas	234
Chastity	176
Cherokee Lane	137
Chewemoff	37
Chicken	125
Chikka	259
Child's Arête	76
Chockstone Crack	181
Chocolate Blancmange Gully	119
Choss	47
Circe	48
Classical Gas	250
Clean Crack	91
Clone of Jeremiah	209
Clothesline	213
Cob	125
Cock or Two	253
Cock-a-Leekie Wall	70
Cointreau	63
Cold Comfort	205
Cold Shoulder	148
College Crack	201
Colonel Bogey	37
Compositae Groove	39
Conclusor	154
Conformist	123
Congealed Chimney	252
Cooper's Route	208

Climb	Page
Corner Crack	164
Costa Brava	73
Crack and Nose	175
Cracked Edge	150
Cray-Pas	92
Crazy Pinnacle Face	197
Crazzled Cracks	91
Critical Town	158
Crooked	188
Cross Purposes	231
Crutch	63
Crux, The	67
Cucklet Delf Eliminate	87
Curving Crack	171
Cut Loose or Fly	148
D'Artagnan	244
Dalkon Shield	124
Damocles	83
Dancing the Hard Bargain	170
Dargai Crack	173
Dargai Variant	173
Dead Banana Crack	56
Dead on Arrival	79
Death Row	266
Death's Retreat	236
Deceptor	211
Deep Thought	250
Deep Throat	250
Delusor	154
Demolition Man	122
Devil's Eye	90
Diamond Wall	201
Diamonds and Rust	77
Diaphragm	226
Diddyogger	188
Dies Irae	49
Diminished Responsibility	185
Dinky Toy	127
Direct Route	181

Climb	Page
Direct Start	245
Disillusioned Brew Machine, The	80
Dismembered	264
Disturbing the Daylight Owl	134
Do Androids Dream of Electric Sheep?	124
Do Nothing	49
Do Up Your Flies	167
Dobbin	170
Doggy's Roof	249
Doing the Business	137
Dome's Groove	79
Double Scotch	63
Down in the Sewer	218
Dragon's Back	182
Dragon's Side	182
Drainpipe Groove	79
Drunk and Disorderly	185
Dysoning	180
Early Bird Wall	246
Easy Action	80
Easy Interloper	127
Easy Skanking	36
Eat the Rich	136
Ed's Wall	136
Edge of Insanity, The	155
Eeonefivebee	188
Egg an' Onion Crack	245
Elbow Ridge	167
Elderberry Crack	181
Elective Affinities	90
Elsanity	40
Emanon	76
Emergency	225
Emmaline	251
Emotional Rescue	83
Enigma	157
Ephemeral Groove	237
Ernie	39
Esso Blue	128

Climb	Page
Evasor	33
Exfoliation	149
Exide	172
Face Value	201
Fade to Grey	185
Fallout	80
Fe Fi Fo Fum	56
Feed 'em	218
Fiat	231
Figment of Imagination	249
Film	173
Fingal's Cave	67
Fingal's Flue	67
First Day of Winter	120
First Day Tower	246
First Offence	187
Fixation	225
Flake and Pillar	73
Flake Crack	181
Flakes Direct	47
Flakes, The	47
Flaky Pastry	89
Flam	173
Flashing Fisher, The	63
Flavour of the Month	57
Flick of the Wrist	139
Flip Side	180
Floating Rib	245
Fluff Pirate, The	41
Fly, The	213
Flycatcher	33
Footprint	126
Fop, The	247
Forbidden Fruits	266
Forging the Chain	249
Forgotten Groove	145
Formic	212
Four Minute Tiler	38
Frantic Manoeuvres	202
Fred	89
Free 'em	218

Craig Smith on the final overhang of Helmut Schmitt, Stoney Middleton.
Photo: Ian Smith.

Ian Riddington finishing Legal Action, Horseshoe Quarry.
Photo: Keith Sharples.

Climbers on Suscipiat, Staden Quarry.
Photo: Ian Smith.

Climb	Page	Climb	Page
French Connection	123	Green Onions	259
Friction Wall	171	Greensleeves	196
Friend 15	189	Griffon	259
Friendly Local	226	Grin Low Crack	205
Frisco Bay	59	Grin Low Slide, The	205
From Here to There	53	Grin Low Wall	205
Frore	156	Gripple	80
Froth	57	Gritstone Transplant	124
Full Frontal	218	Grockle's Gully	126
Funf	181	Groove, The	193
Gabriel	66	Groper, The	66
Galening Crack	124	Grotty Totty	39
Gam	249	Ground Zero Man	227
Gangway, The	176	Growl, The	219
Generosity Exists	226	Gruesome Groove	146
Gentleman Jim	244	Gymnic	147
Gerremdown	36	Hades	154
Gesemini	59	Halcyon Drift	227
Ghost in the Machine	116	Half Way Crack	252
Giant Staircase	226	Hammer into Anvil	235
Gibbet, The	264	Hammer	62
Ginger Man	168	Hanging Garden	179
Girdle Traverse (Ravensdale)		Hangman	248
	157	Happy Humphrey	251
Glory Road	50	Happy Wanderer	39
Gluttony	199	Hart Attack	77
Going Straight	189	Hay Wain	164
Gold Label	126	Haystack	163
Golden Brown	116	Hazy Day	250
Golden Gate	58	Heart to Heart	119
Golden Tights	126	Heat, The	86
Goldfinger	173	Helicon	37
Gollyberry	82	Helmut Schmitt	86
Gorrah	150	Help the Poor Struggler	
Gothic Demarcation	116		264
Govinda	261	Hercules	53
Grauncher, The	92	Heron, The	226
Great Escape	64	Hi-Fi	151
Great Expectations	227	Hidden Corner	208
Great Rocks Girdle	267	High Crusade, The	208
Green Crack	72	Hinges	58
Green Groove	171	Hip Hop, Hip Hop, ...	139

Dave Bates on Gymnic, Ravensdale.
Photo: Ian Smith.

Climb	Page
Holiday Home for Pets Pie Company	252
Horizon	67
Horrorscope	89
Hot Legs Special	258
Hot Rock	135
Hot to Trot	266
Hot Zipperty	126
How Many people who have worked at Ellis . . .	193
How the Hell	76
Hsiao Mieh	265
Hydrolysis	148
Hysterectomy	46
Icarus	82
Ice Cream Phoenix	149
Impendent	148
Inception	198
Indictment	237
Indirect Route	181
Indirect Start	265
Inquisitor	49
Insidious Iceberg	231
Into the Labyrinth	128
Investal	230
Invisible Limits	237
Ivy Corner	145
Ivy Groove	173
Ivy Groove	79
Ivy Grotto Direct	53
J. Arthur	80
Jack Frost	247
Jackdaw's Gully	210
Jackorner	208
Jaggered Crack	172
Jailer's Crack	174
Jailer's Groove	174
Jailer's Wall	174
Jam Butty Mines Crack	198
Jam Sandwich	63
Janbaloo	213
Jasper	86

Climb	Page
Jeremy's Jungular Jaunt	210
Jericho Road	137
John Peel	83
Joint Effort	230
Juggernaut	67
Jungle Arête	70
Just Another Tricky Day	87
Just The Ticket	202
Just What the Doctor Ordered	73
Kaiser Bill	168
Kali	261
Keep Arête	174
Kellogg	48
Kellogg's are on Strike	226
Kelly's Eye	58
King Kong	41
Kingdom Come	48
Kink	48
Knee Trembler	250
Knight Rider	119
Kundalini	265
La Belle et la Bete	38
Lachesis	198
Last Exit Going South	188
Last Stand	50
Lazy Day	246
Lefrack	92
Left Route	219
Left-Hand Crack	87
Lefty	182
Legal Action	121
Leningrad	236
Leper's Groove	237
Leprosy	40
Let Me Introduce You To The Family	260
Lethanol	208
Letter Box, The	175
Levant	237
Lift Off	137

Climb	Page	Climb	Page
Like Ice, Like Fire	123	Menopause	46
Liquid Courage	230	Mephistopheles	156
Liquid Dream	73	Merger, The	260
Liquid Engineering	125	Merry Pheasant	202
Litany Against Fear	121	Metronome	151
Little Capucin	77	Midge Dance	252
Little Crack	73	Midi	77
Little Damocles	125	Mignon	179
Little Lady	188	Millionaire Touch, The	83
Little Plum	36	Mindblind	58
Little Weed	251	Mineshaft	53
Looking at the Blue	148	Minestrone	70
Looking Through Gary		Mingtled Wall	56
Gibson's Eyes	71	Minus Ten	63
Lost Contact	188	Minus Wall	64
Lost Horizon	67	Mitre Crack	209
Lost Monolith	122	Moaning Groove	171
Lucy Simmons	50	Mong Attack Crack	192
Lust	197	More Me than Me	139
Magnificent Concept	194	Morgue, The	78
Maid Marion	253	Morning Crack	76
Main Motor Mile, The	221	Mortuary Steps	78
Malaido	202	Mother's Milk	136
Malaise	202	Mottled Wall	57
Malpossessed	149	Mozaic Piece	234
Man From Delmonte – He		Mr Jagger's Warning	171
Says "Yes"	124	Mr. Blue Sky	128
Mani	71	Much Monkey Magic	221
Marasmus	76	Muscle-Cock Crack	91
Marmaliser, The	259	My Girdle is Killing Me	40
Marmoliser	237	My Personal Pleasure	57
Matrix	38	My Tulpa	232
Matterhorn Face	167	Myopia	151
Matterhorn Ridge	167	Nails, The	231
Mealy Bugs	155	Nancy Boy	247
Mealystopheles	155	Nandin	261
Medusa (Ravensdale)	154	Narrow Gauge	201
Medusa (Stoney)	59	Natty Dread	266
Megalithic Man	121	Naze	76
Megsy	250	Nazi Baby	209
Melting Pot	41	Neptune's Bellows	259
Memnon	42	Nettlerash	212

Climb	Page
Nice 'n' Sleazy	235
Nice Face, Shame about the Ledge	122
Nijinski	127
Niknak	194
No Cure for Gangrene	264
Northerners Can't Climb	90
Nose, The	180
Not a Patch on the Apaches	138
November Wall	208
Nuclear Device	260
Obvious Crack	92
October Crack	259
Okra	56
Old Nick	247
Oliver	83
Om	71
Omelette	71
One Deadly Variant	197
One Night Stand	249
One Step from Earth	227
One	193
Onga	258
Opportunity Mocks	138
Or Perhaps None?	193
Orang Utang	86
Orange-Throated Gonk, The	225
Order Number 59	124
Original Start, The	145
Orrid	43
Ostrich's Throat	245
Our Father	46
Ourobouros	265
Overhanging Face	164
P.M.'s Question Time	128
Padme	71
Pagan Man	149
Parachute	64
Paraplege	233

Climb	Page
Parrot Crack	253
Party Animal, The	127
Pastoral Corner	82
Patience	92
Paupericles	157
Peak Climb	173
Pearly Gates, The	66
Pedestal Branch	145
Pendulum, The	32
Permutation Wall	201
Peter Dale Chimney	185
Peter Dale Staircase	185
Phaseout	222
Phone Home	173
Physical Fizz	120
Pickpocket	59
Pig Sick	227
Pineapple	40
Pink Indians	137
Pinnacle Route	180
Pint of Blood	168
Piton Route	175
Plaque Crack	150
Platband, The	180
Play it again, Sam	187
Plough, The	135
Ploy	156
Ployed	32
Pock Wall	175
Poison Flowers	92
Pollyanna	67
Polymath	248
Popeye	198
Porthos	244
Positive Discrimination	201
Postern Crack	151
Postman's Meander	90
Pot Full	89
Pot-washer's Wall	126
Predator	82
Primrose Path, The	247

Climb	Page
Princess Anne's Crack	192
Private Gripped	230
Private Prosecution	121
Prolapse	82
Psychodimbo	192
Psychological Warfare	227
Psychopath	82
Pullemdown	37
Purple Haze	156
Pussy Galore	259
Puttrell's Arête	175
Puttrell's Crack	175
Pygmies Walk Tall	63
Queer Tree Groove	248
Racial Harmony	42
Railroaded	202
Rain Dance	120
Rainbow Woman, The	57
Rainsong	90
Rainy Day Ramble	258
Rambler's Arête	245
Rated X	249
Rattan	179
Raven Crack	144
Real Thing, The	79
Recessed Corner	181
Rent a Ghost	209
Restive Being	238
Revulva	50
Rhombus	258
Right Arête	214
Right Groove	219
Right Slab	245
Right-Hand Crack	87
Right-Hand Face	164
Righty	182
Ring Bolt Buttress	171
Rippemoff	37
Riser	128
Rising Potential	227
Rite of Way	167
Robin Hood	253
Robin	70
Rockbiter	150
Roman Candle	64
Roman Numeral X	226
Roof Route	180
Roraima	86
Rosehip Wine	70
Rotund Rooley	120
Round the Bend	150
Route 1	236
Rubber Ogre, The	260
Rubbish	82
Run For Your Wife	121
Running Over	89
Runts Grunt Stunt	175
Rupert Bear Goes Hiking	235
Russian Roulette	148
Sad Crack	193
Sagittarius	150
St. Paul	64
St. Peter	64
Samson	218
Sanctuary of Siva, The	261
Sans Nom	212
Say it With Flowers	120
Scabby Buttress	171
Scarab	72
Scaramanga	265
Scavenger's Daughter, The	265
Scent of Spring	250
School's Out	120
Scoop and Corner	172
Scoop Route	180
Scoop Wall	172
Scoop Wall	46
Scorpion	147
Scott's Wall	187
Screwy Driver	122
Scrubber	41
Scurvy Knave	66

Climb	Page	Climb	Page
Second Day Crack	246	Solitaire (Gt Rocks)	259
Second Lesson	245	Solitaire (Stoney)	64
Sensayuma	258	Solo Man's Ploy, The	225
Sergeant Mold	264	Solo	225
Sergeant Pepper	219	Somebody's Trademark	
Seven Deadly Sins	197		234
Seven Deadly Virtues	197	Sooty	184
Shae	189	Southern Man	122
Shaken Not Stirred	266	Southerners Can't Climb	
Shaky Crack	72		90
Shanacie	188	Special K	47
Shattered Crack	148	Speckled Egg Indirect	136
Shellfish Shuffle	52	Speckled Egg	136
Shetland Chimney	125	Spectrophotometry	123
Shot Yer Bolt	122	Speed Kills	79
Sickle	62	Spider, The	213
Side Step	184	Spiron	90
Silent Fear	237	Spring Awakening	123
Silent Manoeuvres	234	Springtime Fable	194
Sin	50	Square Hole, Round Peg	
Skull, The	193		135
Skywalker	259	Stack Wall	180
Slab and Arête	53	Stainsby Girls	187
Slab and Cleft	172	Steps, The	181
Slabbering Slab	125	Stheno	58
Sloane Ranger	135	Stroll Wall	252
Slob Team Special	197	Subsidiary Groove	193
Slow, Like Strychnine	260	Summertime	253
Slurper, The	80	Sun Crack	225
Smoke and Noise Filled		Sunday Sport	122
Room, The	135	Sunshine Superman	260
Smokestack	163	Supplementary Question	
Sneck	149		128
Snerp	87	Surface Plate	213
Sniffer Clarke	92	Suscipiat	231
So-So	145	Swan Song (Staden)	234
Soapsuds	72	Swansong (Stoney West)	
Socket Set	188		89
Soft Mick	236	Sweep	184
Solar Plexus	226	Swine Vesicular	48
Solar Wall	225	Sword and Stone	208
Solitaire (Ravensdale)	151	Sycamore Crack	209

Climb	Page
Sycamore Groove	172
Syntax Error	62
Tank	149
Tantalus	52
Tax Dodge	137
Taxing Times	237
Telescopic Demand	234
Temple of Lara Jongrang, The	261
Tequila Tory	91
Terrace Wall	174
Terrace Wall	214
Therianthropic	208
Thin Crack	176
Third Day Tower	246
Thirty Nine and a Half Steps	202
Thirty-Four Candles	82
This Wall!	71
Thorn, The	70
Throwback	227
Thrutch	63
Thunder Buttress Route	247
Thunder Chimney	247
Thunder Wall	247
Thyrsus	157
Ticket to the Underworld	39
Tiger Trot	41
Timber	208
Tit for Tat	137
Titanic Reaction	231
Titbit	194
To Hell and Back	76
Tom's Off Day Route	252
Tomarwa Groove	87
Too Mellow to Bellow	248
Total Haemorrhage	261
Touch and Go	252
Tourist Crack	166
Tourist Groove	253

Climb	Page
Tourist Wall	166
Tout Comprendre	235
Tower Climb	145
Tower Crack	146
Tower of Babel, The	50
Town Hall Clerk	248
Traffic Jam	63
Tree and Leaf	252
Tria	148
Tricycle Man	201
Troops of Tomorrow	150
True Lime	145
Truffle	50
Trundler, The	87
Turkey-Vulture Crack	91
Twang	91
Two Cave Gully	198
Two Tier Climb	180
Two-Step	181
Ubiquitous, The	189
Unpleasant	144
Up and Coming	258
Upthrutch	197
Upthrutch	201
Urge, The	218
V Groove	172
Venom	213
Venous Return	157
Very Windy Slab	244
Via Vita	154
Vinegar Fly	70
Vintage Two	157
Virgin on the Loose	33
Visions of Vishnu	261
Vulture's Crutch	250
Wall of Jericho	120
Wallop	57
Warder, The	193
Was Harpo a Trappist Monk?	135
Watcher, The	149
Watchtower, The	174

Climb	Page	Climb	Page
Waterloo Road	230	Windy Slab	244
Wee Doris	59	Winter's Tale	194
Welcome To Hard Times		Wipe Out	233
	231	Wry-Necked Gonk	225
Werewolf Crack	193	X Certs	230
What the Hell	76	Xenophobia	231
While the Cat's Away	128	Y Chimney	151
Whispering Crack	189	Year of Living Dangerously,	
White Dove	128	The	58
White Knight, The	66	Yew Cap	151
White Mane, The	172	You Are Only Mortal	43
White Ridge Crawl	172	Yukio	213
White's Height, The	119	Z Victor 1	198
Who the Hell	77	Z.C.T.	218
Wick, The	149	Zany Pop	248
Wide Gauge	201	Zebedee	196
Will O' The Wisp	265	Zen and The Art of Moving	
Wilt	149	Horizontally	192
Windhover	47	Zyklon B	264